Rembrandt's Angel

Rembrandt's Angel

by

Steven M. Moore

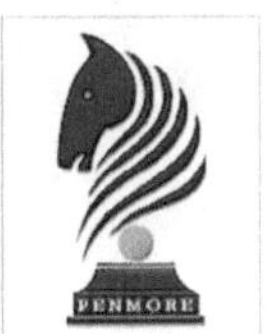

www.penmorepress.com

ISBN-13: 978-1-946409-02-7 (Paperback)
ISBN-13: 978-1-946409-03-4 (e-book)

BISAC Subject Headings:

ART015080**ART** / History / Renaissance
FIC022060**FICTION** / Mystery & Detective / Historical
FIC022040**FICTION** / Mystery & Detective / Women Sleuths

Editor Susan Wenger
Cover Illustration by Christine Horner

Address all correspondence to:
Penmore Press LLC
920 N Javelina Pl
Tucson AZ 85748

Dedication

To all the great classical mystery writers, but especially to Agatha Christie, whose Miss Marple and Monsieur Poirot entertained me for many hours in my youth...and would have enjoyed sharing a novel together!

Cast of Main Characters

Sylvia Bassett = art thief and ex-mistress of an old, rich Italian

Esther Brookstone = Scotland Yard expert on tracing stolen artworks and catching art thieves

George Langston = Brookstone's boss

Reginald Fox = Brookstone's neighbor

Jeremy Brand = counterterrorism expert at MI-5

Count Alberto Sartini = Brookstone's late husband #3, a Swiss banker

Angus MacDougall = deceased Scotsman who leaves Brookstone a castle in his will

Bastiann van Coevorden = Dutch Interpol agent

"Joachim" = black market art dealer

Hal Leonard = American Interpol Agent

Ambreesh Singh = MI-5 techie

Kurt Geiszler = German Federal police inspector

"Ruth" = Joachim's female counterpart and Brookstone's shadow on the Lima trip

Gerhard Dunst = German industrialist

Walther Lietzke = Dunst associate

Karen Lietzke = iconic head of the neo-Nazis

"Jacob" = Ruth's partner, and eventually van Coevorden's shadow on the Lima trip

Ernesto Felipe Lopez Diaz = cartel leader

Rolando Castilblanco = NYPD homicide cop

Introduction

The great detective Sherlock Holmes had his Dr. Watson who observed and recorded his many adventures. Scotland Yard Inspector Esther Brookstone has me. Unbeknownst to her, I began to write about her many cases, many of them more interesting than my own, when I started at the Yard. She was running the Art and Antiques Unit at that time, a position I inherited from her when she had her fill of bureaucracy. She still runs the Unit in many ways, and her cases have become even more interesting.

The facts surrounding this tale were obtained from reading her reports and my conversations with her. To make a complete story, I have had to tinker with that panoply of facts by adding material in the grand tradition of Dr. Watson, material which neither Esther nor Interpol Agent Bastiann van Coevorden—nor yours truly, for that matter—could have known or experienced at the time. I have strived to make the whole story coherent and logical, but I will admit that the real events might have occurred differently.

That said, I hope the remarkable personality and strong character of my dear friend Esther Brookstone, and of her Dutchman, Bastiann van Coevorden, will shine through in spite of any storytelling ability I lack. We are a forgotten section of the grand Metropolitan Police force, and we deserve to be better recognized. Perhaps this tale will help achieve that recognition.

As a further note to the curious reader, I have never called Esther Miss Marple, nor Bastiann Monsieur Poirot. Their public abhorrence to the employment of those nicknames is surely due to their use in a pejorative nature among their colleagues, but they still might be hiding an impish pride at being compared to Agatha Christie's famous sleuths. Sometime when I'm in Scotland visiting her castle I shall ask her, but certainly not in the Unit.

G.L.

London, October, 2023

Steven M. Moore

Prologue

Sylvia's Italian lover ripped her nightgown to expose her breasts and pushed her down on the bed, fist raised to strike. She pushed him off, jumped up, and ran out of the room, tired of his abuse. His proclivity for rough sex had turned more violent of late. He had become a possessive monster.

She knew he would be right behind her. The old man would still be bent on punishing her. He would beat her, drag her back to the bedroom, and have his way with her. *Will I suffocate in the plastic bag this time? What a fool I am!*

She needed a weapon. *Knives!* But the kitchen was too far away. She fled into the nearby library. Once all those books, many first editions, and artwork on the wood-paneled walls, all from past centuries, had impressed her. Now she despised them. The old ogre didn't really appreciate any kind of artwork or literature. He only saw them as investments. She saw the fifteenth-century painting of the saint with her halo and grimaced. *Am I to become a martyr too?*

She heard his wheezing in the hall. She prayed to the saint for a weapon. The saint didn't respond, but the eyes of the bust on the grand piano seemed to be following her. *Is that a wink?* She dashed to the instrument the old man thought he could play and grabbed the bust by its neck, hefting it. She turned as he entered the room, a savage smile on his face.

"My dear Sylvia, you are my mistress. I took you in. I have showered you with my gifts. I own you. You once enjoyed my attentions."

All that was in Italian. In her time with him, she had picked up the language. He was gone during the day, leaving her locked in her room in his mansion. She had nothing to do but watch local TV, developing language skills by osmosis, preparing for her escape.

"That was before I discovered you were a monster," she replied. "You don't own me. No one owns me!" She spoke in her mother tongue, tainted by her working-class roots in northern England. "You pretend to be nobility, but you're as common as my own sleazy father."

He began to approach her. She swung the heavy bust. His arm absorbed some of the blow, but that only deflected it alongside the head, and that was enough to knock him senseless. He sunk to the floor.

She bent over him. *Is he dead?* She felt for a pulse. *Weak, but still there.* She stood and spat on him.

***

She tied up the old man. *What to do for money?* She had none. She then smiled. She knew most things in that library were valuable. If she could just receive ten percent of the value of items she stole, that would do for a while. She made a quick inventory and took what she thought was the most valuable of the portable items.

She carried her stash to her room and threw open the huge walk-in closet's door. The closet was almost empty. She didn't have many clothes besides the hideous nightgowns, chemises, and slips he had purchased for her. Those purchases had been frequent, because he often ripped them off her in his predatory fury. She had a few summer dresses, comfortable shoes, and lingerie. They would have to do.

The mansion was in the Roman suburbs. She left the huge house and walked along the long entrance drive, carrying her bags to the busy roadway and turning towards the city's center. A lorry driver, another old man with a genuine smile, not a leer, took pity on her. Her angel carried her away from her devil. *But where should I go? And what should I do?*

She decided her first goal must be to pawn some minor *objets d'art* for cash. *One step at a time, Sylvia.*

***

With some of the money, she bought an old purse from a street vendor and headed for the train station, stopping at a pharmacy on the way. Like most European train stations, there were public loos and washrooms. She used one to wash up and trim and tint her hair with scissors and an inexpensive dye she had purchased.

She stared at her face in the mirror. Scars from old wounds still showed pale white, but inexpensive makeup hid most of the yellow from old bruises. *I look like a peasant woman. That's good.* She wouldn't be noticed. She glanced at her bulky luggage. *Except for that. What I have left to show for years of abuse!*

Even with an unknown future ahead of her, she was upbeat. *I escaped!*

When she entered the main hall of the station, she looked at the huge marquee. Again the question. *Where to?* She decided a return to her native country was in order. She was tired of continental Europe. But maybe trains were too slow and offered authorities too many chances to find her? She exited, found an agency, and bought a ticket for the airport instead.

Part One

You use a glass mirror to see your face; you use works of art to see your soul.
—George Bernard Shaw

Chapter One
Wantage, Oxfordshire

Brookstone had been to Wantage in Oxfordshire before. Her parents had taken her there many times as a child, sometimes alone with her mother when the train was still in service (now one had to go to Didcot Parkway, nine miles east of town), and other times passing through on their way to family holidays in southern England. She hadn't been in that region for a while but had an invitation from an old friend that justified a getaway into the country.

King Alfred the Great was born in Wantage in 849. She couldn't remember why he was born there, but the place had a bit of history. It was also down the road from Oxford, that famous college town fourteen miles to the northeast. She'd once lived there. Her very own Alfred, her second husband, had been a professor. Compared to London, she found the whole area droll. *But Natalie is a good friend, so I must make sacrifices.*

The estate's iron gates opened wide after the security system recognized her plate number—just as Natalie had promised. She drove her Jaguar XE Prestige sedan around the semicircular gravel drive, did a three-point to back into an area originally set aside for horse-drawn carriages, she imagined— her car was much shorter—and gave a nod and wave to two gardeners who straightened up with astonished looks on their faces as she exited the car.

Somedays, she felt the weight of her life's six decades. Today, although stiff from the ride, she felt much younger. Americans say sixty is the new forty. *So be it!* A woman of forty could still notice a man from the corner of her eye and assess possibilities. She wasn't about to mumble about how good it used to be, either. Life was too short to pretend romance ended with a husband—in her case, three—and children—in her case, none. She waved at the gardeners again.

She tried to imagine what they were thinking. She was always well-dressed when out and about—in this case, a sharp and flattering business suit, a salon hairdo, designer sunglasses, and stylish pumps. She kept in shape, so not much of anything sagged. So far she had avoided the plastic surgeon's knives too, although she felt a bit self-conscious about the few wrinkles on her neck and back of her hands.

She looked like a rich forty-year-old on a drive in the neighborhood around her estate. *Ha! As if I could afford one.* She could barely afford upkeep on her car. *How is it we have a national petroleum industry yet the petrol price is so high?* She had some money in investment accounts and stashed away in banks for her retirement, so she had decided to live a frugal life, making do with her meager salary.

The older gardener looked Welsh or possibly Irish—all Celts looked alike to her. She could see he sported what she called a Fourth-of-July nose—white with blue and red veins, the prominent colors in the Yanks' Independence Day fireworks as well as their flag that looked like a New York City barber's pole. The other man looked like the son whose predilection for drink hadn't affected his nose yet. She admired his rippling muscles and received a smile in return for her appraisal.

She ended the mutual admiration—his might be for the sedan, after all—and set off for what she considered a house of the filthy rich.

On the way to the front entrance, she glanced at the sky and decided her arrival was timely. A committee of clouds enjoyed a private meeting over the manor. They were like an insult to her holiday-like trip; compared to London's bad weather, the countryside enjoyed better, but maybe that was psychological—one was often in better spirits there in spite of the weather. Assuming one was rich enough to be comfortable, of course. She didn't need servants in the city; they often were required for comfort in the countryside. Fortunately, for the estate's owner, they were also less expensive outside urban areas.

Although she was a striking and imperious figure, the car adding even more evidence for her taste for the good life, she didn't approve of the rich and their wasteful ways. Her favorite and last husband had been a count; she had experienced many soirées and other posh events where she'd mingled with the rich and famous, enough to last a lifetime. Most were arrogant, narcissistic clods. As far as she was concerned, they should close Parliament's upper house and be done with the parasites. But she tolerated the royal family, even with their scandals and lavish lifestyle, assuming the middle class and poor needed something to distract them and allow them to keep a stiff upper lip. They were Great Britain's arthritic backbone and had stuck it to that little French corporal and his band of blaggards long ago, as well as to that German madman.

***

Esther Brookstone was an English contradiction. The Scotland Yard inspector wasn't one to suffer fools gladly, mostly spoke her mind, and would never curtsy for the Queen if she ever had the opportunity to do so. Nevertheless, she was refined and the Yard's foremost authority on stolen artworks, often collaborating with Interpol, MI-5, and MI-6, as well as other authorities throughout Europe and the rest of the world.

Even with the FBI and other Yanks. She remembered one recent case and smiled, recalling the brash Puerto Rican detective from New York City. *We're still looking for that ex-Nazi.* Castilblanco would call it a cold case now. She never called any case cold. She was a bulldog when it came to hunting down art thieves, pieces they stole, and collectors of the same. Her colleagues had a hard time reading her, though, because she was anything but simple and nearly always unpredictable.

Natalie Smythe was her opposite. Brookstone knew there wasn't a complex thought swirling in her friend's head. *Not many thoughts at all.* It was a small miracle they were still friends. In public school, the duo had a reputation for being wild, but Esther had always been the instigator. She had introduced Natalie to alcohol and tobacco and had arranged for her first sexual adventure with a handsome stud from another public school. Her friend had married only once, though, and married well.

The door opened before Brookstone had the pleasure of employing the huge door knocker reminiscent of Dickens's in the "Christmas Carol." She didn't like Dickens, but thought that little story and *Tale of Two Cities* well enough done to forget about his verbose and boring other tomes. She faced yet another Alfred: Natalie's butler, not Marley's ghost. He wasn't your typical butler, but his erect posture and uplifted chin gave him away. A modern butler, a bit creaky now with age, a local who had spent a lifetime in service to the well off. She liked his whiskers. *Testosterone is good, whether Beaujolais or well-aged.*

"Madam will see you in the Oak Room," he said.

"Thanks, Alfred." He hinted at a bow and nodded. "I know my way." He nodded and stepped aside, closing the huge door behind her.

He followed her along the corridor but went straight while she turned, went through the dining room with its huge table and chairs for thirty-two—*does Natalie still eat here?*—and entered the Oak Room. It was a large library, its walls covered with old wooden bookshelves stuffed with all sorts of books both new and old, most leather bound, and many from the 18th and 19th centuries; they preened in their perches above even more wood, cabinets cured by centuries of dusting and furniture polish and containing anyone's guess of knickknacks. In one corner crouched an immense desk—more wood and notable for its heavy, ornate legs. *The entire room would give a termite an orgasm. That's why it's called the Oak Room!*

"Look what the wind blew in," Lady Smythe said. She rose from a two-seater leather sofa, stretching—she was much shorter—to give Brookstone a peck on each cheek with an accompanying "Mwaaah!", then hugged her. "Did you have a nice ride from the city, dear?"

Lady Smythe wore a comfortable sleeveless summer dress, its bright red contrasting with her light white sweater but matching her pumps. *Bet those cost her a few schillings,* thought Brookstone. At one time they had been equally poor, their parents always voting Labour. *Wonder how she votes now?* She wasn't about to embarrass her friend by asking.

The BREXIT ballyhoo was long past, but there was still some fallout. Brookstone didn't notice much difference. They were getting along just fine with the E.U., just like Norway. She always thought the whole thing was a storm in a teacup, like Scottish independence. She lumped all politicians together and considered them parasites. Fortunately there were layers of bureaucracy between her and the bloviating fools.

"A Jaguar is a poor substitute for having a man in the saddle," said Brookstone, "but yes, it wasn't bad. Counter commute and all that, as the Yanks say."

Natalie blushed. "You still have a saucy tongue, Esther," she said.

Brookstone ignored the chastisement but continued to prove the truth of the statement. "The younger gardener looked like he might be worth checking out," she said with a smile. "I'm surprised you haven't traded old Alfred for a newer model too, one offering an extended range of services, if you know what I mean. You look relaxed, though. Leaving stressful business activities to your barristers and accountants now?" Brookstone had chosen to sit on the matching sofa facing Natalie's.

"You guessed right. It was getting to be a bit much." She picked up a tiny bell. "I'm ordering some lemonade. It's too early for tea."

"And a bit too warm," said Brookstone. "Spring was short."

A maid half their age entered, Lady Smythe murmured her order, the maid nodded and disappeared, and Natalie took her seat again.

"That's why the desk is clean." *It was tidy but busy last time. How long ago was that?* "But what convinced me were the trips into London. A terrible nuisance."

Brookstone's friend had kept the Smythe family's import-export business going after her husband's passing, and even expanded it. Brookstone wondered how it was doing now that the country had left the E.U. She had always admired her old school chum's fortitude. After an acceptable period of grieving, she had jumped right in and shown a knack for business. Her hard work made up for a lack of brains. It was even related to Brookstone's work, because some imports and exports were legal art deals between legitimate collectors. On more than one occasion, Brookstone had served as a consultant for an authentication.

Chapter Two
Smythe Manor

Brookstone glanced around the huge room, savoring its comfortable grandeur. The portrait of Natalie's husband hanging over the sofa where Natalie sat was the only painting. His stern scowl made it seem like he was critical of the female gossip going on in his work study. Other wall space was available for paintings, though.

"I'm surprised your husband wasn't a collector," said Brookstone. "Did he have properties in London? This room could use some modern art, for example, to brighten it up a bit. A Gauguin, or even that flamboyant South American fellow, Obregon. This place could be taken for a mausoleum after the apocalypse."

"To answer your first question, we had paintings and properties in London," said Natalie. "I sold them all because I prefer the countryside. My husband had also started a collection here. I sold those too. After he died, I was a bit short on cash. I regret that now, so I told my accountant I fancy investing in some artwork to make this place a bit more cheery and refined. You'd be surprised at how that gets out. I even receive brochures from Sotheby's. It's a bother, it really is. I could never afford a Gauguin. Who's this Obregon?"

"One of the big five Colombians. But if you can't afford Gauguin you can't afford him, either. I have a reproduction of his *El Condor*. Botero is another."

She knew enough Spanish to read Garcia Marquez in that language, although when speaking she tended to confuse it with Italian. South American art was more attractive to her than literature. Because that art was less known—Britain focused on its own past and favored the Commonwealth countries—illegal copies were less detectable by the general public, and even by many art connoisseurs. Of course, anyone buying expensive artworks who didn't check for authenticity and provenance was a fool. It was surprising how many of her clients were fools who were preyed upon by unscrupulous people. She called them clients as if she were some insurance company representative. After all, she was there to protect their interests, no matter how foolish and careless they were. Many rich dilettantes hired people to protect them from these duplicitous people; Scotland Yard did it for free, as much as they were able.

Natalie nodded. "The one with fat caricatures of people in his paintings and sculpture," she said with a laugh. "Doesn't sound like I could afford any of those either. My accountant knows London galleries, though, and thinks I might collect some good paintings by artists who will likely acquire a following later on. They would be an investment as well as being decorative."

"Don't take his word on any of them," said Brookstone. "Some modern art requires a preventive antacid; you mightn't want to view it every day. I like some modern pieces, but classics are safer if you have extra money to spend, from both aspects, enjoyment and investment. My work is about as close as I can be to the old masters, though."

"Is that going well?"

"The monthly trip to the gun range is a bit of a bore. I'm not with homicide investigation, counterterrorism, or drug interdiction, after all. Firearms aren't important in my life for the most part. During my years with the Metropolitan Police, I can't ever remember being involved in a shootout or having to take down a criminal in a physical altercation." She grinned. "I wouldn't know what to do with myself if I retire, though. And I can still spot an attractive man and pretend he might be interested in me, so it's good to be out in public and not in a home for the elderly." She winked. "Sometimes they are interested, especially if they think I have money, the louts."

"You always were more interested in those pursuits than I," said Natalie. "However, I know a retired scientist who bought a cottage nearer town. He's a good looking fellow, if you like tweed sport jackets and trilby hats."

Esther thought a bit. "How old?"

"A bit younger than you, I'd wager. Isn't that a good thing?"

"Of course. Old men tend to have things go wrong with their plumbing. And why chase a man who can't get it up and is going to die on you soon?" She thought a moment. "What's his background? Would he be willing to live in London?"

"I've heard he's from there originally." She leaned forward. "I'm also privy to gossip that he worked for MI-6—cloak and dagger stuff. I know his housemaid. She's a dear."

"But a scientist, you say? Not a field agent then. Probably lab work of some kind. I could have a fling, I suppose, but if he's bent on tending his rose gardens here in the countryside, he's not a keeper, at least for me. What about you?"

"Oh, I'm through with men. They're too damned needy." Natalie smiled. "Even my old hubby. His grave's in back, by the way, with the rest of them. I don't visit him much. It's creepy there."

***

Esther and Natalie chatted some more, mostly about old times, and sipped their lemonade. After an hour or so, Brookstone became antsy.

"I should move along. I'm driving to Oxford to talk with an art expert there. He's a specialist in Italian sculpture. I need to brush up a bit. My forte's oil paintings, but some old rich bastard from Florence had a bust stolen, and Italian authorities think it's in England on the black market." She smiled at her friend. "I apologize for killing two birds with one stone. It's been nice chatting with you again. We should do it more often."

"Why don't you return and spend the night?" said Natalie. "We could visit the local pub and admire the scientist. He goes there often." She winked. "He's an eyeful. Black hair with enough gray to prove he's experienced, and the expressive blue eyes of an artist."

"Twelve pence the dozen," said Brookstone. "And many of them narcissistic. Maybe some other time."

On her way out, she spotted brochures and an envelope with a German postmark with a June, 2022 cancellation. *Who still uses ordinary post these days?*

"Do you have a secret admirer in Munich?" she said.

"That's what I was explaining. Some bloke there picked up the gossip that I want to buy a few pieces of art and sent me a description of a painting he's selling."

"Might I see it?"

Natalie handed her the letter. Only addressee and postmark, no return address; inside no addressee and no signature, just a short message and phone number. It was printed in a blocky computer font all in caps—Arial, she thought. The letter offered a private showing of "An Angel with Titus' Features" by Rembrandt van Rijn. She frowned.

"This is either a scam, or it's a black market sale," said Brookstone. "Any chance you can make a copy of the letter?"

"Oh, keep it," said Natalie. "It's trash as far as I'm concerned. It arrived two weeks ago and has been gathering dust."

A fortuitous and interesting coincidence. Brookstone was attracted to art scams like a calico to catnip. She checked the postmark again. "Some kind of bulk rate. He's targeting the ingenuous rich. In the E.U. and the Commonwealth, they're all too common."

"I'm not a wealthy person. I can't afford a Rembrandt."

"Only the filthy rich or a major museum could. But one never knows how rich people really are because they often hide it so well. In particular, he doesn't know how well off you are, most likely, only that you own this estate. In other words, he might have you or your husband on a list of landed gentry in this area. FYI: this painting has been missing since World War Two. The Nazis set it aside in 1943 for Hitler's museum, along with 332 other works, but only 162 have been found."

"You do know your art history," said Natalie. "Shouldn't we turn this over to the police then?"

Brookstone laughed. "My dear, as far as these things go, I am the police, discounting the bloody blaggards at Interpol and your local constables. Of course, I have to bow to those local authorities, being from London, but they'd call our office anyway—they couldn't begin to handle a case like this."

Chapter Three
Oxford University

The A34 to Oxford wasn't busy. On the Oxford University campus, Brookstone found the visitor's space nearest to Littlegate House where the Department of the History of Art was located. Her Jaguar turned the heads of a few students who were chatting nearby, which surprised her—the young were much more into the convertible version. *I wonder what it takes to enter Oxford?* In her years there as Alfred's wife, she'd never discovered a satisfactory answer to that question and, in spite of its size, had always thought the place, which had existed before 1096, was more like a huge country club.

Nicholas Greenly, art professor, was a pompous little twit, not all that different in appearance from Natalie's older gardener, but the Yard had consulted with Greenly before about missing sculptures. He ushered her into his cluttered office. He removed a pile of journals and books from a leather visitor's chair, dusted the seat a bit, and offered it to her with a gallant wave of the hand.

"I know the piece well," he said, jumping right into it. He handed her a replica. "I had this copy made up. We're high tech here, my dear. The original is early Bernini, predating his 'Damned Soul' of 1619. A bit of a prodigy, old Bernini. He's better known to tourists for the fountains in Rome, of course, if they ever think to ask. Most just ogle and snap their pictures with those damn iPhones."

Brookstone turned the bust around in her hands. "I could sit this on my baby grand."

"You can have it. It's an exact replica we made with a 3D printer."

"How's that done?"

"A laser hologram is digitized and the data mapped into printer commands. It's built layer by layer."

"It isn't enough they're making movies with dead Hollywood stars," said Brookstone. "What a boon to art counterfeiters!"

"Well, it isn't marble, so that's a tell," said Greenly with a smile. "It might take the techies a while to pull that one off. Looks like you fancy it, though. Call it a lightweight version."

"Let's say I can see why the owner's upset he's misplaced it."

"Why does he think it's here in England?"

"A tale about a romance ending badly: according to him, his mistress threw a fit and scarpered with a few items. This bust was one, the heaviest; his original could be the weapon she used on the old lecher because it's marble, not like this copy. Others were a first edition, some drawings, and a musical score, easier items to carry. Some of the latter have turned up. The bust and a few other pieces are still missing. I'm guessing the bust is harder to sell."

"They turned up in London, I presume?"

"Exactly. The mistress is from the U.K., wouldn't you know? She hasn't turned up either. An octogenarian Italian man having a twenty-five-year old mistress seems a bit strange, but I'm not sitting in judgement."

"Italians. Always trying to relive their youth."

"So impractical. More logical if it goes the other way."

"You mean...?" Her smile and wink answered him. He reddened. "Hmm, I'm not sure how else I can help you. Especially not with that."

"You said this is early Bernini. I want to know more about his work. I couldn't find much on this piece beyond what the Italian authorities sent me. All the old art connoisseur had was an authentication. Some count in Rome determined that the bust wasn't a fake."

"You've come to the right person then. Want a spot of tea? It's almost time, and I've heard rumors Mrs. Katsaros left some delightful goodies today."

"I'll have some coffee instead, if you don't mind, because I still have to drive back and will need caffeine. Your goodies are probably on my New Year's resolution list of things to avoid to keep trim and fit. But who's this lady, Nicholas? Has she stolen your heart?"

"In a way. Greek pastries are my downfall, I'm afraid."

She followed the mousey little man from the office, carrying her bust in the crook of her arm like a mother would carry her baby.

****

They spent nearly two hours over coffee for her, tea and little Greek pastries for him, during which Nicholas Greenly related an entire history covering Bernini's early years.

At one point he paused. "Shouldn't you be taking notes?"

She tapped her head. "It's all in here. And it will be for a long time. Writing it on paper is like etching it in stone. I can't play with written facts like this—" she turned the bust around in her hands, "examining them from all sides and looking for complex connections. It's the way I work."

He nodded. "Shall I continue then?"

"If you'll be so kind to pour an additional half cup first. The coffee's excellent."

When they finished, he paid the bill and shook her hand. "It was good to see you again, Esther. Some people around here still remember you."

"That was ages ago. Oh, by the way, can you run me off five copies of this letter? You can read it if you like."

Greenly glanced at the letter and then looked at Brookstone. "A Rembrandt for sale? Preposterous!"

"Maybe not so much," she said. "It was set aside for Hitler's museum with other works, but 170, including this one, are still missing."

"I'd wager it's a scam then. Why now? Someone found it in their attic, do you think?"

"It happens, but why the secrecy?"

"Have you called this number?"

"Not yet. I want to leave three copies with you. Maybe someone in your faculty knows something. A secret private cache maybe, where the owner just died?"

"We don't deal in the black market."

"But I bet you hear rumors, right?"

He smiled. "Sometimes. Wait here. I'll print some copies in the annex."

He returned and handed her two copies and the original. "Your work sounds like fun."

"It is until it isn't." She bent and gave him a peck on the cheek. "Thank you for seeing me. I now feel as if the young Bernini were my own *bambino*."

Chapter Four
London

Brookstone took M40 and A40 back to London and pulled into her parking space in the underground garage beneath her apartment building an hour past sunset. *Not a bad day's work,* she thought.

She was tired, though. She stepped from the Jaguar, shook out her short mane of black hair, and reached into the back for the replica of Bernini's bust. *I need a good soak.*

A neighbor was on his way out. "Did you have a nice day in the country, Esther?" said Reginald Fox, standing with the door of his BMW sedan open.

Who told you? "Yes, I did, as a matter of fact." Fox was a bit of gossip. She only told him what she wanted him to propagate. "Are you heading out?"

Fox was a swarthy man with oily, black hair and a pompous goatee. His legs were much shorter than his torso, giving the appearance he was top heavy. The bulldog jowls of an elderly man didn't help there. He was refined enough, though.

"A date, actually. I'm taking Patricia Kelly to a show and dinner."

"Isn't she married to that barrister Kelly?"

"Her husband isn't in town." He winked. "I offer my services to rich widows, even if it's only a temporary state."

Hint, hint. Fox had made a play for her on several occasions. He never gave up. *Maybe he thinks I'm rich?* The joke's on him. She was well enough off on paper, but not in Patricia Kelly's category. She recalled the conversation with Natalie. *Patricia is at least fifteen years younger.* Fox was a dashing figure in his tux, but he was older than Brookstone.

"Did you call the manager about your balcony? I'm tired of sweeping up your debris that falls through the cracks."

"I've been too busy. I'll make a note to buy you a broom."

Is he implying I'm a witch? "And I'll find some way to put the debris back on your balcony. You know the management has to take care of that repair, but they won't do anything unless you ask. I can't ask for you. Why the delay?"

"Because it gives me opportunity to flirt with you, my dear."

Flirt? You mean annoy me! "Have a good evening, Reggie. I doubt Patricia will." She turned and headed for the lift.

***

Brookstone collected her mail in the building's lobby and climbed stairs the rest of the way for exercise. In her apartment, she tossed the envelopes onto the kitchen counter, found a doily, and set the bust on the baby grand. It made a better statement than the glowering Beethoven she had there. *That old deaf bastard will have to go into storage.*

She had wanted a bust of Mozart on the piano but could never find one. Everyone seemed to love Beethoven's scowling face. She supposed he must have been a good pianist, but she thought Mozart's piano music to be uplifting optimism for a world that often sorely needed it. For her, music was like literature, though—they both took a second place to art. Art depended on the eyes, and human beings experienced the world through them. Even Beethoven's bust was a visual experience, not aural, although she supposed a music lover would recall passages from the man's masterworks simply by seeing the bust, hopefully beyond Winnie's "V for Victory."

She then glanced at her mail. There was a letter from some barrister in Edinburgh. She'd visited as a tourist a few times but had no idea why a barrister there would be writing her. She left that envelope with the other unopened ones containing bills, tossing the remainder, mostly catalogues, into the waste bin. *Bills are so depressing.*

She set out some leftover tortellini, uncorked a nice red from a northern Italian winery that had been a favorite of husband #3, and went into the bathroom to draw a bath. After bath and dinner, she was revived, so she opened her laptop and started her search for information about the Rembrandt. She learned the Titus in the painting was Rembrandt's only surviving son. *I can see where a father might think his son is a good model for an angel.* But then she thought of her brothers. *Definitely not angels!* They were off in their own pedestrian world of sons, daughters, and grandchildren. Contact with them had been reduced to a yearly exchange of Christmas cards.

She also learned Titus was named after Rembrandt's wife's sister. The dearth of information about the painting saddened her; all she had was a blurry black and white image she downloaded from the internet. The sadness turned to a bit of rage as she reminded herself that the Nazis had stolen the painting for Hitler's museum.

She was familiar with the history of the *Führermuseum.* It was Hitler's dream to create a museum and cultural center in his hometown of Linz and convert the city into Austria's capital because he hated Vienna. Hans Posse and other Nazi art experts set about "collecting" art for that purpose and other cultural projects. Posse alone "collected" over 2500 artworks before he passed on to enter Nazi Valhalla. The Rembrandt was a later "acquisition," though, its provenance uncertain.

She sipped her wine. The case of the Bernini bust was a distraction from her usual agenda. She found thieves and dealers of stolen art despicable because the cases often involved selfish people who wanted artworks all to themselves, people who felt pleasure when they could view something no one else could. That the case of the missing Rembrandt involved Nazi looting of European culture made it even more desirable to solve.

At least Hitler would have put it in the museum. *That psycho fancied himself an artist and art lover.* Too many high-ranking Nazis appreciated art only for its monetary value; they weren't art lovers but art thieves. It was possible one of Hitler's lieutenants had absconded with the Rembrandt, and it was now in Argentina or Paraguay or some other country that had offered haven to ex-Nazis.

But in the morning she would call that Munich number. She understood Germany and Germans. They ran that economic juggernaut of the E.U., and some of those old Nazi companies still existed. But she had taught Germans to remember their past before. Maybe this would be another chance.

***

"Any luck on that Bernini bust?"

"Not really, but I'm a bit more comfortable with the case," said Brookstone.

George Langston wasn't only a good boss, he was also her friend of many years. At fifty-four, he was still in good shape, a serious man who relished the scent of danger. Both his father and he had served in the RAF, but the Metropolitan Police had been his home for over twenty years. In spite of his rugged good looks, there was also something of the gentle aesthete about him.

He looked more like an Oxford professor than her late husband, Alfred. His natural tonsure begged for a monk's skullcap; old-style glasses, often perched on top of his head or low on his nose, were only used for close work. His demeanor was similar to a professor's too. Soft spoken with perfect enunciation akin to Henry Higgins's, Brookstone could imagine herself as a flirty coed sitting in the first row of his lecture class and showing a bit of leg. She would have targeted him even now if he weren't happily married to a music professor. Brookstone wouldn't have turned the unit over to anyone else.

"That doesn't answer my query, Esther." He sank into her visitor's chair. "Any more leads on the thief who's marketing the stolen goods?"

"The mistress most likely still has the bust," she said. "She'll have some problems. It's more important than the other stolen items. A collector might balk at buying it, especially without a valid provenance. I haven't checked this morning, though. I'll get right to it if a certain handsome but prying gentleman leaves my office area." She smiled to soften her words. She never wanted to use angry words with Langston.

"Right. Just checking." He stood.

"Before you go, what do you make of this?"

She handed him a copy of the letter from Germany Natalie had received. He scanned it.

"Could be someone has a Rembrandt, or someone's running a scam, or the case of someone luring a gullible victim into a bad situation where she or he can be robbed, kidnapped, or worse."

"Or it could be a prank. My old school chum Natalie received it. She lives on an estate in Oxfordshire, so someone might think she's a rich aristocrat looking to buy some art on the black market. She is well off, of course, but also frugal, and not able to afford what these people will be asking, I'm sure."

"And wise to ask you for your opinion. We probably covered all possibilities. What's the history of the painting?"

"Stolen by Nazis for Hitler's museum and never recovered." She gave some more details. "All we have is a black and white photo."

"This isn't going to be another wild goose chase after an old Nazi, is it?"

She smiled. "No wild geese were involved in that case. We nearly nabbed him. He's still on the run, though. And I still have my claws sharpened and ready to grab him."

"I'd leave this new case to Interpol if I were you. We need to close cases, not just make art thieves run. Two days more on the Bernini. After that, I'm handing you another case. The Art and Antiques Unit has quite a backlog for lack of personnel, as you know."

"If I solve your Bernini case in a day, can I have that other day to pursue this?"

He shrugged. "I suppose. What are you going to do?"

"Pose as a rich aristocrat looking to buy some art on the black market, of course."

***

Brookstone was now motivated to solve the case of the missing Bernini bust. But first she called the Munich number. She used a cheap mobile she had purchased on the way in to Scotland Yard, what American authorities would call a "burn phone," untraceable unless you were MI-5 or NSA.

"Leave your phone number and we'll return your call," said the recorded message in English, French, and German.

It had been a single voice for all three languages. She couldn't detect an accent in any language. She left her mobile number and hung up.

Next, on her office phone, she dialed a contact in MI-5.

"Jeremy, old boy, I need a favor."

She had collaborated with Jeremy Brand on several cases peripherally related to art thievery—terrorist organizations selling antiquities they had stolen. He usually dressed like a banker, but he was a successful agent working on counterterrorism efforts.

The Channel seemed to keep the U.K. freer from terrorism compared to continental countries in Europe, more so now with Britain out of the E.U., but the U.K. had enclaves filled with dissatisfied young and unemployed immigrants too. Even Ireland had them. *We want cheap labor but then take away their jobs.*

Long ago, Brand had been husband material. He possessed dashing good looks and, in spite of being MI-5 now, he always reminded her of Ian Fleming's mythical character in MI-6, the British Secret Service. He had also been her handler in that organization before she met any of her husbands-to-be and helped her narrowly escape the clutches of the Stasi. Their relationship had mellowed over the years; he had moved to MI-5, she to Scotland Yard, but they remained friends.

"Maybe," said Brand, "if you'll treat me to dinner in a good curry house."

"It's a deal. I hate to put you out, old boy, but if I follow protocol, I'll receive information too late to act."

"Understood. But no guarantees. Security and all that, you understand. What do you need?"

"I need to know where and when Sylvia Basset entered the country. She'd be arriving from Italy from—" Brookstone checked her calendar and gave the MI-5 agent a span of dates from June 15, 2022, to the present.

"That's easy enough to do. Should I know anything about this Basset woman?"

"She's not a threat to national interests, if that's what you mean. She stole a Bernini bust from her geriatric Italian lover, and he wants it back."

"The old thieving mistress trick," said Brand. "I suppose you don't have time to explain who Bernini was?"

"Your cultural ignorance isn't very Bond-like, Jeremy. But yes, I can do that. Over curry. I received the whole scoop at Oxford yesterday. Definitely not as exciting as terrorists. Or spying on East Germany."

"The mistress sounds more exciting. With all those beautiful Italian women, you'd think the old codger would have picked fruit falling from nearby trees."

You'd think. "One man's exotic enchantress is another's plain Jane." She was remembering her Italian count, though. *Those eyes!* "How soon can you send me that information?"

"Give me an hour. We'll have some techies wandering in, late as usual. Can't complain too much. Many work into the wee hours. They make a mess of everything with takeout cartons and the like all over the place, but we need them nowadays."

"You need to start running that place as if it were a branch of the military."

"That's not possible. They would chafe at that kind of discipline. Their nirvana is the Silicon Valley. I'll email you."

She ducked out for her second cup of coffee.

Chapter Five
London

The English mistress had not had a problem selling most of the smaller items, but even unscrupulous art dealers shied away from the Bernini bust. None would give it an appraisal either, except to say they thought it was priceless. She knew that; the old ogre wouldn't have bought it otherwise. Not knowing what to do with it, she stashed it in a locker at the airport.

She entered the little car she had stolen and pounded the steering wheel in frustration. *I'm on the run because of that monster!* She left the parking lot burning rubber. When the traffic patrolwoman tweeted at her, Sylvia Bassett gave her the finger. In her review mirror, she saw the woman jot down the license plate and smiled. *The bitch doesn't know I already swapped plates twice!*

She needed a place to hide for a while. She could go back to her home town, but she hated it. Always had. She'd spent some good years in Scotland. *Maybe my best years?* No, the years in Italy had been good in the beginning. They had only turned to pigeon shit later on.

She stomped on the accelerator and headed north. The little car was economical. She only stopped for gas once. In that same town, she changed plates again with a similar car parked at a shopping center.

***

Rodney Billings spotted the vehicle even before arriving at his destination. He parked his van near it, spit out the window, and looked around. He saw a woman sitting downslope a bit away from the ruined house. She was staring across the lake toward the horizon. He approached her.

"Excuse me? Who might you be?"

The woman turned toward him and lowered her sunglasses. *God, she's a stunning young bird!* Although a bit wide in the hips, she could otherwise be a fashion model. Her hair was in disarray because of the stiff breeze. An old wool sweater looked a bit tight on her, but he didn't mind that at all.

"Who's asking?"

"Rodney Billings, at your service, madam. I have a contract to fix the old house up a wee bit. Owner's died, he has, and it's not clear what's going to happen to the property, but there are some developers interested in it."

"I was exploring and stopped to admire the view, Mr. Billings. Not your typical *loch*, but it is beautiful." She stood and walked toward him, a tall angel floating among the old stones from the ruins. She stopped, turned back to the lake, and hooked her arm in his. "Now, good sir, doesn't that just take your breath away."

He received a whiff of her perfume. Smiled. "Something sure does. But I need to start work. The day's not getting any longer."

He wasn't a small man, but when she looked at him, her eyes were level with his. She wore a long dress with a floral print. From where the waistband sat, he could tell her legs were long.

"You're not Scottish," she said. "Northern England?"

"That's right. Carlisle born, I am. My parents moved to Glasgow, took me with them, you know. I make me home in Edinburgh now, mum."

"You're a nice fellow, Rodney." She unhooked her arm and offered a slim hand. "My name is Sarah Jones." They shook. "Please, you just go about your business like I'm not here. I hope you don't mind. I'd like to take in the view a bit longer. I need to think through some personal problems."

"I don't mind at all. If I can fix things inside enough, I'll invite you in for a spot o' tea later on."

"I'd like that." She turned and went downhill to her original vantage point.

***

Sylvia Bassett, Rodney's Sarah Jones, watched the congregation of clouds push its reflection across the lake. *With this breeze, how can there be reflections?* She decided the wind must diminish as one headed to lower ground where the lake was and across it. It wasn't much of a lake, and not what people generally called a *loch*, which was more often an inlet akin to a *fjord*, but the view explained why someone in some early century had decided to build on the knoll above it.

I would like to spend Christmas here. It must be beautiful when there's snow.

She'd always been there in spring or summer. Back then it had been a place to drink and have teenage sex. The mere thought caused her to feel dirty, even more so because it brought back memories of her Italian lover, the ogre she had left bleeding on his library floor.

Sylvia, you are a tramp! She hadn't lied to Billings. She did have many personal issues to work out. His seemed a broad shoulder to cry on. He had the physique of her working-class father and the gentle disposition of her poor, suffering mother.

It was hard to figure out who might be after her now. She could imagine her livid Italian lover even calling Interpol! *Maybe every constable in the U.K. is looking for me?* She smiled. She was like a famous highwayman, robbing from the rich but not giving back to the poor. She had no pretensions of being Robin of Loxley. Or that Californian hero Zorro. Instead, she and only she, was the poor beneficiary of this highwaywoman's largesse. The sale of the smaller items had given her a much needed cash infusion, but after that?

Life had turned Sylvia Bassett into tempered steel, albeit a bit rusty now. Like her mother, she appeared sweet and innocent; like her father, she had become a grifter. Her childhood in Newcastle, on the opposite coast from Rodney's Carlisle, hadn't been a happy one. Her father was absent from most of it. Her mother cleaned rich people's houses.

But Bassett wasn't dumb. Working hard and saving to complement money her Mum managed to give her, she had obtained a decent education in graphics arts, only to find jobs were scarce. But she wasn't about to become a cleaning lady. Her life on the dole had seemed to change for the better when her father took her to Italy. She had met a rich man. Paps left her there, happy to save her return ticket to England.

She sifted through more black thoughts for hours and was glad when Billings called her in for tea.

***

"I was so happy when I managed to fire up the stove. I brought fixings with me. 'Tisn't civil to go without a cup o' at four o'clock, is it, Sarah?"

She smiled at Billings and took a dainty bite of scone. A bit stale, but it was her first food of the day. She wasn't about to show him she was famished, though.

"What would developers put here in this old house's place?"

"Beats me. A hotel or resort maybe? You'd think tourists would head for the Highlands, though, wouldn't you? Get out o' Edinburgh fast, shall we say?"

"The city has its charms. Glasgow too. A lot of history around this area."

"I guess. Me, I just work to keep me head above water. What do you do for a living, Sarah?"

"I have no job. That's one of my problems."

"Lots of people lose their jobs around here. Me, I think a lot of noise about Scottish independence has its roots in that. Some of that BREXIT business contaminated people's thoughts too, I'd say. People aren't satisfied with the English keeping all the jobs for themselves for the first, or the French and Germans taking jobs away over the Channel for the second. Independence from the E.U.; now independence from Great Britain. There's a logic to it maybe."

"Profound, Rodney. Yes, economic strife can make people want change. There's always the idea that things would be better with it." *But what change could affect my life more than what has just occurred?* She took a sip of the strong working man's tea. "I wonder if I should retrain."

"There are programs for that," Billings said. "My sister-in-law was in one. She became an x-ray technician. I think I still make more money than she does, though. And I don't have to work all the time." He took a hearty bite of his scone and studied her. "You heading back to Edinburgh? I'm done with what I was sent to do, but I don't want to leave you here alone. You're a pretty thing. No telling what a passerby might do, you know."

"That's gentlemanly of you, but I'd not expecting any passersby, let alone a pervert. You were a welcome surprise."

He blushed. "Thank you, I guess. I think I'll keep it from my wife that I had tea with a beautiful woman, though."

"I'll stick around a bit. I still have some things to work out in my mind."

"OK by me. No one need know. You're only a wisp of mist off the lake, you are, as far as what I'll tell folks."

After he packed up, he came back downhill. "You going to be OK, Sarah? I must head back."

She kissed him on the cheek and then wiped off the lipstick. "We don't want the wife to see that. You take care of yourself, Rodney."

"I'll do that. And back at you, young lady."

Chapter Six
London

In the office canteen, Brookstone, swallowing her guilt along with the first bites of pastry and sips of coffee while daydreaming a bit, jumped in her chair when the cheap mobile's ringtone sounded. The same voice from before rattled off time and place before the dial tone. She knew the establishment, a *bierhaus* in Munich, Germany. *Does he already know that much about me?* The time was three days in the future at 10:30 p.m.

Munich was her favorite German city. The Prussian part of Germany always left her a bit cold, literally so in winter. Bavarians took life less seriously. Those beer halls, filled with food, beer, polka music, and good cheer were symbolic of a carefree lifestyle. A frown clouded her face, though, as she remembered that Munich was where Hitler had joined the German Workers' Party in 1919. *Who could have predicted at that time he would become such an evil monster?* She had known a few men like that in East Germany. The political labels didn't seem to matter when it came to those personalities.

She sighed. She doubted Langston would spring for the ticket. She'd have to buy it. If he didn't give her time off, she'd have to take two personal days. She had plenty of those, but

Langston would prefer she stay in London, working on that caseload.

She'd worked in both the old Scotland Yard and the New Scotland Yard. The latter, on Broadway in Victoria, had been more convenient for her commute, but they had moved the Metropolitan Police HQ back to the Curtis Green Building on the Victorian Embankment. She'd also preferred the office space she had at the Broadway facility, although both her offices were tiny.

The Art and Antiques Unit was considered backwaters by some and not successful in dealing with either victims or art thieves. Some inspectors had left to establish lucrative private practices victims often preferred over the Unit. She thought that would be a hassle for her, though, and a betrayal of Langston's trust and her long career at the Yard.

She stared at the paper cup's residue. *The coffee might be better here. We're lucky to have it.*

Attrition had taken its toll on the Unit too. People retiring weren't replaced. She'd eventually have to retire too. The bureaucratic nonsense of generating the required paperwork to avoid forced retirement—she's an essential person for the Unit, look at her marvelous record, bla, bla, bla—was helped along by Langston, but it was still a bloody bother.

One Yard inspector had called her Miss Marple. The nickname stuck in spite of her discouraging it, but she had never dealt with homicides. No one dared use the name to her face. And, although she still used her maiden name, she was not a Miss, but intense romantic relationships were less important now. There was always the prospect of a fling with a younger man, of course. She wasn't dead yet, after all.

She was a member of a vanishing class of old Yard inspectors. The official suggestion she should retire would be received again in a few months. She would have to defend herself yet again, with Langston's help, running a gauntlet designed to sap energy from any retirement-aged agent as the powers-that-be tried to replace them with younger ones they wanted to promote. It was more a young-blood issue than finance issue, though, because no one had a huge salary at the Yard.

Will I have enough energy to fight that battle again this year?

***

When Brookstone returned to her office, Jeremy Brand's email awaited. Acting on his data, she dialed security at Heathrow. She identified herself to the security agent who seemed impressed at first it was Scotland Yard calling, but his exuberance diminished when he heard she was from the Unit.

"I'm tracking an art thief. I need to view your security footage at Terminal 4 at Heathrow—in particular, Alitalia arrivals on the 16th."

"It would help to have a time window," said the agent.

She provided one and explained what she wanted to do. "I suppose I have to visit you there."

"Not if you send us the woman's picture. That's a short time window. With her pic, we can run security footage through facial recog and get you what you want."

"Give me an email address and I'll make a JPEG and send it to you. Thanks for the favor. I don't need a trip to the airport today. I have to fly to Germany in three days."

She sent the JPEG, barely glancing at the pic. Sylvia Bassett was pretty but forgettable, and Brookstone put her out of mind.

Computers were useful sometimes. *JPEGs and emails— you're not a complete Luddite, Esther.*

Later she found a snippet of video attached to an email message from airport security. She put everything she knew into a tidy package and, before going home, handed a file to Langston.

"What's this?"

"Check out this baggage locker in Terminal 4 at Heathrow," she said. "I'm betting the Bernini bust is in there. She was carrying a heavy old bowling ball bag like Yanks are partial to—the big balls, not candlepin ones. I suppose the woman prefers big ones, international pun intended."

He smiled. "And why are you giving this to me?"

"Because I need time to develop a cover for my trip to Munich."

He frowned. "Not on my timecard."

"George, the day you have timecards here is the day I walk out. You're forewarned. If it makes you feel more frugal with money that isn't yours, I can take one personal day. You owe me one for solving this case in record time."

He waved the folder. "Not solved until we have the bust and its thief."

"So, do you want me to strap on a holster and go after the bust, old man? I'd think you'd prefer to send some bobbies to bob out there and retrieve it. If it's not there, I owe you a curry dinner." *I'll combine you with Jeremy—a geriatric ménage à trois.*

"I never expected such quick action," he said. "I don't want to know how you did it. OK, your curry wager is accepted. Indian food is a weakness of mine, you know, and my wife hates it." He studied her for a moment. "On another note, I received the yearly paperwork from up-high. Do you want me to write another defense arguing to keep you on?" She nodded. He smiled. "Just checking. This Italian case will be mentioned, of course. International success stories always impress the old fools."

***

In the time she took to travel to her flat, Langston had left a message on her answering machine. The Bernini bust was found in the locker. Still no sign of the missing mistress, but Brookstone was sure her Italian Romeo would be happier with the return of his bust than with the return of his prodigal Juliet. *He's likely replaced her already.*

She had talked to Reggie Fox again. He had pulled in alongside her. There were no assigned parking spaces in the garage; just a general permit was required. That meant he could ignore all empty spaces and sidle up to her. *Jaguar versus BMW—two expensive British sedans in a standoff.* She watched to see if he dinged her vehicle as he opened the door.

"You're home early, Esther. Want to join me for some fine wine and cheese?"

She glared at him. "I suppose you haven't called management yet. I wonder how much of your debris will be on my balcony this evening."

"You're obsessed," he said.

"Let me invite you downstairs for wine and cheese instead so you can see your debris."

"I made my offer first."

"And I'll be the first to decline." She studied his car for a moment. "Are you trying to make your old vehicle look better by parking next to mine?"

"On the contrary. You're near the lift. I like that too."

"And that's where I'm heading."

She was in and closing the lift's mesh door before Fox could organize his briefcase and books. He taught French in a girl's public school. *A dirty old man teaching French to young girls? Now there's something to worry concerned parents!* Of course, Fox had been doing it for years, so he likely wasn't a pervert, only a lecherous gadfly.

After listening to Langston's message, she prepared some cheese and crackers and opened an Australian cabernet she fancied, a bit of a comfort snack to put her in the mind frame of an Italian *contessa*, widow of *Conte* Sartini—he would be aghast at her wine choice. That husband's family had fled Italy and settled in Switzerland when the fascists came to power. Alberto Sartini had made a living as a Swiss banker. Because Italy no longer recognized royalty, his claim to the title was dubious at best, but his Italian was refined, and the dashing young banker had swept her off her feet.

Because of the war, it would be hard for anyone to check on her husband's noble bloodlines. She decided to use Natalie's address. *Her country manor is damn impressive.* Possibly a bit rundown compared to the glitzy cinema actors and old rock stars' remodeled mansions in East and West Sussex—talk about *nouveau riche*—but its character had that Goldilocks touch, not too ostentatious but just right. She decided that would be enough. That the *contessa* now lived in England wouldn't be unusual either. War and its aftermath had torn Europe apart, and she was neither Italian nor Swiss. It was reasonable the widow had returned to her home country.

She would have to brush up on her Italian, though. The thief could be a polyglot and speak it well. Her German was nearly perfect, but she'd only spoken Italian on holidays and in the bedroom.

She called for a pizza.

***

While Brookstone waited, she decided to read the Scottish barrister's letter. She dropped it in surprise. *Angus MacDougall? Who the hell is he? Or was?* Apparently he'd just died, and she had inherited a Scottish castle from this unknown relative. *Now there's a conundrum. What do I do with a bloody castle?*

It wasn't even clear where Dughallach Castle was. Presumably near Edinburgh. She had a laptop, though, and used it. Location still wasn't clear, but she was able to study several pictures. The ancient edifice sat atop a knoll covered with windblown lush grass and strewn with old building stones. A lake could be seen in the distance. *Not bad scenery.* Close-ups showed an old rundown stone building, though, that looked like it hadn't survived the last Viking attack. *Oh my.*

Old Angus was easier to find. He had been an Edinburgh businessman. One photo showed him in traditional kilt, frilly white shirt with scarf matching the tartan of his kilt, and tam o'shanter; he was playing bagpipes. She hated them because they always reminded her of funerals. He was into his ancestry without a doubt. *Maybe why he still had the castle?* Not a bad looking fellow, either—strong and manly, even though the knees were a bit knobby.

She read farther into the letter. She inherited on condition she kept the castle. *Huh? Try and make me, barrister!* She tossed the letter aside when someone knocked on the door.

"Giorgio, please come in." She waved a ten-pound note at him. "Do you have twenty minutes?"

The delivery man arched his eyebrows. *What? Does he think I want—what do the Americans call it?—a quickie?* She had always admired his bulging muscles and smooth abs, of course. He was dressed in a muscle shirt, with horizontal stripes that made him look even more barrel-chested, and tight jeans; here was a Venetian boatman trolling for innocent female tourists. Her husbands had always treated her well, but they weren't athletic types. This Italian looked like he should be playing rugby for some rowdy English or Irish team or curling with Angus instead of delivering pizza.

"It depends. I can always tell Giancarlo I was held up in traffic."

Giancarlo must be his boss. "I need you to talk Italian to me, my man. I need practice. Tell me about your day."

They spent twenty-five minutes. Giorgio droned on about the old delivery car, bad London traffic, clients who didn't tip, his demanding girlfriend, and other trivia, Brookstone spurring him on with questions and comments. It was more like a mother-son conversation instead of an older woman trying to seduce a much younger man. *I'd need more time for that!*

***

"You speak excellent Italian, Mrs. Brookstone," Giorgio said at the session's end. "I detect a slight Swiss accent, though, also in your choice of words and sentence structure."

"My count grew up in Lugano. I practiced Italian with him, of course. I suppose my command of the language is influenced by him more than dealing with shopkeepers in the city's boutiques." She smiled and handed him the money. "Thank you so much. I needed to make sure I could converse well enough in an ordinary setting, not just the bedroom." She pointed to the notes. "Is that enough? I feel like I've received a tutoring session from a handsome Italian male model."

Giorgio blushed. "It's more than enough. Most of my customers don't even give me the time of day."

"Their loss, my friend."

He returned to the garage where he'd left his delivery vehicle.

"I'm going to report you," said Reggie Fox, who pulled in to park next to Giorgio's old car. "You can't park in here."

"I always do when I make deliveries," said Giorgio. "I'm never here that long."

"That doesn't matter." Fox got out of his BMW and removed some boxes of wine from the boot. "It's not allowed."

"Even when I deliver to you?" said Giorgio with a smile.

"When have I ever eaten pizza you have delivered?"

"About two months ago. You were entertaining a lady friend. I saw her in your bedroom." He winked at Fox. "Quite the *gambas* she was waggling too. You said she wanted pizza."

"Hmm. Yes, I remember. Gina. The mother of one of my students. Poor thing had just lost her husband. He left her for his secretary. I was consoling her."

"Yes, sometimes a man has to console a woman in that way."

"Indeed. Were you consoling Esther?"

"I was helping her brush up on her Italian."

"An unlikely story." He waved a hand at the delivery car. "I'll forget your blatant disregard for the rules of this building this time, but don't do it again. I'll have your relic towed."

"And tell management to pay for it?"

"You have fair warning."

***

Giorgio had done well, but Brookstone's mind had started to wander. Practicing Italian reminded her too much of her late husband....

Alberto Sartini's funeral had been a sad adventure. The count had been an incurable atheist, if that needed a cure, but he still wanted a memorial service. That wasn't the hard part. Dead husband #3 had also wanted his credo to be read at the ceremony. She found the leather folio containing the version in English to the right of his urn on her mantle. The ashes of #1 and #2 were on the left. She knew most of the credo by memory.

"I apologize to whomever is reading this credo. She or he will have a rough time with it if she or he has swallowed all the mumbo-jumbo from any modern religion that pretends a deity or deities look after the welfare of human beings. That's swine breath, pure and simple. There is no God—Jewish, Christian, or Muslim, or any other deities, for that matter. I'm sure of that. Religion has swindled human beings through the ages by demanding we believe in such tripe. Our only heavens and hells are found on this planet, they're manmade, and we'd better make a good go of it here because there's nothing waiting for us on the other side. There is no other side. I go to my death confident this is true, and yet I will embrace the darkness of sweet oblivion even knowing that I should have lived a better life, but also at ease knowing I did the best I could. To my sweet Esther, love of my life, if she outlives me, I wish her well. To others whose friendship I have cherished, please be assured fond memories of you accompany me to my grave. And to all I have maligned, please forgive me. My remains will become one with sweet Gaia once again, so please take care of this planet—it's the only one we have right now. Farewell."

At the funeral, Brookstone had to read her husband's credo in English, French, Italian, and German, the last three the "official languages" of Switzerland (the real language being money, of course). By the time she reached the Italian version, she could barely speak. She had never kept her promise to sprinkle his ashes in Lake Lugano, making his comment about sweet Gaia a lie. *Maybe someday. But then #1 and #2 might be lonely.*

She was more an agnostic, mostly because Alberto had created tremendous doubt by being so sure of himself. She was a regular visitor to the Atheist Alliance International website always with the intention of understanding him better. *You'd think at my age I'd want to be done with it all and ascertain what the afterlife, if any, is all about! But I'm following Alberto's advice: if this is my only chance, I'm going to make the most of it....*

***

After she reread the credo, ending with tears in her eyes, she reheated the pizza in the microwave—she liked it piping hot—and went at it, accompanying the fast food staple, a complete meal when it had several toppings, with another glass of cabernet, while still sobbing at the laptop.

She now decided she couldn't use Natalie's address. First, the letter had been sent to Lady Smythe, and she didn't want to assume her friend's identity. Second, she didn't want to cause problems for her dear but guileless friend either.

She had a better idea. She performed a search and found another estate in Oxfordshire for sale. Such sales weren't uncommon in Great Britain. Upkeep on such estates was expensive; so were taxes. Of course, now she had her own castle in Scotland. *How am I going to pay for that?*

Some estate owners covered expenses by renting to tourists. Some estates became national historical monuments and guided tours were conducted for a fee, even with owners still in residence, who sometimes conducted the tours in period costumes. Other owners sold their estates, often to *nouveau riche*—people with money who often wanted to make a statement, and a country estate with a Rolls or Bentley parked in front did the job nicely. Many estates in East and West Sussex shared the latter provenance, although the actors and old rock stars living there most likely preferred other cars to English ones. In any case, an expensive estate wasn't something just anyone could afford, whether old wealth or new.

The one she found would become *Contessa* Sartini's for the purposes of her cover. The German art thief might see it for sale like she had and wonder, but she'd have a story ready: she had decided to move back to Lugano, so she put it on the market. Unless he called the real estate broker, he would have no idea who the seller was; that was something not divulged for such upscale properties until the sale went through. The connection to Switzerland would also be useful in convincing the thief she had oodles of money stashed away there, enough to buy a Rembrandt and more.

Am I ready? No, she needed to upgrade her wardrobe. She couldn't be in the market for a Rembrandt looking like a commoner, could she? She smiled. She hadn't been shopping for a while.

Part Two

People who say it cannot be done should not interrupt those who are doing it.

—George Bernard Shaw

Chapter Seven
Munich

Flights around Europe are often short. One spends more time in airports than on planes. As a consequence, people often prefer trains. Brookstone flew to Frankfort, then caught the train to Munich, adding to both sets of statistics with a late plane in London and a pleasant train ride from Frankfort.

Germany is a mixture of its past and future; many Germans still wallow in their World War Two guilt for the war and its atrocities, yet enjoy their status as Europe's economic powerhouse. *Both cause national angst*, she thought.

The *Hauptbahnhof* on *Bayerstrasse* in Munich is a modern building devoid of any old world charm. The old building had taken several hits during the war and was put out of its misery by allied bombs in 1944. She walked out wheeling her overnight bag, hailed a cab, and was soon installed in a comfortable hotel not far from the *bierhaus* where her meeting was to take place. After tidying up a bit, she took the lift to the lobby. A short man rose from a wingchair and walked toward her.

"My dear Esther, lovely as ever," said Bastiann van Coevorden, her favorite Interpol agent. He took her hand and kissed it. "I trust you had a good trip."

I might remind people of Miss Marple, but he reminds me of Hercule Poirot. The agent was a bit shorter, more muscled, and less rotund than the actor who played the famous detective, but the tidy handlebar mustache was just as prominent. He was also more energetic and in better shape. He was Dutch, not Belgian, although she knew there were Dutch immigrants in Belgium, so family trees in the real world were mixed.

Their lives were intertwined from work and more. She was fond of him yet not sure where to take their relationship. They enjoyed being with each other. Their trysts in Europe were more frequent than in England, though. With his work in Interpol, he was restricted mostly to cases on the continent. *Long distance relationships are such a hassle!*

In the old Interpol, agents didn't make arrests. That was still generally true—they worked more with local authorities—but now agents could arrest criminals and act alone if necessary. Van Coevorden was based in Amsterdam, but he was often in France, especially at the HQ in Lyon. He also had worked with that NYPD detective and Brookstone on a case involving stolen art.

The two, Brookstone and van Coevorden, shared similar cultural tastes. Their European dates often began with a concert or visit to an art show followed by dinner. *But sometimes it goes beyond that.* She frowned. *Tonight we won't have the time.*

"You know I hate planes, dear Bastiann, so the trip is never good. I'm so happy you could make it."

"I concur. No planes for me either. I drove from Salzburg."

"I hope I didn't inconvenience you."

"On the contrary. I'm between cases and took a few days off before heading back to Amsterdam by way of Lyon. Munich was a good place to stop *en route*. Please sit and tell me about your case."

He ordered coffee for both of them, and she brought him up to date.

"I don't approve," he said after she finished. "You should have called us. This could be dangerous, just like that cruise lines case." He was referring to yet another case where Interpol hadn't been involved.

She had seen his frown growing as she talked. "Oh, please. Imagine: recovering a Rembrandt!"

"How will you explain how you obtained this criminal's number?"

"From a friend, of course, who knew I was eager to buy a masterpiece. You Interpol folks would only botch the works, I'm sure."

"Pass me off as your husband. I speak Italian."

She framed his face with her two hands. "My apologies, Bastiann. You're a dear friend and have given me excellent company during some continental trips, but you're not husband material." She winked. "At least, not yet."

"So... I'm only backup for your other paramours?"

"And dinner companion this evening, assuming you're available."

He nodded and smiled. "I feel so used. I'm a Dutch gigolo."

"Can't we just enjoy each other's company? You're a charming man. And I can be charming too, if I'm among pleasant company. Let me tell you about the Bernini bust now sitting on my baby grand."

"That should be interesting. Have they increased Scotland Yard's pay that much?"

"Patience. Let's decide on a restaurant first."

***

Unlike the French, Italians, and Spaniards, Germans eat dinner at reasonable hours. They might play outside afterward, especially in summer months, but dinner hours are similar to those of Great Britain and the U.S. The British manage a decent hour in spite of substantial breakfasts and teatime snacks; the Americans were forced into it by horrendous commutes in metropolitan areas. Fancier German restaurants took longer to prepare and serve your meal, but Brookstone was still standing outside the *bierhaus* fifteen minutes before the appointed time.

She figured her art thief would spot her as the only lone woman in the hall. She found a table for two as far away as possible from the traditional polka band and ordered a stein. She didn't plan on having any of the usual accompaniments. She liked bacon, as most British do, but she had avoided sausage all her life, especially the authentic Bavarian kind—she considered it uncouth to eat the intestines of livestock. She also didn't like heavy cheese. *But to each his own.* She made a mental note to look up the statistics for the incidence of German heart disease, especially in Bavaria.

The singer onstage—the stage was an open kiosk in the center of the hall—seemed to be eyeing her. Dressed in *Kniebundhosen*, traditional leather shorts that looked like a Welsh farmer's overalls cut off above the knees, she could tell the latter were knobby and he had varicose veins. *Old age hits us all.* She liked his smile, though, and he was otherwise in decent shape—a large elf from the Black Forest singing traditional German drinking songs. Polkas were interspersed, but no one danced... yet. She raised her stein to him and he nodded toward her. *Yes, definitely eyeing me.*

She had dressed more for dinner with van Coevorden and not the beer hall, so she felt a bit overdressed for the venue. Black evening dress, faux pearls, high heels—not too high, because she had no desire to sprain or break an ankle at her age. The scent of her expensive perfume was lost in the busy place's traditional Teutonic aromas.

She looked around and saw what looked like a 40-60 split between tourists and locals. She thought it was a good sign there were many locals. *Of course, I look like a tourist—a rich lady with too much money.* That was intentional, of course.

A much younger man approached, pulled out the other chair at her small table, and sat. His pasty skin was unpleasant in the bright light of the hall. He looked like an old-fashioned funeral director from a Sherlock Holmes novel. *How I love those tales!* He extended a hand across the table, carefully avoiding the half-full stein.

"A good evening to you, madam," he said. She shook the proffered hand. It was strong but clammy. *Maybe from working with embalming fluid?* She smiled. "I understand you are interested in acquiring some priceless art."

"Right to the point, aren't you? If what you're offering is truly priceless, we need talk no more."

He smiled and shrugged. "A figure of speech. Call me Joachim, by the way."

"A nice Jewish name, but if you're selling black market art, you didn't benefit at all by being 'raised by God,'" she said.

Now a frown—he knew what she was referring to in her verbal parry. He removed his old-style eyeglasses and cleaned them. With his slicked back hair and charcoal-gray conservative suit, complete with vest, he looked out of place in the 21st century. *Definitely a Conan Doyle villain. He only needs a top hat if a funeral director, or a homburg otherwise. Or did they come later?*

"That's not my name, of course. And I'm not Jewish. But your comment proves you're cultured. Tell me about yourself."

"Will you also tell me about yourself?"

He frowned. "No. My only aim is to ensure the painting will have a good home."

She smiled. "I would think your aim is to ensure you make a tidy profit on some stolen art. Don't tell me about yourself then.

Tell me about how you came by the painting instead. Provenance is always important."

"I'm afraid I can't do that either."

"Can you tell me your price for this priceless painting then? I might be rich, but my funds aren't limitless."

"One-half million euros will allow you to play."

"To play? Is this some kind of sporting event? I'm not a gambler. Never have been. My father occasionally bought a Sweepstakes ticket, though."

"In a way it is a sporting event—an auction, to be precise. Bidding starts at one-half million euros, to be deposited in a special account in Zurich."

"If I lose in this bidding, what becomes of my money?"

"It's wired back to your account, of course."

"Sorry. I'm not playing your game. I don't trust you."

Joachim stood and nodded. "It's the opportunity of a lifetime."

"On the contrary, I see no opportunity but risk. Why should I trust an art thief?"

"I'm not a thief. I'm an art dealer."

"Do you have any other players?"

"For this painting, you would be the first. That is all I can say at the moment."

"You might have a difficult time interesting other players, although I suppose a half-million euros is nothing to some. I made my money the hard way, so I'm frugal about my spending, even if it's at a level beyond the average person's."

"And how did you make your money?"

"I won't discuss details, because you were less than forthcoming about your own background. I'll only tell you what is public knowledge: I married an Italian count who was also a

Swiss banker. Good night, Joachim." *And that's the whole truth!*

The art dealer frowned, spun on his heels, and left the *bierhaus.*

That went well, she thought.

***

"He'll be back," Brookstone said to van Coevorden over the mobile. "He made that offer to see if I'd take the bait. I think he's a Nazi."

"Not an original, for sure, at that young age. And not with the name Joachim."

"There was a twinkle in his eye when he said that—a private joke, and a telling one. He was unhappy when I caught him at it. He might be speaking for a group. We need to dig into your databases. I have his pic, by the way."

"Did he see you take it?"

"I pretended I was talking to someone on the mobile as he approached my table. I'd turned the flash off. There was plenty of light. We should try facial recognition. The name Joachim won't help us much."

"So, it's 'us' now. Are you officially requesting Interpol's help?"

"No, I'm asking for *your* help. My superior won't touch this, I'm afraid. I had to badger him unmercifully to obtain two days off."

"Understandable. You're a small unit. Can you download the mobile pic to your laptop and then send me a JPEG? A computer programmer owes me a favor, so I'll collect on it. He'll be able to enhance it and use facial recognition."

"He'll have to go international. I don't think this fellow is a Yank, but he could be South American. No accent. Of course, he could be from anywhere." She thought a moment. "This is an organization. He's only the Liverpool agent representing the boys' rock band. Maybe you can search for active groups. This one has enough sophistication to open Swiss bank accounts for participants in the auction. That's smart, by the way. They open an account in the bidder's name and the latter makes a deposit. Looks to be on the up and up. Interpol would never guess."

"Hmm. I suppose not. Swiss banks don't appreciate us. They're still reeling from Hervé Falcioni's leak of account files in 2007. We'd be extremely lucky if they told us anything."

"I'm not sure I approve of whistleblowers. That fellow Snowden left a bad taste in my mouth. Putin's welcome to him. The Yanks should throw Snowden in jail and lose the key if he ever returns to the U.S. But I suppose some whistleblowers are useful. I loved that all those VIPs were exposed when the Panama Papers went public. That showed how rotten the world is, my friend." She hesitated. "My Swiss accounts are legit, by the way."

"That's news. I mean, that you had Swiss accounts. So... you're a rich old lady?"

"A cougar, as Americans would say, who needs her play money. Mine's all for retirement, of course."

"This gigolo might have to look into your finances. Marrying you might allow me to retire too."

"Don't be absurd," she said. "Marriage would deal a terrible blow to my playtime. But I'll keep you informed."

Her inner being smiled. She'd always been chummy with Bastiann van Coevorden. He was an agent, but also a gentleman. *The Belgian Poirot made more money as a private investigator for hire. Interpol's salaries are as bad as Scotland Yard's. Given my seniority, maybe worse?*

Chapter Eight
Munich

Hal Leonard swirled his single malt beneath his nose and then took a sip. "She's asking for trouble, old man," he said.

Van Coevorden nodded. "You're probably right. I worry about her."

Leonard, a colleague in the Interpol bureaucracy, cultivated the shabby American tourist look that was good cover in many situations.

"She thinks they're Nazis," Leonard said. "I wonder if they're among the groups I'm considering in my case." He was querying van Coevorden about gun shipments to criminal elements in Europe and the Middle East—specifically rightwing groups and terrorists.

"She always thinks they're Nazis until proven otherwise," said van Coevorden. "It's a bit of an obsession. Stolen artwork is her specialty, and they stole lots of it. You saw *The Monuments Men*."

"A good flick," Leonard said, "but this painting is among many still lost. It's possible, you know, that it's all a bluff, they don't have the painting, and just want to scam a bunch of old people. Not to say the fools wouldn't deserve it, dealing with the black market."

"Of course. But let's suppose they have this painting. Why go through a bidding process?"

"To have access to buyers' bank accounts? To drive the price up? I'm more interested in the following question: are they acquiring funds for illegal arms purchases? That money comes from somewhere. By interrogating buyers, I can find the sellers."

Van Coevorden studied his friend. Where the Dutchman wore a tie even in the bar's informal setting, Hal was wearing a short sleeve shirt not tucked in, khakis, and sneakers that made him look younger than his years. Hal's tanned face had wrinkles on the forehead and in the corners of his eyes; a receding hairline complemented his thinning hair. He was not a young man—just a bit younger than van Coevorden, in fact—but he had the appearance of a hard-living, well-traveled American, which he was in many ways.

"We'll have to answer that question later," said van Coevorden. "I have to decide what to do with Esther."

They were both treating the single-malt like cognac, sipping it from inverse bell-shaped Glencairn glasses and enjoying the aroma. Good whiskey could serve in that role.

Van Coevorden put down his glass. "She can kick butt, you know."

"I suppose anyone at the Yard has to be prepared to do that," said Leonard. "But you think she's too confident? I like that in a woman, my friend."

"So do I, to a certain point. I don't want someone I'm fond of to be hurt, though. Exuberance and over-confidence can be the death of you."

"Well put. So, what are you going to do?"

"Play along with her for a bit, I guess. What else can I do? She's too stubborn. If I nag her too much, she'll tell me to bugger off and do what she damn pleases."

"I have a sister like that. She's in gay Paris, and I mean gay. She and her lesbian lover had tickets to that rock concert where that massacre took place, but they missed it. The lover had eaten some bad shellfish and took sick. The only time I've ever appreciated bad shellfish."

"Where are these people getting guns?"

"Anywhere they can. It drives us nuts. Know what drives us nuts even more?" Van Coevorden shook his head in the negative. "That authorities in the E.U. countries don't collaborate. Countries in the Union are too independent. We saw that in that other Castilblanco caper."

"His foe was only one psychotic Palestinian," said van Coevorden. "The terrorists in Paris and Brussels were better organized, as the recent ones have been."

"The gun buyers aren't just fanatics bent on *jihad*. Nazis, ISIS, al Qaeda—what's the difference? Illegal arms dealers are having a field day getting rich off fanatics. Especially in Europe where the demand is high and tough laws make for short supplies."

"Your assignment is a bit more complicated than mine, but I share your frustration. I mostly interface with local and national authorities, but there's not a whole lot of collaboration. I'm sorry I can't help you."

"Just keep your ear tuned for any gossip about illegal arms, especially about rightwing groups like neo-Nazis. Good intel is hard to come by. And I'll hear it from you faster than from anyone else."

Chapter Nine
Munich

When van Coevorden returned to his hotel, the man at the desk had two messages for him. One was from Brookstone giving him her return flight information that had changed slightly. The other was from Lyon HQ. He had a new case; files had been sent to his laptop.

He returned to his room, figuring he had enough of a nightcap with Leonard, undressed, smoothing his clothes and hanging them up for the drive to Amsterdam the next day. He sat in his boxers and accessed the laptop.

Not quite Amsterdam, but Rotterdam, the busiest port in Europe. He was to meet a French-speaking agent who needed help with a kidnapping. *Why not use local authorities? That question will have to be answered tomorrow.*

He would be driving through France. He considered French his second language. His mother had spoken it to him, both mother and father firm in the belief that any citizen of Europe should speak three or four languages. He spoke it better than he wrote it, though.

His mother had died in Paris....

***

"Yes, that's her," the younger Bastiann, a university student, had said to the coroner. "What did they steal?"

"Her purse and jewelry. I'm told she was working a case. She was headed to the theater where she was supposed to meet a suspect."

"She what? A case? Absurd. My mother was a retired university professor."

"You didn't know? She worked undercover for the Sûreté. Perhaps I shouldn't have said that. I don't see that it makes any difference now, though. She's dead, after all."

"I live in Amsterdam. She returned to Paris after my father's death."

"Hmm. Possibly the police can give you some background to give you closure then. I'm sorry."

It took van Coevorden a week, but he managed to meet his mother's superior.

"Your mother is a French heroine, young Bastiann."

"Let's get to why in a moment. Have they caught the person who killed her?"

"No. We're sure it was the suspect she was going to meet. Somehow he discovered she was working undercover. He tried to make her murder look like a mugging gone badly. I'm sorry."

He hadn't listened to the rest of his mother's story. He had felt numb when he received her diary from her superior. He decided then and there to go into law enforcement.

Some ten years later, they caught his mother's killer.

***

Van Coevorden went to his nightstand and found his wallet. He took out the old picture taken at Christmas in 1998, the year before his mother's death. He was standing beside her. He smiled. He went to his suitcase and found her diary. He always carried the picture and sometimes the diary, both for good luck.

He turned to where a leather bookmark indicated a favorite passage.

"I do what I do to respond to a greater calling. Many struggle to make ends meet and suffer many hardships while criminal elements of society try to steal what they have worked so hard to obtain. Many innocents even die at the hands of these criminal elements. That is my greater calling: protect the innocents. I hope my son one day understands this as well. If one can protect those innocents from harm, we give real meaning to our lives. Those who are able should do this."

"I have failed my son by avoiding this aspect of his education. Instead, I have tried to shelter him from the evil in the world. I would not want him to follow my path, for there lies danger. I want him to be safe. What more could a mother want? Nevertheless, I think of all those mothers who have seen their sons and daughters die before they do, for whatever reason. I am so lucky in that respect. Whatever my son becomes, I shall love him always and pray that their fate is not mine. That's a terrible fate for a mother."

No, you didn't succeed, mother—I followed your path. He brushed away a tear, remembering her face and personality. *A similar personality to Esther's.* If it's true women look for men like their fathers for relationships, does the same apply to men? *Brookstone even looks like her a bit!* He laughed. A therapist would have a field day with that.

Of course, he wasn't about to see a therapist about his relationship with Brookstone, even though he might need some sound advice. His experience with therapists after shootings—required by most law enforcement agencies everywhere—had never been productive. He didn't expect a relationship counselor to offer much help either.

And, if I'm crazy, so what? His immediate problem, of course, was trying to keep her safe. *She makes that almost impossible!*

Chapter Ten
Sardinia

Hal Leonard met his contact Hussein in a small café near the international container terminal in Cagliari, Sardinia. He was waiting in a back booth, nursing a beer, and facing the door.

"*Salaam alaikum*," said Leonard, sliding into the booth opposite Hussein.

Hussein responded to his "peace with you" by saying, "*Wa alaikum salaam*," meaning "and peace upon you."

"You have information for me?" said Leonard.

Hussein, a Muslim, was what authorities in the U.S. would call a snitch. He was skilled at moving amongst the Middle Eastern groups digging up dirt on what was going on in the strange world of terrorists, gun smugglers, mercenaries, and more common thugs, especially those who professed to be followers of Islam. Unlike a cop's snitch, though, Hussein was almost a devout Muslim; he just happened to like alcoholic beverages. He did what he did because he abhorred people of his faith who really didn't follow the principles of the Koran.

"Some of your gun smugglers are working through this port," said Hussein. "They're quite organized. Their clients in the E.U. are outnumbered by clients in the Middle East and Africa, though. There's one shipment about to go out which would interest Interpol more than normal. Maybe the Israelis too." He said the last with a smile.

"I don't want the buyers necessarily, just the suppliers, but am willing to let the buyers lead me to the suppliers."

"You'll need help here. I don't know where you'll get it. The Italians don't worry too much about Sardinia except for its lovely beaches. Like I said, these smugglers are organized. Don't fight them alone."

Leonard nodded. "Who are their suppliers?"

"Americans, by way of some cartels. Some of that is simply payment for raw product, but they're making quite a killing selling arms too."

"Probably not as lucrative as selling drugs in the U.S. and Europe, but there might be fewer middlemen between them and their arms clientele. Any names?"

"Some Peruvian infidel named Ernesto Lopez is the kingpin, but some American henchmen run this little side business. It's a huge organization, my friend."

"And what's of interest to Israel?"

"One client, big by German standards, but small in the grand scheme of things, is an Austrian-German neo-Nazi group. I have no particulars, but there's a rumor they partially finance their purchases by selling old masterpieces the Nazis stole in World War Two. Cute, huh? I hate Nazis, by the way, almost as much as Jews. They both believe they're the master race." Remembering the conversation with van Coevorden, Leonard frowned. Hussein misinterpreted his expression. "OK, I'm out of line. Not all Germans are bad, not all Jews are bad, and not all my brethren are bad. Far from it. Unfortunately the evil ones do a lot of damage in this fucked-up world."

"I'll have to plan on how to go after the smugglers," said Leonard. "I have contacts in the *Carabinieri*. Maybe I'll expand the Italians' interest in Sardinia beyond fun in the sun."

***

At his hotel that evening, Leonard pondered what Hussein had told him. First, he didn't like the expansion of a drug cartel into arms smuggling. They had to get their weapons from somewhere—the thugs in Juarez had nearly killed him—but becoming suppliers was a new twist. Making money from selling illegal drugs wasn't as profitable anymore, with the legalization of marijuana in many places and an overabundance of cheap heroin. Human trafficking and other sidelines had become popular, but the arms smugglers and cartels had always seemed to operate apart.

Second, he was worried about arms dealers supplying terrorists and criminals anywhere, but especially those living in Europe as citizens while plotting their crimes. Most E.U. countries, unlike the U.S., had strict gun laws. You could buy a firearm on a street corner in Manhattan, but they were harder to obtain in Europe, and therefore more profitable for the smugglers.

Third, he would have to help van Coevorden out. Was the Nazi group the same one he and Esther Brookstone were trying to bring down? It seemed like it. But he wasn't going to cry wolf until he had more facts.

Chapter Eleven
London

Next morning Brookstone caught the fifty-minute flight to London's Heathrow. She was back at her desk after a leisurely lunch near Trafalgar Square. The *kebob* picked up her spirits enough to face what awaited her back at HQ.

"Back early, I see," said Langston. "In case you're interested, we still haven't nabbed the mistress. She was last seen in Edinburgh. Turns out she went to school up that way. We'll apprehend her eventually. Good police work, Esther."

"What will happen to her?"

"We're not sure. The old duffer in Italy won't press charges now that he has his beloved Bernini back. The case is in hands of courts and barristers once she's in custody, and that's local police's job. Our case is closed. You might be called to testify later, though. How'd Nazi hunting go?"

"Not every shady art deal involves ex-Nazis, you know. I made contact with the art thief, though." She filled him in. "Snapped a photo with my mobile. Van Coevorden is processing it with facial recognition software."

"You involved Interpol? We could have done that."

"After fighting through layers of bureaucracy? Bastiann is willing to grease wheels, as they say."

"And you don't think I'm able to do that?"

"Yes, if it were only up to you, but there are too many wheels to grease here. The Yard isn't immune to the grand British tradition of stultifying bureaucracy. And we don't have programmers per se." She studied him for a moment. "You'll also have to admit you didn't express any interest in the case."

"I thought it was a long shot."

"And, now that I've made contact, you want in on the action? Oh, please."

He sighed. "That's an unfair comment. But you're right. Any case that's satisfactorily closed helps prove the worth of our Unit. You've closed some big ones."

"Thank you for the compliment, if I can interpret your comment that way. This one's far from closed, though. We might be left hanging like in that case involving the Gardner Museum's paintings. I'm sure that old rascal Richard Metzger is here or on the continent somewhere. He wouldn't dare return to the States."

She was referring to a case where she had consulted with two NYPD homicide detectives and the FBI; it had involved stolen and still missing paintings from the Isabella Stuart Gardner Museum in Boston, Massachusetts. The main culprit had managed to elude the Yanks and British authorities. He was still high on Brookstone's list of people she wanted to apprehend, and for multiple reasons.

"What will you do if this art thief contacts you again?"

"Tell him I'm still interested if he gives me some guarantees." She waited to see his expression and decided to broach a new topic. "Can I ask for your advice?"

"Not romantic advice, I hope. I'm a bit out of practice."

She smiled. "No. We were talking about the Bernini thief from Edinburgh. I inherited a castle up that way."

"You're kidding. What are you going to do with a castle?"

"Precisely my problem." She told him about the conditions for inheritance. "I'm not sure what will happen if I don't keep the castle."

"Talk to the barrister. Maybe it just reverts to the state?"

"And the state might demolish it. It could be classified as an eyesore."

"And you wouldn't want that to happen?"

"I'm not sure. I wouldn't want old MacDougall's ghost to haunt me."

"Do atheists believe in ghosts?"

"I'm not an atheist most of the time. I was speaking metaphorically. I would be going against that old man's wishes, you know. In a sense, I shouldn't care, but I learned enough about him to admire him a little."

"Like I said, talk to the barrister. Get your facts straight first. You might not make enough at the Yard to even pay taxes."

"What a dreadful thought. Thanks for bringing that up!"

He shrugged and smiled. "I'd focus on Rembrandt's Angel. But do try to dispatch some other cases too, if you would be so kind. And keep me better informed."

She gave him a salute.

***

That evening she ate dinner late and was attempting to play a Chopin nocturne at her baby grand while admiring her faux Bernini, when her mobile's ringtone destroyed the mood. She stopped, stood, and decided to finish the wine. After blowing out the candles, she made her way to the desk, her flowing nightgown swishing along the hardwood floor. She checked her hands to make sure there was no cabernet on them. Smiling and thinking of Lady Macbeth, she picked up the mobile.

"Deposit the funds. We have established an account so only you will be able to release them to us if you win the bidding."

"I'll confirm that." But the art thief had already hung up.

She could cover the initial bid with her retirement funds. She wondered how high the bids would go afterward. The painting was indeed priceless. The sky was the limit.

She expressed her doubts to van Coevorden during the next call.

"I'll see what I can do if it comes to that," he said. "There's a way to make it appear funds are there when they're not. We've used it on some kidnapping cases. There's no real money now—it's all electronic, you know."

Yes, it is a bit like a ransom. "Swiss banks have changed some, haven't they?"

"They've been smacked around," he said. "They're still a haven for absconding tyrants' funds after they rape a country, underworld barons, and tax cheats, but yes, times are changing. I prefer their chocolates."

"A man after my own heart," said Brookstone. "So the initial bid is on me. A bit risky, but I want to recover this painting and nab the thieves."

"Understood. I'd make the first your number one priority. The second could be dangerous."

"You know, this could be only the start. Maybe these people have all the paintings that were bound for Hitler's museum and are still missing. It would be a master stroke to recover them. Very exciting, my dear Bastiann."

"If that's the case, danger increases by a factor of one hundred," said van Coevorden. "You need to be careful."

"Back at you, my handsome Dutchman."

After she hung up, she went to check her Swiss bank account data to see how high she could go in the bidding. *It's only money.* She'd never arranged for electronic exchanges, though, not trusting online banking when a large amount of money was involved. A quick trip to Zurich was needed. *I should have gone from Munich.*

***

Next morning she called Langston at home. He agreed to give her another day. She caught Swiss Air's eight o'clock flight from Heathrow, landed, and took a cab to the bank. She always thought it might be the model used by J. K. Rowling in her *Harry Potter* series, complete with goblins, but there were plenty of London banks that looked just as gothic, and they were run by the same wizened creatures. She went through the process of making the transfer of funds, put all the paperwork in her large purse, and returned to the airport.

While waiting for the plane, she remembered how much Alberto Sartini loathed Zurich in comparison to his beautiful Lugano. She'd always thought the commercial capital of Switzerland to be ugly too. Banking there was a matter of convenience for her. Flights to Zurich were easy; to Lugano, not so much. She justified keeping her funds in the country, an inconvenience, by thinking there was no reason the U.K. should be able to tax what she and Alberto had earned during their years working in Switzerland. It was possible she was breaking the law; she'd never checked. She couldn't remember if the British government had considered her legally married to the man, and she didn't much care.

Of course, Alberto was Italian, so he'd be more at home in Lugano. Zurich's airport passengers reflected the polyglot country's three languages, though, providing an interesting experience comparable to Belgium, Canada, and Ireland, other countries where there were more than one official language. Nothing like New York City with its eight hundred languages, but one could only call English official there, and American English at that.

She was no expert on world cultures but found them interesting. The stranger a culture was, the more interesting. *Funny I don't feel that way about Swiss culture, and it is strange. They seem to be an anomaly—part of Europe, yet aloof and withdrawn.*

She knew her melancholy often reared its ugly head when she was in Switzerland. *Maybe it's because the only Swiss citizens I've ever respected were two: Alberto, my beloved count and that little Jewish clerk in the patent office in Bern, both immigrants.* She smiled. Her Alberto had put all others to shame.

Chapter Twelve
London

Brookstone drove to work fuming. Her Jaguar had a ding in the right rear wheel-cover. Reggie Fox's BMW had stood beside it. Sure enough, a smear of blue metallic paint from her beloved car was on the BMW's left bumper. She snapped a picture of it with her mobile. He would receive the repair shop's bill.

"You do get around, don't you?" said Langston when she returned to the office. He handed her a computer printout and winked. "You might be interested in this."

She read the essentials and then smiled. "I suppose that's justice in a way. We still don't have the paintings, though. And now someone has a homicide case to solve."

The bulletin indicated Richard Metzger, the old Nazi they were looking for from the case with the Yanks, was dead. Dutch police had found his body floating in a canal in Amsterdam.

"Considering what that git did besides steal a few paintings, good riddance, I'd say," said Langston.

I suppose for my purposes I can now count that case as closed. "No time for backslapping." She pointed to the pile on her desk. "When will we achieve the paperless office?"

"Never. Besides, a pile of cases reminds my inspectors there are always more to solve."

"Then toddle off and let me return to work. Chatting with you is entertaining, but I'm sure you still want me to justify my meager pay."

He nodded. "Want me to inform those two American detectives?"

"I'll call tonight. I'll catch them in the afternoon there."

***

"He's out of office right now on a case," said Detective Dao-Ming Chen from NYPD homicide, Castilblanco's partner.

"Just pass him this FYI then," said Brookstone. "They found *Herr* Metzger floating dead in an Amsterdam canal. That brings some partial closure to that awful case."

"Except for the missing art," said Chen. "It's been a while. How are you, Esther?"

Brookstone realized she hadn't begun with the usual social pleasantries. *Damn!* "I'm OK. More arthritic every day. How are you and Rollie?"

"Still trying to solve murders. We sometimes split the caseload and look for quickies to solve. Everything's about stats now. Our superiors want to see more cases solved. It's a bit like the doctors' situation, especially internists, going crazy trying to take care of all the new patients who are now covered. Same personnel, more clients."

"No different here, but everyone is covered in our single-payer medical system. You Yanks need to do away with the insurance companies and restrain the big drug companies." *Take that, you conservative bitch!* Brookstone had never liked Chen much. She seemed to be a good cop, but she was too conservative. She couldn't understand how the progressive Castilblanco could work with her. "Give my regards to the big guy."

She hung up. She would never warm up to Chen. *Maybe just my jealousy?* What a body the stoic Asian woman had! She looked like an ex-model. Castilblanco was more her opposite. Yin and yang, to keep the Chinese metaphor going. She smiled. She considered herself to be neither leftwing nor right. She'd rather be in the middle of the plane went it went down.

Chen's partner reminded her of her count, not in looks but in personality, although the big fellow was now a Buddhist. *Maybe a Buddhist is an old-style atheist?* Castilblanco was just a genuinely good fellow, while Chen was cold and aloof. *I guess that has nothing to do with politics, only personalities.*

She sampled her stir fry. *Too much ginger?* She didn't often cook when she ate alone, but that evening she wanted some spicy roughage in her life to accompany her white wine. She remembered Castilblanco had promised her Indian cuisine. *Maybe I should have gone out?* There was a curry house less than three blocks away.

Her mobile rang.

"We are at five," said Joachim. "The others didn't make the cut."

"I thought it would go to the highest bidder?"

"We adapt the rules as needed. A real auction allows everyone else to outbid you until everyone declines to bid except the winner."

"That rule makes the winner pay too much. I never liked it. Real estate pariahs use it all the time to increase their commissions."

"Are you withdrawing?"

"How much time do I have to think about it?"

"Forty-eight hours starting at Greenwich midnight. If your next bid isn't made by then, you're out."

"Does the extra over my existing deposit have to be in that Swiss bank account?"

"No. With your first deposit, we'll assume you're honest. Call this same number and place your bid."

You're honest? This from an art thief? "And if I make the new bid and don't win, what happens?"

"You'll take your deposit and enjoy your money elsewhere. We'll keep you in mind, though. We have other paintings we will auction off."

All the missing paintings destined for Hitler's museum? "Thank you for that offer. I'm an art lover, not an investor, though."

"I understand. We have more paintings needing some love, madam."

There was a click! as he hung up.

OK. I won't need any more money...until I do.

But she didn't want the painting. She wanted to return it to its rightful owners and put Joachim and his gang of art thieves in jail. *But, as Bastiann says, the painting is the priority. And the rest is dangerous.*

Chapter Thirteen
London

Next day she took a long lunch followed by a walk to Trafalgar Square where she found a bench. She lamented the state of Admiral Nelson's statue. *They should clean the pigeon poop off the poor fellow more often.*

She took the cheap mobile from her purse and placed the bid, doubling what she had deposited in the Swiss bank account. She winked at Nelson. *You beat the Spanish and French fleets, old boy, and made the British navy master of the seas. Can I beat the Germans?* Old Winston had, in spite of the French.

She maintained a private mental war with historians and their recording of history for consumption by others. First, she knew the adage was true: victors rewrite history for their own benefit. Cromwell might have tried to make the Empire more democratic, but he also murdered, plundered, and tore apart families. Just ask the Irish. And Wellington should never have fought the battle of Waterloo because old Bonaparte had returned from exile and no longer had a taste for empire. At the end, the little corporal would have been content making needed reforms in France that could have been a model for reformers in oppressive European countries, possibly heading off the mad slaughter in World War One.

She kept her thoughts to herself for the most part. Historians were as stubborn as other academics, if not more so. They were the ultimate "spin doctors." She smiled. She liked that American terminology. Twisting everything around for public consumption was spin in the Yanks' vernacular. But English aristocrats, politicians, and historians had invented the technique centuries ago before Columbus even reached North America. *Maybe even before the Vikings?*

The most egotistical of all were those who wrote about themselves. Churchill, a bulldog of a man, had been one of the worse. Yet, whether good or bad, he had usually devised some plan of attack. Like Churchill, she needed such a plan now. She was almost certain Germans or Austrians were involved in the auction. If not, the thieves were still devious people and dangerous. Her one ace in the hand was that she was stealthy—the bad guys wouldn't suspect an old, rich, and aristocratic widow. *Unless they discover I work for the Yard!*

Her present plan, besides being incomplete, had a fatal flaw. She had no idea what to do if she won the bidding. *Bollocks, I don't know what to do if I lose!* She had to track Joachim and his gang before bidding closed. That Plan A was a work in progress; Plan B was nonexistent.

She called her friend Ambreesh Singh.

"I have a tiny problem," she said.

"And a good day to you too, madam," he said.

The British are too damned polite! She smiled at that thought, though—Singh's family had origins beyond the present U.K. She had tried many times to train him to be less obsequious. Most people didn't deserve politeness. *Quite the contrary!*

"Yes, yes, but cut the pleasantries. If I bring you my mobile, can you locate a caller?"

"No, not if his mobile is without a locator chip. I might be able to locate nearby mobile towers. Where did this person of interest call from?"

"Germany? Not here anyway."

"All the better. A com satellite might have been used as a waystation. I can retrieve some information from that too. Where do we meet?"

"I'm in Trafalgar Square right now. Where are you?"

"I can't say, but I'll catch the Underground. I'll be there in half an hour."

Brookstone liked a Greek pastry shop near there. She would have just enough time for a *baklava* treat. She smiled. Nicholas Greenly wasn't unique in his love for Greek sweets. She figured she'd burned enough calories lately jumping across the Channel to compensate for her indulgence.

While eating the Greek delicacy, she made a call to the barrister in Scotland.

***

"I'll have to give you credit," Brookstone told the barrister, George Cearrach, after connecting and explaining who she was. "You were able to find me. I had no idea I had Scottish ancestry."

"I didn't find you. Angus did. He was into genealogy." He explained the relationship. "You see, no matter how tenuous, you're his only remaining relative."

"It's a bit curious he was younger than I am." *Which makes me feel more mortal!* "You said the castle is mine as long as I use it. What does that mean?"

"Let me see. Oh, yes. You have to take possession of it, live in it at least one week each year, maintain it, and pay taxes."

"Thank you for maximizing the pain. What happens if I don't meet those conditions?"

"The castle and its surrounding property are turned over to the government. It would be an albatross for them—too many old castles in Scotland, you know, and most are larger and in much better shape. They'd likely sell the land to developers. A hotel chain has already shown some interest."

"How much are the taxes?" He told her. "That's not too bad. How about maintenance?" That figure was zero. "But to live there for a week, I suppose I'd need to make some repairs."

"You might want to improve the plumbing. Angus used a privy." She groaned. "Sorry. He couldn't bear to give up his castle, but he didn't want to put money into it either, besides taxes, that is. There are some back taxes due, by the way. I didn't count those."

"Why am I not surprised? What do I need to take possession?"

"Sign the papers I send you and return them."

"And who makes sure I spend my week there?"

"I do. It doesn't have to occur all at once. You have to inform me when you're coming, though. They say it's beautiful in the winter. There are some rooms with heat."

She sighed. "OK, send me the papers. I might have to be in and out of the country during the next few days, so be patient."

"No worry. You have six months to sign and return papers."

***

"I guess your bonnet keeps pigeon poop off," she said when Ambreesh appeared.

"It's a turban," he said. "But you're only pulling my leg. Do you have the mobile?"

She handed it to him. He handed her another.

"What's this for?"

"It's a cheap and temporary replacement. I'll need some time. But this one is a burn phone too."

"I needed to be discreet," she said. "The caller in question is a man named Joachim. It's probably the only German number on that phone."

"Are you sure he's calling from Germany?"

"It might be Switzerland. Austria? I don't know. I don't remember all the international codes. Not from here, like I said."

"Is this for a case?"

Like Jeremy Brand, Ambreesh Singh worked for MI-5. *Maybe Singh is one of those uncouth programmers he had mentioned?* She doubted it. He was as anal as they came. And she knew he wasn't going to risk his job on a whim.

"Yes. Stolen art, as usual."

They had met on a case involving some stolen Sikh relics. She'd liked the young techie and had supped several times with his family. He had a lovely wife and three kids. He also was brilliant in a quirky sort of way.

"It's sticky," he said, showing her phone to her.

"*Baklava.* A half hour was too much for my sweet tooth."

"I see." He smiled, using his handkerchief to wipe the mobile clean. "Good thing I don't need prints. I'll call you. I have to return to the office now."

"Say hi to the family. You're lucky to have them."

"Yes, but I'm dreading when the children become older, especially the girls. Young people can find so much trouble nowadays."

Not only now. She was thinking of her escapades with Natalie. They had mooned the royals from a rooftop once. *Bet she never told her husband about that!*

Chapter Fourteen
London

The mobile gambit with Singh was a shot in the dark. But Brookstone had other ideas to try. She first made a call to Ludwigsburg in Germany, the home of the Central Office of the State Justice Administration for the Investigation of National Socialist Crimes—a typical German bureaucratic name so long everyone shortened it to Z Commission. The office was about eight miles north of Stuttgart. The two cities had competed for attention by Bavarian royalty since the founding of Ludwigsburg; Stuttgart eventually won.

Dietfried Hofer answered her call. "Do you know you only call me when you want a favor?"

"When I'm there in person, I let you take me to dinner," she said.

He laughed. "Are you coming to peruse our archives again? I know a new restaurant I've been itching to try. We can both be lab rats."

Hofer was a confirmed bachelor. His playground was more Stuttgart than Ludwigsburg, though.

"Some other time, *mein Herr*," she said. "No damsel has captured your heart yet?"

"Too many have gravely wounded me, madam. But one IT lady is now giving me the evil eye. I might have to make an exception to my rule against office romances. What about you? It's been almost a year. No new men in your life?"

"Slowing down, I'm afraid. I think I'm smitten but then think better of it. I've had too many husbands."

"You're a high maintenance woman. And you might have to lower your standards. All the rich old men are looking for twenty-year-olds now. I find that amusing."

Hofer was well off but not that old. *Mid-forties like Bastiann?* She couldn't remember if she'd ever known how old the German was.

"Are you going to keep insulting me, or do you want to hear the favor I'm asking?"

"No insults intended; they're only barbs, my dear lady who sounds so sexy in a verbal battle. I'll assume that's an exclusive or, by the way, and go for the last."

"Rembrandt van Rijn's 'An Angel with Titus' Features.' Do you know anything about it?"

"You're the art connoisseur. You tell me." She told him what she knew about the missing painting. "Hitler's museum? That's a myth because it never existed. Those old Nazis made off with the artworks unaccounted for. No telling where they are now. You might as well chase the Himalayan yeti or the Yank's big foot. That said, how can I help?"

"There are efforts to recover the ones still lost. I'm interested in the paintings, of course, but to find them I need to discover if there are any neo-Nazi groups trying to finance their mischief by selling paintings one-by-one to the highest bidder, which is what I expect is going on. That would require time digging into your archives, time I don't have right now."

"I'm not sure our archives are recent enough to help you. Talk to Kurt Geiszler. He's in the Federal General Police Office and is likely privy to more recent events. He's an upstanding fellow and will be happy to cooperate."

Brookstone noted the number, said her goodbyes, and made the call.

***

"You need Interpol involved in your case," Geiszler said after hearing Brookstone's story.

"They are," she said. *But not officially.* "But I want to work other contacts too."

"I've only had a few beers with Dietfried. I'm pleased he remembers me. Of course, I'm not in Stuttgart that often since the capital moved from Bonn to Berlin."

"Dietfried remembers everything, including how many times he's taken me to dinner so he can tell me it's my turn to pay. Was he right in thinking you can help me?"

"You've come to the right person. At least one of them." He gave her some background on what they had on neo-Nazi groups without going into classified information. "And now for the best part: A rich industrialist from the Stuttgart area came in not long ago while on a business trip to Berlin to inform us about this same auction. The painting offered to him wasn't your Rembrandt, though. He's a cautious type and figured he was dealing with black market characters. His is still an open case for us, although we haven't given it a high priority, and it might be related to yours."

"What do you know about the group running his auction? Did your industrialist talk to a man named Joachim?"

"No, he spoke to a woman named Ruth. You realize these are probably fake names, right?"

And both Jewish. Nazi humor. "Of course. But sometimes aliases, if used consistently, can be traced back to a real person. Do you have any Ruths or Joachims on file?"

"I'm sure we checked on Ruth, and a search for Joachim is unlikely to match anyone either. We agreed to monitor the industrialist's phone, though. His request. Next time he's called, we'll try a trace. They're handling that locally."

"Not likely to work. Can I speak to this industrialist?"

"As a matter of fact, you can. You will only have to lift a phone. He's in London right now at a pharmacological convention." Geiszler provided the name and telephone number of the London hotel.

She thought it odd that Geiszler would have that information. *Are they keeping track of this man?*

Chapter Fifteen
London

"Please sit, Mrs. Brookstone," said Gerhardt Dunst.

The industrialist had agreed to meet Brookstone in the Corinthia Hotel's Bassoon Bar. The hotel was located two minutes from the Embankment tube station and six minutes from Trafalgar Square. It was an ornate Victorian building with a glass-domed lobby at Whitehall Place.

She arrived a bit after seven p.m.—too early for music, too late for tea, but a charming site to interview the man.

Dunst was imperious even while sitting, a tall, balding man with wide shoulders. One Rachmaninoff-like hand held a glass containing an amber liquid, probably single malt from the shape of the glass; his long fingers were wrapped around it. The right hand rested on the table. He was trim and well-fit, but his icy blue eyes made her nervous.

He looked like a politician who worked out to maintain his public persona, oozing a false charm and self-serving affability, and he was dressed casually but in expensive clothes—not chic but cosmopolitan. She didn't like him or his kind but hid her reaction. She'd been wrong before about first perceptions, even about her own father...

***

Thomas Brookstone had often scared little Esther when she was a small child, especially when the vicar would launch into his sermons from the high wooden pulpit. She read about Moses when she was four—the bible reading suggested by her father, of course—and she imagined her father to be the prophet in the tale about the descent from the mountain when Moses, filled with wrath, chided the Israelites for worshipping false idols. That was the public face of her father, though.

At home, her father was stern but loving; he and her mother managed to make ends meet as they raised three children. Little Esther became the tall man's favorite, although their relationship was always formal and a bit distant—not many hugs or kisses from either father or mother. All the children went to public school. At holiday time, Esther's older brothers instigated typical boyish mischief, but she often participated in it with gusto. Her older brother almost created a scandal when he got his girlfriend pregnant. The vicar married them immediately after ensuring that the two families would forever keep the reason for the hasty wedding secret, the girl's parents more than happy to do so. That older brother had become a successful businessman. The next in line joined the military upon graduation from public school and made a career in the RAF. Both brothers were now retired.

While Esther loved her father and felt the stern man loved her, she never saw much love expressed between him and her mother. In discussions with her mother, it was clear that the plump, mousy woman was generally happy with her lot but felt a God-fearing woman's duty to her husband was to attend his needs and bear his children.

Her father loved art and music. She remembered the reproduction of Leonardo da Vinci's "Adoration of the Magi" on display in their sitting room at the vicarage. Bach's cantatas were his favorite pieces, but the music from other classics often permeated their humble abode. She would often go to sleep listening to a classical piece, for example. Mozart's Linz symphony was her favorite, but she loved Mendelssohn too.

Except for my love of art, I'm not like my father or mother. She wasn't like her brothers either. *They're all conformists.* Thinking about her brothers' retirements brought to mind her own need to retire someday. She felt she could still do some good in her Unit, but some higher-ups with personalities like Dunst or Thomas Brookstone, whether good-intentioned or bad, probably thought of her as an anachronism, one of those antiques she and others in the Unit tried to track down when stolen. *Do you retire when you no longer feel needed, or do you retire when they say they no longer need you?* She ignored the latter but worried about the former.

***

Brookstone took a chair at Dunst's table. "You can call me Esther."

He nodded and smiled. "Only if you call me Gerhardt. Would you like a drink?"

She thought a moment. "Vodka and lime, please."

He waved to a waitperson who could have passed for a Buckingham Palace maid. When she had her drink, Brookstone raised her glass.

"To a fellow art connoisseur," she said.

"Cheers. Geiszler said you were approached too. I suppose it's against rules for us to be chatting together about the auctions, but I was offered a different painting. I also bowed out. To paraphrase that illustrious Prince of Denmark, something seemed rotten to me."

"I always take the side of Ophelia. She's only one of two female characters in the whole bloody play."

"The latter is an unintentional pun, I'm sure," he said with a smile. "You aren't one of those raving feminists, are you, channeling some old, radical suffragette?"

"At my age, I can choose to be many things, but I wanted to buy a missing Rembrandt. I'm careful about my investments, though. I'm trying to learn more about these art thieves."

"You'd play their rotten little game?" He seemed scandalized. "These artworks are Nazi loot, I'm sure. Stolen during the war from rich Jews. It's a disgrace what happened." The outraged expression had turned into a smile, though. *Does he mean what he says?*

"Be practical, Gerhardt. If I buy the painting, I'm only paying ransom for a kidnapped art treasure. 'Donated by Mrs. Esther Brookstone, *Contessa* Sartini' beneath the painting in the National Gallery or even Amsterdam's *Rijksmuseum* would be a more fitting way for future generations to remember me than a simple grave in Lugano, don't you think?"

"Ah, you'd buy it and then donate it. Admirable. I see your point. I should have done the same. It would be a wonderful PR coup. But what's your fear, madam? Just put in the highest bid."

"My innate paranoia warns me they could take my money and not deliver the painting."

"I understand. I had similar thoughts, but I lusted after the painting they offered for my own private collection, Esther. Rather selfish, I suppose, but I came to my senses. I was not about to reward unscrupulous art thieves. I've tried to put the whole incident behind me."

"I thought you told Geiszler you were allowing him to trace your next call with them."

"I changed my mind. I didn't want to soil my hands by negotiating with hooligans. I'd think you'd also be reluctant to do that in spite of your altruism."

"I'm ready to stay the course in spite of the shadiness." *Lies, all lies, but so what?* "Shall we compare notes? I want to learn enough about these people to be confident this isn't a fraudulent offer."

"I suppose. I met this Ruth in Berlin. She explained the rules of the game."

His story was similar to hers. But she thought she might have only discovered an alias for another art thief. Assuming the two auctions were related, two art thieves confirmed one thing: this was a group, if only two, wanting to make money by selling stolen art. *What am I getting into?*

Chapter Sixteen
Berlin

Geiszler perused the personnel file on his screen. Esther Brookstone had an admirable career at Scotland Yard, although she had started late. He wondered what she was doing before that. He found her an interesting character. *I should have told her more.*

The file on Dunst was even longer than he had remembered. They had nothing specific on him, but Jewish organizations with their justifiable paranoia had read between the lines of his public pronouncements. Sometimes he criticized Hitler for making mistakes, though. Of course, most historians agreed creating an eastern front against the Soviet Union had been a strategic error. Others argued not invading Great Britain in a timely fashion had compounded that error.

He smiled. *Hindsight is 20/20, and historians are as guilty of abusing it as anyone else.* He thought of things differently. *If the German people couldn't resist one madman, would others have their day in the Teutonic sun?* With migrants who came from Syria and others arriving from that and similar trouble spots, rightwing extremists were daily adding new people to their ranks in Germany and elsewhere in Europe. To curry favor among voters, right-leaning politicians were stirring up things even more.

He sighed. Dunst was an example of the new right in Germany. He hadn't liked the man when he met him. Brookstone didn't realize the forces she was dealing with. Dunst might be an innocent, but he had demonstrated sympathies for some scary fringe elements. Phrases like "I wouldn't have done that, but I can understand their motivations" supported the Jewish paranoia. But perhaps he was no different from the majority of German magnates; they often put profit and power above anything else. *But such an attitude had also helped bring Hitler to power!*

He realized he was trapped in the national psychosis. Even people younger than he was still lived through the bad days of the war because their elders wouldn't let them forget.

I think it's time for a beer.

***

"Kurt, you are a bit too pensive to be listening to polka music."

Geiszler looked up and shook his head. "No quotes from a reliable anonymous source today, Helga," he told the reporter.

"I was only wondering if you'd buy me a beer." She smiled and sat.

Helga Schmidt often frequented the watering hole populated more by media types than cops. Geiszler frequented it for its extensive selection of beers on tap and tolerated the reporters, who often became vocal and rowdy as they came off their beats.

She helped staff a small newspaper. She focused mostly on crime, but all the paper's reporters multitasked. She even wrote obituaries. She'd once done one for Geiszler long ago in order to create a cover story. In return for the favor, he'd become a "reliable anonymous source" for the story, and for some stories that followed.

Her angular face, short blond hair, and thick glasses that made her blue eyes seem larger and brighter gave the impression of plainness. *The look of a schoolteacher?* She had a sparkling personality, though, and he knew her fellow workers liked her as much as he did. She was one reporter he didn't find annoying most of the time. There was no amorous interest on his part or hers. They were only friends working in somewhat similar occupations.

"Off the record, I'm mulling over my guilt."

"Oh? Off the record, I'm listening." She waved at a waiter and asked for a beer and a slice of *leberkäse* with black bread. "Breakfast and lunch," she said to Geiszler. When her order arrived, she told him to go ahead. She ate while he talked.

"I'm taking advantage of an old English woman. I've had a hunch about a guy for a while. He might be involved in something that will affect her."

"And I'm supposed to condone that?" she said, mumbling with the bite of bread and cheese. She washed it down with some beer. "Are you using her as an undercover agent?"

"In a sense. From what I've heard and read, she's stubborn enough to proceed no matter how much I protest. But I feel guilty about my possibly benefitting from her actions."

"Without knowing the person, I'd guess you can mitigate your guilt by offering a lot of support." She gulped at the beer and wiped off her lips. "Is there a story for me here? I want an exclusive."

"Maybe. Eventually. But off the record for now."

"You haven't given me enough details even to justify saying that. You're thinking she can do things you won't be able to do in the case, I presume?"

"And that's why she could come to harm."

"Does she have a superior?"

"She does."

"I'd talk to him then, off the record. If he's not a complete ass, he'll not wish her any harm either."

"That's good advice, I suppose."

The conversation dissolved into chitchat. Schmidt lived with her ailing mother, a frail eighty-three-year old. The woman had performed the impossible by sneaking her children into the West in her capacity as a Communist party apparatchik, but she'd also spent several years in an East German prison until the two countries were unified, a stay that hadn't been good for her health. Like many East Germans, she'd been a Communist in name only. All that made Schmidt's family life much more interesting than his.

***

Geiszler returned to his HQ feeling a bit better. Schmidt was a good friend. They shared confidences shared with no one else. And now he had a mission and the resolve to complete it: convince Brookstone's boss at Scotland Yard she could be in danger. And he would find the Interpol agent she was working with and tell him the same thing.

He was enchanted by Esther Brookstone, though. She was smart and competent. He felt guilty about working to remove her from the case. *I can't win.*

It was always difficult when civilians became involved in police work. While Brookstone was an inspector, hardly a civilian, but she wasn't the usual policewoman. True, he supposed she had to pass periodic tests of competency in firearms and minimal self-defense. She was also in good shape for her age, her voice on the phone seeming to indicate an energy he hoped to have at that time in his life, so she probably worked out. But her years of experience living in the genteel art world made her an innocent. She could be hurt in the long run.

Her boss, George Langston, was receptive to his suggestion to rein her in enough to increase her chances for survival as she pursued her case. Geiszler could only leave a message for Bastiann van Coevorden to return his call.

That night he left the office a bit more at peace. He had done all he could to keep the woman safe. Schmidt had been a good friend to suggest it.

His mind turned to other cases as he drove along in his Saab. He had on light classical music but smiled when he heard Lehar's overture from *The Merry Widow. How appropriate!* But then he frowned. The Viennese Lehar had trouble with Nazis because he tended to use Jewish librettists. His wife, at one time a Jew until her conversion to Roman Catholicism, hadn't helped his situation. *An omen?*

Geiszler shuddered and turned off the radio.

Chapter Seventeen
Amsterdam

Interpol Agent Bastiann van Coevorden entered his apartment ready to collapse. During the train ride from Lyon, he had also been scheming about how to keep Esther Brookstone safe until a young female passenger boarded the train when it stopped in Brussels.

She reminded him of a classmate from his student days at the university, so he struck up a conversation. Initially it was pleasant—she was a graduate student going home for a long weekend—but the encounter had turned sour when she learned he was Interpol and started to express her fears about terrorist attacks, which she blamed completely on the European acceptance of immigrants from the Middle East over the past years.

As a Dutchwoman living in Brussels, van Coevorden supposed she had a right to her paranoid opinion. Brussels and France had the largest Muslim populations in the E.U., many of them citizens. Like most western democracies, the two countries also had many soft targets. It was almost impossible to keep on top of the threat. A rash of attacks, many engineered by ISIS or its sympathizers, hadn't been surprising in hindsight. Almost as sad was the constant flow of people from Western Europe to the Middle East to join the terrorists. Even women.

His fellow passenger just couldn't understand it all. Because he wasn't directly involved in counterterrorism, though, he could offer her little solace. What little he knew was classified.

He did manage to convince her that legitimate refugees made up the majority in the wave of immigrants. While it was an established fact that one of the Paris terrorists had infiltrated as a refugee, and that had been taken to imply a general trend in response to paranoia, ordinary families of men, women, and children were still just looking for any escape from the chaos and violence that sprang up in many areas. It made for a delicate situation, though, because a few unscrupulous people gave others a bad reputation.

Reactionaries had closed off borders and stranded entire families in new refugee camps in Europe, so close yet so far from a normal life, albeit with a slightly improved existence. A few camps were seven-years-old already, their continued existence caused by new arrivals replacing those who left. The situation had worsened over the years. He wrote off BREXIT, which happened several years ago, in part as a paranoid reaction to a worsening situation. Nothing had been done to mitigate the causes of the grand migration. People kept dying on those boats, fleeing even more squalid conditions in the Middle East and trying to reach Europe.

"It's a mess," he had told her. She had nodded her agreement. *An educated person. She listens. Many don't.*

The conversation ended abruptly when his traveling companion rubbed her right eye. Through a series of questions, he ascertained that something strange was going on with that eye. She complained of floating specks, flashes of light, blurred vision, and a curtain-like shadow. *Can it be a stroke in one so young?* But she didn't feel any pain, and her pulse was normal. He made calls on his mobile. In Amsterdam, an ambulance was waiting at the station. The EMT diagnosed her condition as a detached retina.

He watched the ambulance pull away with lights flashing and siren bleating, and wondered about the vagaries of human existence. It could have been worse. You never knew when the Grim Reaper's sickle would find you.

He found a cab, not an easy task at that time of night. After giving his driver a good tip, he entered his apartment, which seemed a welcome respite from an uncertain world. To enhance that perception, he made tea, left it steeping, and went to his small bedroom to change. He could obtain a few hours of sleep before the morning when he had to do favors for Brookstone.

When next morning came, he found the teapot on the table still full of cold tea.

***

Favor for Brookstone #1: Van Coevorden followed the Amsterdam adjutant into the morgue. An inspector and coroner were waiting for him. After introductions, van Coevorden waved his hand and the coroner removed the sheet. Never handsome in his old age, Richard Metzger lay on the exam table, his pale, naked body fat, bloated, and ugly.

"Time of death?"

"Hard to say because of the time in water," said the coroner, "but I'd guess not more than two days ago. It's difficult to imagine they wouldn't have spotted the body early, though, so let's say max twenty-four hours."

"Cause of death?"

Inspector and adjutant smiled. The coroner turned the corpse to its side. The rear of the man's head was gone.

"Explosive round?" All three nodded. "That sounds like military ammunition." The inspector nodded again. "And illegal for the most part. I'll have to check if we have any similar homicides on file. I suppose you've done that as far as the municipal police go?"

Inspector and adjutant nodded again. They all looked like gray ghosts pretending they were one of those dashboard dolls with the bobbing heads. Everyone looked sallow under the strong lighting.

"We haven't had one like this in a while," said the adjutant.

"Did you determine where he was living and do forensics?" When the two cops nodded, van Coevorden said, "Did you find any evidence connecting him with a support network? What about evidence for his killer?"

"He had a fake passport, using that to rent his apartment—better than I can afford—and a bank account under the same name," said the adjutant. "It's possible he had a support structure, but he didn't need one—he had funds to live peacefully."

"He didn't die peacefully," said van Coevorden.

"With all that money, he should have done some plastic surgery," said the adjutant. "Someone recognized him. Probably someone who became judge, jury, and executioner. He would have been better off if we discovered him first."

"Satisfied?" said the inspector.

"That Metzger is dead, yes. But his death leaves us with a lot of questions, don't you think? Are you pursuing this as a homicide?"

"You might say that," said the inspector, winking at his colleague. "Considering he was wanted by everyone from Scotland Yard to the FBI, and considering what his crimes were, I'd say we won't spend a lot of energy on it. Someone saved everyone concerned a lot of time and money."

"I might buy that if we or the police killed him, but that's not the case, so I'd like to know who did the deed. It could be the case of big fish eating little fish. That's important to pursue."

"Maybe big sharks and little sharks would provide a better metaphor," said the inspector, who now winked at the coroner. "With swastikas painted on their foreheads." He coughed and jerked a thumb toward the cadaver. "Not our problem. Madame Justice has found *Herr* Metzger, and that's the story's ending for us. Case closed."

"I'll agree with that as far as it goes," said van Coevorden, "but I insist: for me another case has opened. Who killed Richard Metzger? This isn't a mugging. It's a professional hit. Send me copies of all the forensics."

He handed his cards to both cops and the coroner and left the morgue.

***

Favor for Brookstone #2: Van Coevorden returned to his small office and opened his laptop. With various national and international databases available to him, he could begin a search for Gerhardt Dunst.

He learned Dunst was a shrewd businessperson who was respected by employees for the most part but a tyrant in the boardroom. He owned several companies not known for their diversity and sat on the board of directors of others, including some American firms and Swiss banks.

More interesting to van Coevorden was a bit of family history. The grandfather was *Oberst* Dunst, the equivalent of a Group Captain in Goering's *Luftwaffe*. Father Dunst was trapped in East Germany when the war ended but escaped to the West as a teen, where he married an Austrian. Both husband and wife became neo-Nazi sympathizers. Yet their only son, Gerhardt, seemed apolitical.

Most of that history didn't bother van Coevorden. Europe was full of families whose past involved direct or indirect involvement with Nazis because that had been a life or death decision for so many. Not for Jews, Communists, and homosexuals, though—they had no choice because they were Hitler's scapegoats. And so much artwork was destroyed because it was deemed perverse and not Aryan enough. *America still has its legacy of slavery; we have the Holocaust and Aryan Supremacy. Hard to tell which is worse, although American blacks and Jews worldwide would have differing opinions about that.*

What made Brookstone suspicious of *Herr* Dunst, and van Coevorden had to agree with that reaction, was that the man who had an extensive history of investing in artworks had passed on the group's offer of a famous painting. She thought it might be misdirection to give the appearance that Dunst was squeaky clean when he really wasn't. *Maybe we're giving too much credit to him?* To follow that up, they needed to know more about Dunst's art dealings. He couldn't find much about those, though.

Maybe I'm going at it the wrong way?

He broadened his search to Dunst's known associates, board members and executives of his own corporations and those where he was a board member. The list was a veritable who's-who of E.U.'s VIPs, especially German ones. One name stood out, though, an Austrian.

Walther Lietzke, born in Linz to German parents, was CEO of a holding company for various chemical factories, not an unusual association with Dunst, the pharmaceutical giant. But Lietzke's wife owned galleries in several cities in Austria and Germany and provided artwork for auctions aboard cruise ships.

After digging around more, the Interpol agent discovered *Frau* Lietzke was Dunst's half-sister. And Walther Lietzke boasted that his maternal grandfather was none other than

Hans Posse, the first "curator" of Hitler's Museum. Van Coevorden couldn't confirm that. *Some people claim to be related to serial killers, though, just for the notoriety.*

At the very least, he seemed to take pride in it instead of shame, which was curious. Of course, there were no records that showed Posse was a murderer who supported killing Jews either. In fact, he had originally been persecuted by the Nazis and forced to join the party to survive, as had so many others.

The perils of fascism, mused van Coevorden. *Would I go to prison or die for my principles?* He was glad he'd never had to make such choices.

The Dunst family's history was intriguing, though. *Possibly all coincidental, and none of it damning or necessarily relevant to present-day events.* It was clear that the family was involved in the art world. Lietzke's wife, the half-sister, might even be selling artworks to Dunst. *Could some be stolen? That would be like money laundering.* And was there any relationship between the wife and the group trying to sell the painting to Esther?

He pulled open a drawer containing a half dozen mobiles, all throw-aways, what the Yanks called burn phones. He chose one at random and punched in the number he saw on his laptop. The call went to voicemail.

"*Guten Tag, Frau* Lietzke, I'm Gustav Hofmeister, an art dealer in Amsterdam. I have a client who's inquiring about Rembrandt's 'An Angel with Titus' Features.' I thought you might know something about its availability. If so, please call me at this number."

A wild chance, but what the hell!

Chapter Eighteen
London

"We have confirmed the deposit of your funds and registered your next bid," said Joachim over the phone.

Brookstone looked at her mobile's tiny screen, seeing Joachim's grin. *Damn! I should have traced this call.* She jotted down the number. "I want some insurance," she said.

"Pardon?"

"I've already met a person who refused to play your little game. How do I know I'm not the only one left, and I'm bidding against myself?"

Joachim laughed. "I must admit we never thought of that. That's a diabolical idea. I'm afraid you'll have to trust us."

"That's a remarkable suggestion coming from an art thief. Here's another question: do you have any other paintings? You offered a different one to the person I talked to. Maybe there's something else in your gallery, for want of a better name, that I might be more interested in. Even a better investment with a less dubious provenance. Why don't you offer your entire catalog of paintings and let us choose? Smart dealers would do that."

"We've selected the painting that's a better fit for you."

"I'd like to determine that. Next question: before I bid any higher, I'd like to see the painting's condition. Or paintings, if you can show me others. You can blindfold me or whatever so I don't know where the paintings are located, but I don't often buy anything sight unseen."

"Hmm. Maybe we can arrange that. We were afraid our rich patrons might think it a trap to hold them for kidnapping and ransom."

"My turn to say I never thought of that. That's diabolical too. I guess I *will* have to trust you. I don't have any relatives left, though, so FYI: such a plan would be futile in my case. So, what's the next step? Can I see the painting?"

"I'll get back to you."

***

"That might put the old kibosh on your bid," said Langston, who was sitting in front of Brookstone's desk in one of her visitor's chairs and had been able to fill in some of the unheard half of the conversation. "Or put you in danger. You're acting like an MI-6 field agent, Esther, but you're only a sweet old lady. I can't recommend it."

"Why, George, only my husbands called me sweet, so I'll take part of what you said as a compliment. The part about being an old lady puts you on my black list, though. I had to say something. They could have had me bidding against myself."

"That would be smart of them, I suppose. I'm talking about your wanting to see the painting. I still say it's a bit risky, don't you think?"

"David walked into the lions' den and left unscathed."

"David had a sling and stones at least."

"You're confusing your biblical stories. The sling and stones were for Goliath. Of course, I might be fighting Goliath, not lions. We have no idea how big an operation this is. Are you still backing me?"

"Let's now say we're interested. It would be fun to obtain a list of the other bidders. We'd be even more interested if there are U.K. citizens on that list besides you. I could get MI-5 involved then."

"It's too international for that, but there might be some locals in the gang, I suppose. Van Coevorden is helping me out."

"Interpol? Is that official now?"

"Not yet. He also toots his own horn sometimes—what his superiors might call a loose cannon. They like to talk like Americans. I suppose we all do. They watch BBC shows; we watch American ones. They have the better part of the deal, although I suppose BBC America adds commercials."

"I empathize with his superiors," Langston said with a smile. "I could order you to back off, you know."

"And I could say what I do on my vacation time—and I shall take it—is my own business."

He shrugged. "Do be careful, won't you?"

"I never shy away from a good fight." Her phone rang. "Sorry, I have to take this."

Langston nodded and left.

***

Even when he had exciting news, Ambreesh Singh never sounded excited. *A serious family man doing a serious job,* mused Brookstone. His wife was sweet and expressive, though, and his kids were intelligent little imps.

"I have a partial trace on that call. It was made in the Stuttgart area."

"Interesting." *Were some of Singh's colleagues at MI-5 listening in?* She didn't care, but he might. *Right in Dietfried Hofer's backyard.*

"Maybe. Do you have any more information about the location?"

"No, but that's close to a certain someone's pharmaceutical plants. Did you use satellite information?"

"Let's say I used other means."

No divulging secrets of the trade. "Is your information reliable?"

"For a computer connection, no, and it's possible they used a computer to bounce it all over the world. That would be sophisticated, though. Assuming only a mobile was used, you have my best guess. I suppose NSA could give you a better fix."

"I don't know anyone in NSA, but I expected a certain Dr. Singh to help out here at home. Never mind. I'm a bit leery of taking this farther and getting someone else involved. Spooks react strangely sometimes when you ask them a favor." She heard his polite cough. "Spooks who aren't close friends, that is."

"I hope the information is helpful. It's all I can provide and still avoid risks. You surely understand that as far as my bosses are concerned, you're just another civilian. One more observation, though: Your Mr. Joachim could be moving all over Europe, and he might have only been passing through Stuttgart, say, on his way to Paris."

"Moving from point A to B, and I'd like to know A as well as B. I need more information about these people and fast." She went pensive for a moment. "Is there such a thing as a long-distance wire with a GPS locator?"

"You mean one you wear that transmits? I suppose that could be arranged. You only need to transmit the RF signal to a repeater with a comsat link. An interesting idea, in fact. Why?"

"I might be going to a meeting where it would be nice to have that."

"Sounds dangerous. Want me to check into it?"

"I'd prefer to keep officialdom in the dark. Do you have any tech-savvy friends who aren't government employees?"

"Plenty. I can hook you up with one. My friend might consider it a challenge too. I'll get back to you."

"Thanks. Hi to the wife and hugs for the children."

Chapter Nineteen
Berlin/Mannheim

Geiszler studied the bodies and detached heads and then turned away from the garishly color images. He was used to gory crime scene pictures, but beheadings weren't common in Germany. That pointed the finger to one group, ISIS. Or, at least, to some radicalized Muslims who believed the Koran called for beheading infidels.

He found his desk phone.

"I have a peripheral interest in that pharmaceutical factory. One owner is on our radar."

"Who would that be?" said the man at the other end.

"Gerhard Dunst."

"We're planning to interview him. Is this line secure?"

"I can make it so. From your end or mine?"

"I'll initiate, you handshake." There were squeals and screeches as the old outmoded top secret encryption went live. "Now, as I was saying, we're planning to interview *Herr* Dunst."

"Any particular reason?"

"We're tentatively blaming this on ISIS, which is consistent with the butchery—they're into everything now—but they haven't claimed this attack as theirs, or of any group or persons sponsored by them or acting on their behalf. Besides the general mayhem and murders, something serious was stolen from a compartmented government project."

"Details? We're on a secure line now, remember." The agent online provided a brief description after defining the level of security. "That's all I can say. If you want something more scientific, you'll need special clearances. Be forewarned: I don't even have them."

After chitchatting a bit about their personal lives—Geiszler had known the agent for years—the German inspector disconnected.

What the hell is going on?

***

About the same time, Gerhard Dunst was having a telephone conversation. The woman on the other end of the line was irate.

"Security in Europe has become a joke! We must change that."

"We will, never fear. For now, though, be careful about what you wish for. We take advantage of inept security. Our own is top grade, but all Germans have become complacent, so attacks like this one are never expected. Don't worry. We have people on this problem. They're efficient and competent. Patience is a virtue. We have other fronts to occupy our attention, as you well know."

"Yes, look at the big picture, Gerhard. Everything is important if we are to succeed. Remember that!"

He was about to reply when the dial tone interrupted him. She had hung up. He stared at the mobile phone and smiled. He supposed even his half-sister might have PMS. *Or early menopause? Women!*

He made another call to Amsterdam. "Any news, Jacob?"

"They found him. It took them long enough. They'll likely be happy to close his case. The old man was a liability for us and the authorities. You made the correct decision, Gerhard."

"A difficult one, nevertheless. It was only a matter of time before they caught him, of course. He knew too much. He had a good run. It's better this way."

"I agree. I'm also moving forward on that other issue. From what I heard on the news, we might have a bit more time?"

"Don't count on it," said Dunst. "That's only a minor setback, and we have to be ready to move when the time is right."

No way I'm going to tell him about the missing scientists— second string, but still capable. He decided that it was one of life's ironies that one group out to rule the world interfered with a program aimed at doing just that for another group. He had no love for terrorists. They were ruthless murderers and religious fanatics. *My people are more logical and more focused on achieving a world order where those who deserve to rule are the rulers.* Chaos and lawlessness would never occur on his watch! And they would exterminate terrorists like an infestation of roaches in a city apartment.

***

Later Dunst was sipping sherry on his veranda when a call came in from London. "I saw the news from Mannheim. This is getting too hot for me. I want out."

"Oh, please, this is no time to have second thoughts. You'd spend the rest of your life in prison. Think of your contribution as a little bit of industrial espionage."

"Somehow I think it's more than that," the woman said, her contralto voice more like a growl over the landline. "The attack indicates a lot more is going on. I don't want to be associated with it."

"Your role will be minor, my dear. We're doing the heavy lifting. One day we'll be on a pleasure boat floating along the Danube or Rhine, drinking a fine French wine, and laughing about these exciting days. For now, consider it the most marvelous adventure of your life."

"You're a dreamer; I'm a realist. I should never have slept with you."

He laughed. He thought it was the first time ever that he had been called a dreamer. That described his half-sister better. "With that old doddering fool as your husband, how could you not? Do you use an IV to drip Viagra into his veins? I wish him a long life, by the way."

"Why?"

"You know the answer."

"You'd lose your leverage."

"*Jawol*," said Dunst. "We're on the same page. Now, do you want some phone sex?"

She disconnected and he started laughing, almost spilling his sherry. *That would be a terrible waste*, he mused. The woman was only a tool, one he had carefully chosen.

***

That night Geiszler had insomnia. He was uneasy about the attack on Dunst's factory in Mannheim. *Why had the man come to see me? Was it only a distraction?* In the dark, murky world of the fascists, things were often not what they seemed. Although his paranoia was often unrealistic, his hunches still nagged him. They often proved wrong, but they still drove him crazy.

The burning question: why would the German government trust such a man like Dunst? *Or, maybe only certain members in the government are doing the trusting?* His government's bureaucracy was as complicated as the Brits', and nearly as complicated as the Americans'. He wasn't even sure of NATO's exact involvement and didn't know where to find out. All this meant the right hand in the government often didn't know what the left was doing.

He smiled at the hidden meaning in that statement, recalling the Nazis' right-handed salute for Hitler. Hitler, and to a certain extent, Mussolini and Franco, had defined 20th century fascism, with Stalin and Mao refining it to further their own agendas. It was amazing to him there were idiots who still considered these men heroes. And that support didn't die off, because the old fanatics taught newcomers to hate too.

I'll need a lot of coffee tomorrow morning if I'm going to be functional at work.

Chapter Twenty
London

It was too cold to sit on her balcony—she would have to sweep up Fox's debris again anyway—so Brookstone sipped her wine inside her sliding glass door and stared out into the night. *Maybe George Langston is right—this is too dangerous.*

Joachim hadn't called yet, but she had one added piece of information: Dunst's company HQ was in Mannheim, a town a direct shot via the ICE high-speed rail, which also extended to Stuttgart. Considering the industry there, which included BASF, Bochringer Mannheim (the Hoffmann-LaRoche diagnostic group), and other companies, she guessed Mannheim would be her first candidate for Joachim's initial location, thanks to Ambreesh, but the art thief could have been anywhere between Frankfurt and Stuttgart.

Her mobile's ringtone interrupted her thoughts. "I'm assuming you're not just calling to bolster the spirits of a lonely woman who's sitting here sipping her wine and looking at fog."

"No, but a good evening to you too, Esther." Van Coevorden filled her in on what he had discovered. He also told her about Metzger.

"Good riddance to that old goat, I'd say. He deserved it. That other correlates well with what Singh discovered as far as

Dunst goes, but I didn't have Linz in my radar. The Lietzke pair makes sense too. How do we approach the half-sister?"

"I already have. I pretended to be an Amsterdam art dealer interested in the Rembrandt."

"She would have to be stupid to bite on that one. Still, it's sometimes useful to take the cricket bat to the hornet's nest. Mere mention of the painting might put them in a tizzy." She filled him in about her conversation with Joachim. "Do you think it's reasonable I want to see the painting?"

"Reasonable but dangerous. They're going to have you at their mercy. I don't recommend it."

"Oh, please. They think I'm a stupid, defenseless old woman."

"They won't think you're stupid anymore but a smart buyer instead. I like that you mentioned Dunst. If he and *Frau* Lietzke are involved in this caper, that will stir things up. Let me know what happens with Joachim. Maybe I can be your backup."

"I'll keep you informed."

***

Brookstone couldn't sleep, so she turned on the tele. As usual, the news was mostly unpleasant. She didn't pay much attention until she took notice of the terrorist attack in Mannheim.

"Sod it! Those ISIS monsters are crazy."

She leaned forward, but the BBC reporter didn't repeat the location. She couldn't even confirm it was ISIS, although there were blurry security camera videos of groups of well-armed men dressed in black with black ski masks moving toward the plant.

As usual, "terrorist experts" were interviewed. They pontificated, reinforcing the popular definition of BBC as "Bloody Boring Coverage." After she finally turned the tele off, she went and turned on her laptop. There she was able to confirm from other news sources, including German ones, that authorities claimed it was ISIS and the location was indeed an industrial park near Mannheim. *Mannheim?* Some connection was alluding her.

She did a bit of searching and found the exact attack site was a pharmaceutical factory. She remembered the attack on a chemical factory near Lyon a few years earlier. *Is this factory partly owned by Americans?* She didn't know how to check that, so she shrugged, finished her wine, and headed for bed.

As she dressed for bed, she remembered Dunst's plant was in Mannheim. *Coincidence?* No one had mentioned the name of the factory. *Journalists nowadays skip over details. They can't write in the Queen's English either!*

Terrorists of various persuasions had made Europe a prime target. The horrendous attacks in Paris and Brussels some years earlier had still left everyone nervous. Rumors abounded that MI-5 and the Yard had stopped various attacks from occurring in London and other English cities. With desperate migrants still looking for a better life hopping the Channel every month, she knew England would soon be more in the crosshairs too as savages with ISIS proclivities filtered into city slums to live amongst legitimate immigrants and produce more malcontents. That meant more Yard personnel and budget dedicated to counterterrorism; same for MI-5. MI-6 was already in the thick of it.

She remembered Langston and van Coevorden's warnings. Her work was tame in comparison with counterterrorism, though. *In the ice cream shop of crime, there are many flavors.*

She was dozing off when the mobile sounded. *Who'd ring me at this hour?* It wasn't Joachim.

***

"Want to hear something unusual?" said Bastiann van Coevorden.

"I never like guessing games," Brookstone said, "so tell me. And it had better be good. I was finally nodding off."

"ISIS hit one of Dunst's plants. At least their evil flag was there and two security guards were beheaded."

"Gross!" She remembered the news story. *Had they withheld details on purpose, or had she missed them?* The reporting had been sketchy, whether from BBC or otherwise. "That's something new. Why would they bomb a pharmaceutical laboratory?"

"Not bomb, my dear. Steal something. They had just left a secure area when the German *SEK* swooped down on them. At least, that's the official story. You never know with the Germans. But I'm guessing ISIS scarpered with a major bioweapons heist."

She thought a moment. *SEK? Spezialeinsatzkommando, the equivalent of an MI-5 counterterrorism SWAT team.* "What's in that secure area?"

"It's secure because it's classified and restricted by order of the German government. I'm still trying to determine what was inside but not having much luck. I don't imagine it's anything I'd like out in the public, though, considering this was a pharmaceutical plant. Thought you might enjoy the coincidence."

"Enjoy isn't the proper word. And maybe not a coincidence. I doubt those mad dogs in ISIS have any love for the Nazi's stolen art considering what they did to those monuments and antiquities in Syria and Iraq years ago and their contempt for anything from the West, so either they were after something else as you say or maybe they're falsely accused this time. Did they claim responsibility?"

"Smart question. The answer is no. Not yet. Do you think it's a Dunst-Lietzke distraction? That they're planning something and are passing it off as terrorist-related?"

"I'm thinking something else. Metzger's death might indicate a squabble among thieves, and he was on the losing side. If Dunst and the Lietzkes were on that same losing side, we have an explanation for the attack. Maybe Joachim and Ruth work for a rival gang."

"Mmm. You have a devious mind."

"Just indicating it's too early to jump to conclusions. It's hard to imagine, though, that artworks could lead to such violence. The beheadings are over the top, don't you think, if my theory is correct?"

"But not if it is ISIS or their sympathizers."

"Is Interpol involved?"

"A bit. It's the German government's party, though, and Interpol isn't invited to it, at least not completely. I know they were a bit embarrassed by that Chen and Castilblanco caper."

"Rightly so," she said. Van Coevorden had been almost a spectator in that case. It was his first introduction to the NYPD homicide detective Castilblanco. "They were caught with their knickers down. European countries without any nobility have no idea how much others love their royals...and tradition. I can't stand our ones here, but they've improved. The red-haired royal was in Afghanistan, after all, and might be OK for a good roll in the hay."

"As a Dutchman, I'm ambivalent too. Maybe Germans consider their rich industrialists and bankers their royalty. That seems to be the common sentiment in the U.S., although many Yanks are smitten with the British royals too."

"Mostly women reading silly romances, imagining they'll kiss a frog who will turn into Prince Harry." She looked at the clock. "We're going off topic, and I'm tired. Let me know if you learn what's in that secure area and if it's truly missing, or whether there's any connection to stolen artworks. The former is only me being curious; the latter would be astonishing but also important."

It seemed like she'd just fallen asleep when her wakeup alarm sounded.

Chapter Twenty-One
London

It was still dark outside when Brookstone awoke. She shook her head to clear her mind. Before she prepared breakfast, she put in a call to Kurt Geiszler.

"Even though it's an hour later here compared to where you are, this is too early to call."

"My apologies," she said. "I'm curious. You put me on to Gerhard Dunst. Don't you think it's odd his pharmaceutical plant was attacked by ISIS?"

"Not my case," he said with a growl, "and what are you inferring?"

"That maybe it wasn't ISIS. I don't know what was stolen from that plant, but it seems to have strategic importance if the *SEK* was involved. Could someone be using those rabid dogs as a smokescreen to remove something critical from the plant?"

"*Frau* Brookstone, you're sounding a bit like those conspiracy theorists in America who claimed years ago their President Obama murdered Justice Scalia."

"Hmm. I do remember Mr. Obama, that nice African-American man. Who was Scalia again?"

"Never mind. This has nothing to do with your painting, I'm sure. Did you meet with Dunst?"

"Yes I did. I think he's hiding something, especially after last night. I'm not sure what it is. For all I know, he's about to cover Europe with the Black Plague."

Geiszler made choking sounds but then laughed. "See. You prove my point. The world's full of conspiracies, right? Please, go back to your mundane case of art thievery. Sometimes coincidences are only coincidences. If you'd never met Dunst, you wouldn't have given the attack in Mannheim a second thought, I'm sure."

He has me there. We're becoming inured to terrorism, but blame the terrorists for many inexplicable crimes. "More than two thoughts now. First: No British citizen wants their head lopped off. Second: We don't do enough to stop terrorism—not here, not overseas. We tend to let the Yanks fight our battles. We've lost that World War Two resolve."

"You're speaking for all of Europe there, I'm afraid, considering the resistance in Vichy France and Nazi Germany. But do you understand my point?"

"Yes. You think I'm just another meddlesome old woman."

"I didn't say that."

"It's the truth. I don't care what you think. Meddlesome is my middle name. Esther Meddlesome Brookstone, at your service. But keep what I said in mind. You'll see. Sorry for the wakeup call."

"Apology accepted, and I was already awake. I was in the shower. I'll try to finish now if you don't mind."

There was a click and a dial tone. She smiled. She wouldn't mind watching that hunk take a shower. In spite of his Teutonic gruffness, she liked Geiszler. She knew she had planted a seed. *Can't hurt to sow a little doubt.* It wouldn't be the first time she drove a foreign cop nuts. She did it all the time with Bastiann. *Of course, he might take it better than Geiszler.*

***

After doing the best she could to get her body in shape for the coming work day, Brookstone was about to leave her flat when her mobile rang. *I'm going to have to learn to turn that damn thing off!* Of course, she'd been the one who called Geiszler. *Is he calling back?*

"My name is Carol Underwood," said a woman's voice. "Am I speaking to Esther Brookstone? Ambreesh Singh told me to contact you."

"Did he say what it was for?"

"I'd prefer not to say. I'm on a mobile, and I see you're on one too. Can we meet?"

How can she determine that? Techies! Brookstone described a coffee bar near the Oxford tube station. She didn't mention the latter directly. And, in describing herself, she said, "I like red berets and my husband used to work at Oxford. Do you understand?"

Carol Underwood laughed. Brookstone liked that laugh. "Yes, I understand your meaning. I will watch for you."

"And how will I recognize you? And when will we meet?"

"This Underwood goes like sixty but uses a lot of ink." There was a click as the girl disconnected.

Just fine. When do we meet? And what's this about ink? Brookstone thought a moment. *Cute! She's referring to the old typewriter—my Oxford husband owned one, not that Underwood could know that. She'll meet me in one hour, and she has many tattoos.*

She remembered to put on her red beret before she left her flat. Unfortunately, she met Reggie Fox in the garage.

"You look like you're going to a meeting of Young Communists," he said. "I'm not paying for your scrape, by the way."

"Then we'll go to court. I have a photo of your bumper with three inches of my Jaguar's paint on it."

"That's not possible! There's no paint there."

"Not anymore. You must have cleaned it off. That's why I took the photo. I work for the Yard. Who do you think the judge will believe? You're mixing it up with the wrong lady, old fellow."

His last zinger was over the top. "Why don't you retire and mellow out? You're only padding your pension, you old witch."

She hopped into her auto and backed up, missing his foot by only inches. *That proves my driving skills are still sound!*

She was smiling all the way to the office, already planning Fox's comeuppance in court. She parked in the Yard's lot with the sniveling Reggie Fox mostly out of mind and thinking of her coming meeting with Underwood. She paused when she used the rearview mirror to check her beret's position and lipstick. She liked the jaunty, artistic look, but the beret reminded her of Fox's comment. The man was like a stubborn odor in the kitchen, impossible to eliminate.

Young Communists? Fox had a nerve. She had never swallowed that debunked ideology, thinking it was historically tantamount to exchanging one set of fascist despots for another, and now only a way to perpetuate entrenched, oppressive oligarchies. She had no use for the fascist capitalism of China either. The leaders in Moscow and Beijing thought they could rule the world economically, although old Putin still strutted his military might occasionally.

The woman's face in the mirror now wore a scowl. That face belonged to a woman who looked to be in her early fifties, not mid-sixties, a woman with an expensive coiffure under the beret, sparkling eyes, and an impish if not flirting smile. Her Oxford professor-husband always had said he had robbed the cradle, although that gentle soul was only five months older than she was when they married.

Her reaction to his death in a traffic accident was to go on a three-month binge of nightclubbing, alcohol abuse, and wild sex. She had come to her senses one morning when she awoke in a stranger's bed with a crippling hangover and multiple bruises. His name was Ralph; he tried to stop her from leaving. She had kicked him in his privates, decked him, and left.

MI-5 had been tailing Ralph because he was a commie. Thinking she had created that illusion and seeking revenge, he implicated her. It took her awhile to straighten that all out. The incident left scars and a lifelong paranoia about possible abuses by government authorities.

And yet I've worked for the government most of my life. She smiled and smacked her lips to make sure the lipstick stayed put. *So long ago.*

She left her Jaguar in the Yard's lot, took the tube to Oxford station, and walked the short distance to the coffee bar. At the late hour, there was plenty of space at the counter.

*****

Brookstone spotted the girl when she entered. Early twenties, leggy but good body—*Ambreesh's associates are interesting.* She came and sat next to Brookstone.

"The mohawk and ring through the nose would have been enough," Brookstone said.

"Doesn't mesh with the Underwood-sixty-WPM-ink metaphor," said the girl.

"What's all the ink for? If I had breasts like those, I wouldn't want to distract potential lovers with tatts."

"I actually had them shrunk a bit—the breasts, that is. Back problems. My yoga instructor recommended it."

"Let me talk to that yoga instructor. He's an idiot."

Underwood smiled. "We should go somewhere more private." She stood and offered a hand. "We'll pretend you're my Mum. As we walk, tell me Harry's terrible for me and I should throw him out."

Brookstone took her hand. "Who's Harry, other than the redhead prince? He's the only one of them I like, by the way. He does good work with veterans."

Underwood nodded her agreement. "To answer your first question, Harry's my yoga instructor. You'd like him. Ever do yoga?"

"Can't say I have, although I used to be quite limber. At least my husbands said so. My sex play is limited now compared to yours most likely."

Underwood laughed. "OK, Mum, come along."

Outside they hooked arms together and strolled off, Brookstone berating Underwood about her choice in boyfriends, adding a bit more color than Underwood probably would have liked. The Archbishop would have loved her fornicators-go-to-hell speech spoken loud enough to generate some astonished looks.

***

"That's a wee bit of a challenge," said Underwood, referring to the Wi-Fi wire. "I think I can do it, though. Do you mind my using black market products?"

They were sitting at a high-top table in an arcade. Young people, some with more ink than Underwood, were obsessed with game machines. Brookstone thought they could have all that on their laptops now, so why bother? *Maybe some kind of attraction to retro? Or, in spite of appearing left in a trance by machine graphics, maybe there's some social interaction?* She saw some where little packages were exchanged for money. *Hopefully only weed and not the addictive stuff! Kids!*

"For the equipment? No, but I don't want to know where you obtain it. The less I know, the better."

"I understand. And I don't want to know what you want it for. Ambreesh said it's important, and that's all I need to know."

"You need to show me how to use it too. I can't wear it and go through airport security, right?"

"It will be portable but not wearable in that case. And I'll package it so they'll think nothing of it when your carry-on or suitcase goes through a scanner. It's not hard to disguise, but it has to be contained in something. Any suggestions? What might be in your carry-on?"

"Condoms?" said Brookstone with a smile, getting a laugh. She thought a moment. There'd be some electronic components. *What would an old woman be carrying?* "Can you pack it all into an old-fashioned electronic calculator, one with big keys for arthritic hands and old eyes?"

Underwood smiled. "That should work perfectly."

"Do I need to return the equipment to you?"

"You're paying for it, so it's yours. Maybe you'll find further use for it. When should we meet?"

"Whenever you have it ready. Give me a call and say, 'same time, same place, same beret.' I'll meet you here in an hour. At your convenience, of course. I don't know what kind of job you have."

"I derive my steady income from running a recording studio, herding a lot of baying boy bands whose pubescent members ogle my tits and tatts and try to hit on me. Building neat devices is a sideline, but I'm actually better at that and prefer doing it."

"Understood, Underwood. Any estimate on the time you'll need?"

"A couple of days most likely." She stood.

"I'll schedule my appointments accordingly."

Brookstone offered her hand. To her surprise, Underwood bent a bit and gave her a kiss on the cheek.

"If I had a Mum, I'd want her to be just like you."

Brookstone was misty-eyed as the girl trotted off. She'd never had any children, but yes, she thought she might have been a good mother. *Of course, daughters are complicated.* She thought of her escapades with Natalie and smiled. *Innocent Natalie. How I corrupted her!*

Chapter Twenty-Two
London/Stuttgart

It took a bit of cajoling with Joachim to schedule a meeting to view the painting. There was a general agreement, but Brookstone had to haggle for details. They settled on a meet at a hotel in Stuttgart, a trip in a car with a hood on, and her being left in a room alone with the painting. Only the one. *They'll probably be watching me. Can I hide my emotions?* Worse, it could be a trap because they might know she worked for the Yard, but they would still take her money by holding her until she released it to them.

She didn't tell any of this to Langston, but she told van Coevorden, who was aghast. He imagined the same paranoid scenario but had to move on when she wouldn't budge.

"I'll have as much trouble getting to Stuttgart as you will," he said.

"OK, don't help. I don't need you. I can leave the recording device in my hotel room, you know."

"No. I want to hear what's going on. I don't want them to toss your body into a wood chipper. I'd like to have something to bury, if you don't mind."

"Why, Bastiann, that's romantic of you. You can monitor my visit with the painting then. I intend to describe it in such detail that they think they're dealing with an old lady who knows her artwork, and I do, of course. The elderly often speak to themselves, you know. You can even follow me and be near where the painting is. That way my blood won't even be tacky by the time you get to me."

"Oh, please. They're not likely to kill the goose that lays the golden eggs, meaning they'll hold you until they have your money."

"Why are you and Langston so worried then?"

"You told Langston?"

"Not after he campaigned against it. I'm not stupid, you know. I'll be sure and file an extensive expense report when this is all over with, though. And you, dearest, will only be there out of friendship, not in any official capacity. Understood? I'll take my lumps with Langston, but I'd hate to see you get into trouble."

"All right. Give me the details."

***

Brookstone was waiting in front of the Althoff Hotel on Schellerstrasse wondering whether Titus the Cherub deserved all his famous father's loving attention when the black Mercedes stopped beside her. She tried to peer inside, but the windows were tinted. A man dressed in a chauffeur's classic gray uniform came around the car's front and opened the rear door, gesturing for her to enter. She did. He shut the door, reversed course to take the wheel again, and took off.

Three blocks later he stopped. A man in a ski mask entered and sat beside her. He showed her a black velvet bag. She nodded OK, and it went over her head. He took her arms folded in her lap and placed a zip-tie on them—not too tight but snug enough.

"Are you blokes mute, or do you speak some Indo-European language I don't know?"

"Ruhe, meine Frau," said her seat companion.

She decided it was better to obey the thug's command to be quiet, so she nodded and sat back, trying to keep track of minutes elapsed and turns they made. She had confidence in Underwood's techno-savvy, but devices could fail, so she wanted to have an idea how far she would have to walk if she had to flee the art thieves' hangout. On the run in a strange city and not knowing where she was didn't appeal to her.

Her workouts in the gym were always more frequent than trips to the gun range. She didn't have much occasion to use a firearm, but she might be in a situation where she had to practice the old caveman tactics, fight or flight. She did some trotting on a treadmill and time on the different torture machines designed to maintain muscle mass, always more difficult for an older person. Every visit to the doctor resulted in the assessment that she was in great condition for a person her age, though. The "for a person your age" qualifier bothered her. She always thought the gym was diddling her because it cost a bomb, but it was better than sweating in front of younger colleagues at the Yard in the facilities they provided. *But can I outrun a nasty Nazi?*

Streets became rough. The Mercedes, for all its creature features designed to allow the rich to enjoy a comfortable ride, bounced her around. She estimated it was a half-hour later when the Mercedes came to a halt. She had the numbers of left and right turns filed away in her head. *I hope I don't need any of that information.* It seemed like it would be a long walk back to downtown.

One man helped her out, turned her, and marched her forward. She knew she'd entered a large building when she heard a sliding door open and then shut behind her, and then began to hear the echoes of their steps.

"Warten Sie hier, bitte," the same man said, pushing her into a chair.

Where do you think I'd be off to, idiot! There was a seat cushion but no back cushion. It was chilly. There was a musty odor as well as remnants of diesel fumes. *Spartan accommodations. Maybe an old warehouse?*

***

Brookstone waited as she'd been told. Five minutes later the bag over her head was removed. She rubbed her eyes and blinked in the bright light and then was able to see a blurry Joachim standing in front of her. As her vision cleared, she decided he looked like a thinner, younger version of the evil dentist from *Marathon Man*—she liked Dustin Hoffman but remembered the villain more, imagining that classic film set back dentistry several decades. A slim index finger lay alongside his nose as he studied her. His spectacles flashed like mirrors. *Is this place cold, or is he icing me with his eyes?*

"Madam Brookstone, *Condessa* Sartini," he finally said with a twisted smile. "You'll have as long as you need to inspect the painting. When you finish, please wave your left hand. My associates will then return you to your hotel."

"I appreciate the opportunity you've given me, but what happens if I discover you're trying to sell me a fake?"

"That won't occur, assuming you know your art. If you use such a claim to renege on our deal, that's another question. My associates and I wouldn't be happy in that case because, as you know, time is money. We've reacted positively to your whimsical requests, but there's always a limit." He waved his hand toward the wall. A curtain rose and she gulped as she saw the masterpiece. "I'll be leaving you now. Please don't touch the Rembrandt, madam. It was a bit battered and needed some restoration, but I think you'll find it in excellent condition considering."

She walked toward the painting as Joachim left the room. She heard him lock the door but never even bothered to look. She knew she was trapped, but she had a role to play. She stopped a few meters in front of Rembrandt's masterpiece, joy sweeping over her. It soon turned to rage, though, as she thought of the years it had been hidden from public eye. *The bastards!*

The first item she studied in detail was the signature. She was surprised it had one. She'd only seen a black and white picture of the painting but couldn't remember a signature. The painter's signature wasn't unique and had changed through various periods in his life. The one on the painting seemed to match its period, if she remembered correctly. *But maybe that's the easiest item to falsify!*

Next, she analyzed the style. It looked like Rembrandt's, with a bit more emphasis on pastel shades perhaps, but a clever forger could copy that same black and white photograph mimicking that period's style. The memory of the photograph didn't allow her to critique those colors either.

That led her to consider the age. She peered at the texture, but only a chemical analysis of a tiny chip could confirm the paints used were popular at that time and not of more recent origin. *I don't have enough information! Had they known she was an art expert? Had they selected this very painting so she couldn't authenticate it?*

The frame told her nothing—the painting had been reframed. She walked back and forth in front of it, scrutinizing every brush stroke and choice of color. It looked authentic, but she couldn't perform a complete authentication without the input of several experts and testing, the kind of authentication Sotheby's might do when selling a masterpiece. A glance at the back of the painting might tell her more—for example, an idea about the age of the canvas material--but she refrained from touching the painting, as Joachim had commanded.

Knowing Dunst was offered another painting went far to convince her this one was authentic. *But none of this matters!* She knew where the painting was, real or fake, authorities could recover it, and the tests could be done. She couldn't be expected to do any more than that. She had seen into the eyes behind Joachim's glasses. The man was a psychopath, and she was in danger. The sooner she was away from there, the better. A clamminess washed over her, and it wasn't just from the climate control in the room for the painting.

She sat and studied the painting a bit more, trying to fix the image in her mind. She then waved her left hand. Joachim reentered. *Hidden camera for CCTV?* It might be a security system for the painting. Along with the climate control, that could be another point for authenticity.

***

"I'm not convinced it's authentic," Brookstone told Joachim. "I'm leaning toward that, so I'll be willing to take the risk. My doubts might temper my bids, of course."

He frowned. She saw a bit of flame in the cold eyes. "What is the problem, madam?"

"It's stolen art no one's seen for decades," she said. "I've only seen an old black and white picture of the painting, so I have to base my analysis on many other details I'm sure you won't want to hear about with your lack of patience."

"But you're still in the bidding?" His tone was hopeful while a bit threatening at the same time.

"Yes. I said I was willing to take the risk. At worst, it will be an expensive conversation piece hanging somewhere in my residence; at best, I can lend it in perpetuity to a reputable museum and receive credit for saving it from the likes of you and your accomplices or other buyers."

"That's a bit harsh."

"It is what it is. You can take me back to my hotel now."

"As you wish. I will be in contact soon."

"You'd better be. I don't like to waste my time either."

Now Joachim managed a smile. She could amuse even an art thief.

Chapter Twenty-Three
Stuttgart

Van Coevorden and his team maintained surveillance at the warehouse until Brookstone phoned to say she was back at the hotel. He gave the command to move in.

The warehouse was now empty except for the painting that still hung behind the curtain.

"It must be a fake!" she said over her mobile. "They would never leave the original. It's only a good copy, but I had no way to confirm that until now."

"And now your cover's blown," he said.

"Maybe not. You fellows didn't mention my name, did you?"

"Why?"

"If you said, 'Esther was here and wore a wire,' that would blow my cover, as you say, and maybe make me Joachim's target for wasting his time. They must have a CCTV hookup, probably Wi-Fi too. I thought they'd need it for the painting, but maybe only to see who's in the warehouse. So, did you mention my name?"

"I'll query the SWAT team members, but I don't think anyone did. There was no reason, and only a few even knew you were involved."

"Where are you calling me from?"

"A few blocks away from the warehouse, from my hire car. What do we do with the fake painting?"

"One thing we can do is prevent them from selling the real one. Authorities can perform an analysis—that might tell us something because forgers that good often leave some clue about their ID. We'll then declare it's authentic and broadcast that over the newswires. That will make other bidders do a double take and it might delay Joachim's little auction."

"Devious."

Of course, he knew one had to be at least as devious as the criminals to beat them at their game. Or more so.

***

Van Coevorden continued to work with German authorities, especially Kurt Geiszler, who had arranged for the SWAT team. Brookstone returned to London. She figured if Joachim called, her cover was still good. That might be an incorrect assumption, but it was her only chance to continue her pursuit of the painting.

"I can't believe you did that," said Langston. He was sitting on the edge of her desk. "You rarely listen to me, you know."

"Feeling superfluous today, George? Van Coevorden and the Germans were watching all the time. I was worried but not too worried."

"So they'd find your body before it was cold? Small comfort. That's no way to retire from the Yard, you know."

"It was a bit risky, I'll admit, but at my age a bullet in the head might be the best way to leave this world. I don't want to die in a hospice, and if I can recover a valuable painting for posterity, it makes the risk worthwhile. I'd love to kick some Nazis in the goolies."

"What a pile of horse excrement! I think you're trying to be fired so you can sue the Yard for age discrimination." He said it with a smile, though. "What's next?"

"I'm waiting for a call from my gothic friend Joachim. If he wants a bid, I'll have to give it to him. He did what I requested, after all."

"But if he knows you're from the Yard?"

"No reason why he should. He's checked my background, I'm sure, but that's all legit. I am Countess Sartini, after all, not that the title will get me an appointment with the Pope anytime soon. My worry is that neo-Nazi might think I triggered the visit from van Coevorden and Geiszler's friends, another reason for them to wait until I returned to the hotel. But Joachim and his friends must have anticipated something like that because they left the fake painting in the warehouse. That doesn't bode well for continuing on this case, of course."

He shook his head. "Not necessarily. Maybe someone spotted the authorities moving in, and they scattered like a pack of rats, not bothering with the fake painting. They might think you still believe it's authentic."

"Possibly. There are a lot of unknowns. I'm going to call Gerhard Dunst and tell him I saw the Rembrandt and think it's fake, no matter what the authorities say. If he's involved at all, he will tell Joachim, and the little twit will think I'm still interested."

"More deviousness. OK. Just be careful, old friend. Sometimes spiders can get caught in the webs they weave."

"I'll confirm that with an arachnologist. And not this spider. I'm a black widow." She paused a moment and smiled. "For the criminals, that is. I treated my husbands well."

"Yet you outlasted them all."

"I can see the metaphor took you to a dark place, sir. Please come back to me and the light."

He smiled. "To change the topic, what about that castle in Scotland?"

She pondered the question. "I'm signing papers and sending them back to MacDougall's barrister. I'm taking it sight unseen, or should I say S-I-T-E unseen, but I don't have time to travel there to make a home inspection. Web pics can be so misleading. I can always bail later on."

"Sounds like a plan. With the other, do be careful, Esther. I value our friendship."

As he left, she found her desk phone.

Chapter Twenty-Four
London

Brookstone had to leave a message for Gerhard Dunst, but the call went to voice mail. She told the industrialist to call her. She needed to finish writing a report on the Bernini sculpture, so she decided to begin. She put on her headphones and loaded a collection of classic hits by the rock group Queen. She was humming to "Bohemian Rhapsody" when the phone rang. She nearly missed the call.

"*Allo, Frau* Brookstone," said Dunst. "My apologies. I've been somewhat busy."

"ISIS does keep Europeans busy these days," she said. "I saw the news. I'm sorry for your losses, whatever they were. I'm particularly upset by those ghastly beheadings. What savage animals! But I called for another reason. I saw my painting." She smiled for her phone's camera. "It's hard to be sure, but I think they were trying to sell me a fake. Who knows why they're trying to pass off the copy as real if they truly have the original? Thought you'd like to know. You were lucky you made no bid for yours."

"If it was truly fake, you are correct. In any case, there'd be lots of publicity if I'd donated it to a museum. Even at my age, I must continue to learn by my mistakes when I make them. I take it you will now bid on the real painting if they offer it? Do you now know how many other people are involved in the bidding?"

"No, and that's a problem. Real estate brokers do the same thing. They like to create a bidding war where no one knows what others have bid. I'll make a reasonable bid. If I don't win, I might go to authorities. They would like to know about these art thieves, I suspect."

"They already do. They recovered the fake painting yet say it's authentic. I have no idea why unless their art consultants are completely incompetent. Your contact is deceiving you, or maybe it was only his test so he knows the painting will be in good hands. I'd ignore what authorities say. You can't trust them either."

"Assuming I was right. I don't know who to trust now. It's not like I can have the painting they offer authenticated. My trip with a bag over my head was wasted, I'm afraid."

"They did that to you? How uncivilized!"

"Not as much as lopping someone's head off. What do you recommend, *Herr* Dunst?"

"Considering your philanthropic goal, I guess I'd assume they wouldn't dare try to show you a fake again. But be careful in any case."

"You don't have any contacts among German authorities? I need more information."

"I can make some calls. I suppose you want to know why they're saying the painting is authentic if it isn't. Give me a couple of days. At the very least, I should find someone for you to talk too. My half-sister runs a gallery in Linz. I'll query her too in case she's heard any rumors. Any idea what the thieves plan to do with your money?"

"No. Is that important?"

"It could be. It depends on their agenda." He laughed. "Maybe they're only going to retire to a Caribbean island." She heard another phone ring. "Excuse me a second." She waited until he returned to the phone. "I'm sorry. I have to go. I'll get back to you when I have some information. Stiff upper lip, as you Brits say."

As she ended the connection and put her mobile back in her purse, she was thinking Dunst sounded like a helpful gentleman during that entire conversation. But many times a criminal knew how to use subterfuge to commit a crime even though he seemed to be a respectable person. *Especially in my line of work.*

Her mind took a sharp detour. She tapped the Bernini report with an index finger and frowned. *Did the Yard ever check on the background of that old Italian lothario? Maybe he isn't what he seems either!*

Chapter Twenty-Five
London

"Not a bad hunch," said Langston, looking across the table at Brookstone.

She was sipping coffee; he was drinking tea. Tea time between them was unusual, but he had invited her.

"Let me guess. He or his ancestors have some relationship to Mussolini."

"No, but he was no Italian gentleman. He was in Tito's army and escaped into Italy through Trieste when that old bastard went to whatever section of hell is reserved for Communist despots. The Bernini was purchased on the black market, and the buyer wasn't even Italian."

"No wonder he didn't pursue the mistress. I bet she knows. We won't know that until we catch her, but she likely figured he wouldn't make a scandal about his stolen artwork for fear of exposure. She was wrong, of course, although he didn't care about losing her. Love among thieves—it's such a bloody farce sometimes."

He nodded. He was going to give her lots of credit about that wild guess when her retirement proceedings came up. It had been a fabulous epiphany. "Still no call from Joachim?"

"Not yet. I talked to Dunst, who's not likely involved as my first guess, but the jury is still deliberating. He didn't go out of his way to convince me the recovered painting is a fake, but he was ambivalent about whether I should proceed, so maybe he's OK. I'm expecting a call from Joachim in any case. He'll want me to rejoin the bidding. If Dunst is involved, Joachim will think he has more evidence of my desire to buy the real one. It's like a tangled potful of sixty-year-old linguine."

"Joachim might want you out of the bidding because he sees you as a troublemaker."

"He would be right," she said with a smile. "Nevertheless, a good thief who's trying to unload stolen property might see a troublemaker as being the more dedicated buyer. He knows my money's good."

"If I were Joachim, I'd try to snatch your money and still hold onto the painting so I could sell it to someone else."

"Van Coevorden and I talked about that. Dunst worried about it too. For some shady clients who are willing to purchase stolen art, such a tactic might put a contract on the seller's head. For all Joachim knows, I have contacts with the Italian mafia or some member of the royal house of Saud."

"Do you?" said Langston with a wink.

She smiled. "Privileged information." She took a sip of her coffee. What they served in the little coffee bar wasn't bad. *At least it seems to be pure Colombian brewed in the Italian style.*

After Langston returned to his cave, she received a call from Scotland. A developer gave her a spiel ending with an offer for her castle property. She thought it might be a fair offer, although she figured they would benefit far too much from the deal. She thanked the developer for calling but turned down the offer.

During the drive home, she continued to think about Scotland, second guessing that decision.

The call motivated her to kill some time researching Angus MacDougall and Dughallach Castle some more. She went at it on her laptop after a light dinner.

Angus is quite the dashing fellow was her last thought as sleep overcame her....

***

"Esther, I'm off," said MacDougall in Brookstone's dream. He was dressed in his RAF uniform, cutting a dashing figure. "The British Empire needs me!"

She turned in the bed, surprised to find she was young and naked. She raised the sheet to her chin.

"You're crazy, Angus. Scotland wants to be independent from Britain, and you want to run off to be shot down by Nazi pilots on their behalf?"

"Independence? What are you talking about? We're at war with the Nazis. We can't allow them to bomb London at will, you know."

He saluted. She giggled. Not long ago her man was naked and saluting her in a different fashion as she tore off her clothes to hop into bed with him. She could never get enough of him, nor he of her. They knew each other's erotic spots so well by now. How could she let him go off to fight?

"Winnie should fight his own damn war, I say. Come back to bed."

"I shall return to you, my love. We're taking it to the Germans this time. They bomb us, we'll bomb them. That's Churchill's motto, and I'm all for it. There will be no future for our children otherwise." She stood in the bed so she could reach his lips, but he kissed her aroused nipples instead. "I'll be back soon. Wait for me."

She spent the whole damn war waiting. She knew where he was—he just couldn't come home.

The letters were always from the Netherlands, arriving in stealthy ways.

"I'm helping the resistance," MacDougall had said in an early one. "They broke me out of the POW camp. I'm staying with one of the leaders of a resistance cell, a fellow named van Coevorden. We smuggled another RAF flyer out of the country who agreed to take you this letter. That system seems to be working."

Idiot! Why doesn't he smuggle himself out of Holland? He's probably humping some busty resistance fighter. I have needs too. Who's this van Coevorden? What right does he have to order Angus around?

"I'm going to ask you for an immense favor, Esther. Take the train to Edinburgh and go to my castle nearby. We're going to send some other refugees across from Denmark. They need a place to stay while you put their paperwork in order for them. I know this is a big favor to ask, but you're the logical person for this task."

A list of names followed with the date the refugees would be arriving. She frowned at the inconvenience of it all, but she couldn't deny Angus's wishes.

She made the trip to Edinburgh during the night. The Luftwaffe's bombing raids had turned cities dark, although London was always the principal target. Train schedules had been decimated by the war, but she arrived at the castle on time, even with the snow.

A man named Gerhard Dunst led the refugee group. They were all tired and hungry, so she helped unpack them while they feasted on provisions she had bought in Edinburgh. She unpacked Dunst's luggage first. Shaking out a suit coat, papers dropped to the floor.

She picked them up, thinking to return them to the coat pocket, but she stopped in her tracks. The credentials were those of a Gestapo agent. *Did Angus send me a spy?*

She heard old boards squeak behind her and turned. Dunst was covering her with a German Luger.

"I'm afraid you've discovered our little scheme, Mrs. MacDougall," said Dunst.

"I'm not Mrs. MacDougall yet," she said. "Are you all Nazis?"

"More than Nazis, madam. We're all spies sent here to create mayhem and murder. As much as possible."

"How could Angus ever permit such a thing?"

"It was easy to convince him. He and van Coevorden are both dead. I wrote that letter."

The gun fired...

***

Brookstone awoke in a sweat and cursed. *I hate dreams!* Good or bad, they always made her wonder if her life was all just another dream.

She glanced at the laptop. MacDougall's RAF record, mostly in his own words, was still on the screen. *Nothing wrong with my imagination, I guess.* She decided the lusty bedroom scene was worth remembering, though.

Are you going to haunt me, MacDougall? Maybe his ghost had been in the castle and was now following her around? *But how did he find me?*

As the phone rang, though, she wondered if her subconscious was reaffirming suspicions once held about Dunst.

Chapter Twenty-Six
Linz, Austria

Karen Lietzke parked her Mercedes in back of her gallery in Linz. She had washed it and vacuumed inside. *Someday I will have a chauffeur who will do that for me!* It would have to be a striking young man, well-formed, blond, and blue-eyed—maybe an *Oberleutenant* in the new SS, her very own bodyguard. She smiled. *A man who will make passionate love to me when I want and keep his mouth shut about it!*

The owner of the neighboring shop, *Herr* Moore, who sold rare and used books to the Linz elite, waved at her. He was smiling; she frowned. He removed a box of used books from the backseat of his car and carried it into his store.

She knew the bookstore owner's story. He was an old fool who had visited Austria for *Oktoberfest* some years back. He liked the country so much, he said, that he had stayed and opened his store in Linz. She didn't know him that well, but the times she had visited his bookstore, she was taken aback by the background music—always Haydn or Mozart, never Wagner. Besides Moore sounded Irish to her, and she didn't like the Irish, whether Protestant or Catholic. She had objected to her half-brother's hiring of the two ex-IRA mercenaries.

The E.U. has made the Fatherland soft. There are too few real patriots. And too many foreign elements!

She expected her day to be slow. Although paintings in the gallery covered a wide range of prices, it was an upscale place frequented by upscale Austrians. Many of them came by appointment, sometimes at odd hours. She still opened Tuesdays through Saturdays, 10 to 3 and Sundays, 1 to 4, excluding most holidays. She would sell to anyone who had the money, of course, even a Jew. *Yes, for now, I'd sell to a Jew who has the means. Not later.* Her plans involved purifying the Fatherland by eliminating all the Jews and immigrants, everyone who was currently ruining Austria and Germany.

She had brought a book with her to pass the time, not one from Moore's bookstore, a recent tale of erotic love she had chosen from another used book store. After opening shop and turning on lights, she poured a glass of red wine and made herself comfortable in a recliner she kept in the rear. But she couldn't read.

Romance and erotica books often had more upbeat plots than what was often swirling through her head. *How this world would have changed if Hitler had won!* The little Austrian was her hero. He represented a chance lost, a chance for future Teutonic greatness. *I will make Austria and Germany great again! Unity and purity. Those concepts are key.* She could imagine herself giving a rousing speech from a balcony like some 21st century Eva Peron. The people would love her too, because she would make them masters of Europe again. Europe? No! The world.

The Jewess who had given birth to her was long dead, only a faint and bitter memory now. There were no pictures of her. She remembered a stern, older woman, although she preferred not to mentally revisit that bit of her bleak past. *Forget the past, Karen. Glory doesn't reside there. Where Hitler failed, I will succeed.*

She had given up a chauffeur and many other things to make that happen—much more than her half-brother. Her husband had indulged her until he believed that the siblings just might be successful. Walther Lietzke was lucky—he seemed to always choose the winning side. *He made his millions without any talents whatsoever.* He might be one of the first victims of her purge!

The phone rang. She had to go to the desk in front. Cursing, she struggled from the chair. It rang five times before she reached it. *Maybe a client? Otherwise, why not call on my mobile?*

***

"I'm having second thoughts about all this," said her husband Walther.

Speaking of the fool! He has my mobile number! The man wasn't too bright, just lucky. Once that didn't matter. Now it was more important to her.

"You have no backbone," she said, "and you're paranoid. But what are your doubts?"

"People will die."

"That's the idea. Some people have to die. Some people should die. We are the avengers, my husband. And, by avenging our past, we will create a magnificent future."

"Noble thoughts. But our actions imply risks. In the art deal, we cannot screen buyers completely, for example. Every time we bring someone onboard, by any manner whatsoever, we run the risk of being discovered and exposed."

"Don't be stupid," she said. "It's like playing the stock market. Those who win big are the ones who take risks. You know that better than I do. That's something you do well."

"That's a bit different. And why Oslo?"

"I like the chalet there. It needs some improvements, but it's the perfect summer home and an ideal venue for an art auction. And we can arrange things so we can watch the buyers like hawks. That should mitigate risks. We'll kill anyone who looks suspicious. Simple as that."

"I guess. That risk is insignificant in the grand scheme of things, I suppose."

Precisely! "You worry about details. Let me worry about the grand scheme. I have it under control. I always do, no thanks to you."

She hung up.

***

Karen Lietzke couldn't remember when she'd last slept with her husband. An older man, he had lost interest years ago. At least, interest in her. She knew for a fact that he liked little girls. That old Prussian pig in the U.S. who had managed many connections in Europe had provided them through his human trafficking business. *A pervert!* At least he wasn't gay. Neither is Walther, but they now slept in separate rooms in their sprawling mansion.

She decided she was now ready for her novel. She began with a sip of wine. She then found a juicy section she had marked about one-third the way through and started reading. Soon her hand went between her legs.

After her orgasm, she fell asleep, and the book dropped to the floor.

Part Three

We don't stop playing because we grow old; we grow old because we stop playing.
—George Bernard Shaw

Chapter Twenty-Seven
London

Brookstone's next call from Joachim was an invitation to a real auction. She spoke to van Coevorden and Geiszler afterward. Both agreed she should make the trip to Oslo, the auction site. She had enough time to take some vacation days, drive to Edinburgh, visit her castle, and then fly to Oslo.

The trip to Natalie's estate had reminded her of how enjoyable it was to tour in her Jaguar. Alberto Sartini had loved touring too, especially in the Swiss and Italian Alps. If not by auto, on train, because he had no love for planes. Both train and auto touring were easy on the continent where less than a day's travel often took you into a new country.

The long trek to Scotland was mostly on M1 and A1, but it started badly. She nearly hit Fox's BMW leaving the garage. He stopped beside her and lowered his car window. She did the same, staring him down.

"You should slow down upon entering the garage, Mr. Fox. No wonder you dented my vehicle."

"On the contrary, Mrs. Brookstone, I shall mention this to my barrister as proof you are incapable of driving and should have your permit to drive rescinded. I'll see you in court."

She fumed during the first two hours of the journey. She then got into it, becoming one with her car, ding and all, woman and machine conquering miles of highway.

The trick to touring was to take bite-sized chunks—no more than a half day of travel followed by some exploring in a nice place and a night in a hotel. She stayed in Harrogate at the Grafton Boutique B&B—the town and area around it was a lovely respite too, and the owners of the inn knew her from previous visits.

Next morning she left for Edinburgh. Some hours later, she pulled into a parking garage near the Edinburgh barrister's office on Frederick Street. One of many at the firm, George Cearrach was affable enough, an old curmudgeon with Victorian era whiskers. He recommended The Raeburn if she stayed the night in Edinburgh and gave her a copy of the keys to her castle.

"Esther, do you understand I have to keep a copy in compliance with Mr. McDougall's wishes?" She nodded. "I'll credit you with one night's stay at your property. With the keys you can visit anytime, of course, but please inform me so I can add the days to your total."

"Of course. Now, if you don't mind, I'd like to have a late lunch and rest a bit. How far is it to the castle, by the way?"

"I'm not sure, but I probably have that filed here somewhere." He searched through the file folder, found a paper, and photocopied it, handing the copy to her.

"I'd love to stay and chat. Maybe on another trip you can take me to dinner. I'm not a frequent visitor here. I'm sure you know some good places."

"You'd be surprised how many tourists want to find the places in that mystery writer's books." She said his name and the barrister nodded. "My sister Minerva and I would love to have you over to dine with us. You'd make quite the splash, my dear. Imagine, a dinner guest from Scotland Yard!"

These people need to get a life! "I'm sure you'll not find me all that exciting. Thank you for all your help."

***

Brookstone headed to the castle before the evening commute and after buying some non-perishables and other items like a broom, dust pan, and trash bin. *One never knows where the next meal will come from, and I'm not going to eat in a filthy kitchen.* The barrister's directions were acceptable, although he hadn't indicated any distances.

Her vehicle was a time machine as she headed northwest. Bustling Edinburgh became Scottish countryside. She could imagine she was in the 17th century as the miles rolled by. The weather turned cool. She didn't think the altitude had changed all that much, so she wrote it off as heading toward the interior.

A bit more than two hours and many winding miles later, she turned off the tarmac onto a narrow gravel road. She could see some ruins perched atop a knoll and wound her way toward them, downshifting to take the grade. *Ruins? My castle!*

She had left Edinburgh with no preconceptions—no idea what to expect at the castle, except for the privy. Pics were deceiving, especially when it came to real estate transactions. But she hadn't expected to find the castle occupied.

Squatter? She guessed the Mini Cooper parked in the back wasn't Angus MacDougall's. He'd never have fit in it, for one thing. She had spotted it a ways back on the entrance road, parked her Jaguar, and studied the situation with binoculars she always carried in the auto. The only sign of the Cooper's owner was found in a few fleeting shadows moving behind some dirty curtains on the second floor of the old house.

She didn't carry a gun, but this was one time when she thought she might need one, only because the person inside her castle might have one.

She decided her first step would be to examine the intruder's vehicle. Except for crunches of gravel as she made her way to it in stealthy fashion, she was soon kneeling by the passenger side, the car between her and the castle. She cracked open the door, rummaged around in the cubby, and found a rental contract.

On it was a woman's name, Dejah Thoris, but it didn't ring a bell. In fact, it sounded fake for some reason. *An opera singer maybe?* She hadn't been to one in years, but she often listened to selected arias at home and even played a bit of the music on her piano. She liked Puccini best. Good English opera composers were as rare as unicorns, as was most acceptable British music—only Vaughan Williams appealed to her. And Handel, but he was really German.

She listened, still in a crouch, but hearing nothing, she stood to prevent cramps. She flexed her legs, knowing she hadn't spent enough time at the gym lately and the ride had been long. Because the small vehicle was otherwise empty, she put the rental agreement back into the cubby and closed the passenger's door.

Still no sounds. *No way around it, Esther. You have to go claim your property.* She hoped the squatter wasn't a violent person. She imagined a psycho high on meth. *Maybe he's even making it here?*

***

Brookstone left the intruder's hire car and went around to the front door of the castle like a Viking princess inspecting the damage her men had wrought to yet another defenseless Scottish abode. The heavy wooden door wasn't too functional— the lower hinge was held fast with only one bolt, the rest of the hardware having rusted out. She decided her keys weren't necessary but also that opening the door would likely warn the squatter. She circled the castle some more, found a ground-floor window partially opened, raised the sash, and slipped inside.

The room had once been a library. Floor-to-ceiling bookcases now sat empty and sagging, some warped wooden shelves resting on ones below. *What a dump!*

She went to a doorway and peered around the corner into a hall. At the bottom of a wide stairway, a young woman with a gun beamed a smile at her.

"I'll give you to five to tell me who you are," she said.

"I'm the new owner come to claim my property. What are you doing here?"

The squatter lowered the gun a bit. "The property was abandoned when I arrived. Maybe you're lying, and you're the intruder." The gun wavered some more. She bit her lip.

She looks unstable. I better bide my time. Unlike other police, she had zero experience in dealing with the criminally insane. She had audited a few courses, but no direct experience. Now she wished she had some.

"I'm a distant relative of the previous owner. He died and left me this place. I wanted to see what I'm getting into. You haven't answered my question."

"The answer is simple: I'm in hiding. I'm wanted by the police."

Could it be? Brookstone smiled as the realization gave her a mental slap. To confirm her hunch, she tried to remember the JPEG image she had sent to Jeremy Brand and the security man at the airport. The airport security tape had been even grainier. But the similarity couldn't be coincidence. *Just my luck! Shall I try to arrest her?*

"Let me guess. You're Sylvia Bassett, not Dejah Thoris, and you ripped off your Italian boyfriend by taking some of his artwork."

The woman frowned. "That's no guess. You must be the police. Throw your purse over here."

"No purse, sweetie. It's locked in my Jaguar in the entrance drive. And I am the owner of this castle, so don't add trespassing, kidnapping, and murder of a Scotland Yard agent to your criminal history. You're in enough trouble."

Brookstone's jaw dropped at the woman's next action. The mistress from Italy turned art thief let the gun fall to the floor, sat on the stair step, and started to cry.

"I've made a mess of everything! He turned into such a brute."

Chapter Twenty-Eight
Near Edinburgh

Brookstone walked over, picked up the gun, removed the clip, and tossed it back into the library. She handed the empty gun to the woman.

"I'll second your first statement," she said, sitting beside the woman and putting her arm around her. "You had the safety on, by the way." The woman sobbed again; Brookstone squeezed her shoulder. "Normally I'd have to call the local constable and have him arrest you. But my mobile's in the car, and I don't know how good reception is here." She looked at the anemic late afternoon sun managing to filter into the old castle. *How did Bassett find this place?* "You've been here before, haven't you?"

"We used to have parties here. It was a secret place where teens could come and get away from our parents. Especially in my case. My father was a scam artist who beat my mother and me when he was drunk, but he thought he had to protect me from men like him. Old man MacDougall was never around."

"OK. Let me call you Ophelia. We can pretend we're in Elsinore, although that castle in Denmark makes this one look like a hovel." Brookstone became pensive for a moment. "Darling Ophelia, because you know this place so well, walk with me and show me around my castle. We can talk. We'll then fix some supper and talk some more. Be assured you can stay here a while longer, but I have to leave tomorrow morning. When I return from my overseas trip, though, I want you to be gone. Do you understand?" Ophelia nodded. "Good. That's settled. Let's first bring my Jaguar nearer the house. Your little Mini Cooper hire car might feel inferior next to it, but I'd prefer to have my car parked nearer the castle, if you don't mind."

***

The tour of the property with Sylvia Bassett as guide showed Brookstone it had potential. No wonder the developer wanted it. Vistas, while bleak, were typical Lowlands ones and worth a lot of money by themselves. The lengthening shadows caressed the land as if Nut and Gaia were performing lesbian foreplay. She smiled. *Nicely mixed mythology, that.*

She doubted any developer would leave the castle standing, though. It was indeed more like a ruin. During their meager dinner, a light rain fell, and water leaked from the roof. Because they were on the ground floor, it meant something was leaking upstairs too. The thought of expensive repairs wasn't a happy one for Brookstone.

Dinner conversation didn't exactly sparkle. The girl seemed lost in her thoughts; Brookstone struggled to put order into her own that meandered farther beyond the bucolic setting with the girl. But Ophelia must have sensed the conversation lag; she broke her silence.

"How does one become a member of Scotland Yard, Mrs. Brookstone?"

"Mere happenstance, for the most part." She smiled. "I married Graham, my first husband, right out of public school. He was a flamboyant and charming older man whom I dearly loved. He was a philanderer, but we separated amicably. Within three years, he died of a massive heart attack doing what he did best."

"And that was?"

"Seducing young girls. Am I boring you?" Ophelia shook her head. "I came to my senses, studied criminology, and discovered art. I can't paint or draw worth a damn, but I love art. That's how I met Alfred, my shy professor. Graham wooed me; I had to seduce Alfred." She winked. "Now number three, Alberto, my Count Sartini—that, my dear, was mutual physical attraction, like an electron and positron colliding, I imagine. It wasn't all about sex; it never is. After the sparks fly, you must learn to live together."

"I'd love to meet someone and have that happen."

"You will, my dear. Shall we do the dishes?"

***

Their meal had been simple and based on the non-perishables Brookstone had brought, so there weren't many dishes. The chipped place settings were a hodge-podge collection from various sets, the cutlery corroded stainless.

"You seem to like this place," she said as they finished putting dishes away.

"It's a magical place. It's where I first made love with a young man, Mrs. Brookstone."

"Ah, such memories can blow away bad ones as long as everything went well. That first experience can be a bit painful for the woman, though. If he was gentle but dashing and handsome, maybe you should have snagged instead of shagged him, my dear."

She laughed. "He was gentle. Dashing and handsome, not so much—he had a bad case of acne, I'm afraid. It was a party. I was a bit tipsy, I'll admit, but he was drunk. He also came too fast. He didn't remember much the next day. It was still special for me, though. At least I learned not all men are brutes. I told you about my father."

"Parents often try to control their children's lives because they can't control their own."

"Do you believe in God?"

Where'd that come from? "Not in the conventional way, I'm sure. There's definitely no room for a vengeful God in my credo, and I often wonder how a loving God has time for all the sinners in the world. Alberto was a staunch atheist, in fact. I'd like to think there's something beyond our mortal existence, but I'm not going to bet on that poker hand either. And I partially agree with my husband: one has the moral responsibility to make the most of our time on this planet, whether we believe in an afterlife or not. That implies helping others do the same, by the way, which is why I'm giving you a bit of leeway, my dear. I'd like to see your life straightened out."

She nodded but looked sad. "I might be swimming in deep, dangerous waters. Like I said before, I've made a mess of things."

"Nonsense." Brookstone saw tears forming in the doe's eyes. "There, there, don't get all teary on me again, feeling sorry for yourself. Yes, you've made a mess of it, dear, but you can change that. Do you hear me?"

"I guess."

***

Next morning Bassett walked Brookstone to her vehicle. "I suppose you want me to turn myself in?"

"After visiting with you, dear, and knowing you better, I don't know what I want. It's your choice. You know it won't be all that convenient for you to remain a wanted fugitive. But I have other fish to fry, as they say, so I don't give a damn what you do. All I can do now is wish you a good life. And please improve on how you select a man to share that life with. Too

160

many are cads who think about that triangle between your legs and not about you as a person. Your father was right in that respect. Keep that in mind."

Ophelia smiled. "The voice of experience?"

"I've been lucky, but luck comes to those who work for it too. My only regret is that I tend to wear the dear old fellows out." She winked and then kissed her on the lips. "We do have to feed what's between our legs occasionally, don't we? One must be smart about it, though."

"You sound like my mother."

"I'm sorry she died on you. She would have provided some balance for your old man. You're lucky he didn't make you wear a chastity belt, you know."

She nodded. "But, if I'd listened to him, I wouldn't be in this fix."

"I suppose, but don't ever forget he basically sold you to that Serbian devil. Apply a bit of reason and logic to your future choices. That will turn your life around." Brookstone entered the Jaguar, and Bassett closed the door. "Remember your promise. Drop me a letter when you're settled...as Ophelia, of course. Good luck."

Brookstone saw the woman waving at her via her rearview mirror. *An interesting experience. I wonder what Oslo will bring?*

Chapter Twenty-Nine
Oslo

Back in Edinburgh, Brookstone stored her car and took a taxi to the airport. The old barrister's recommendation for that was useful too, but she was always worried about leaving her Jaguar anywhere outside its home garage, a bit contradictory now considering Fox had dented it there. She sighed. Things could become so complicated.

She thought of Sylvia Bassett during the short flight on Norwegian to Oslo. Would the woman be gone when she returned to Dughallach Castle? She hoped so, because that would mean her new protégé had decided to choose doing something proactive over sitting around and wallowing in self-pity.

At journey's end, she took a taxi to Oslo's Grand Hotel. The bellhop there pretended to struggle with her bags. *He's looking for a good tip.* He belied the Nordic stereotype. With his dark brown hair and flashing brown eyes, he oozed Latin charm instead. She thought of her Italian count. It was so easy to fall in love with an Italian.

She was tired. *Joachim is making my life difficult.* She realized it was her own doing, of course, and winks from a swarthy young man flirting with her couldn't make it more appetizing. The business with Ophelia had been stressful too.

As she made her way to the registration desk, she nodded to Bastiann van Coevorden, who sat reading a paper. He'd flown in from Amsterdam. Expenses were always an issue, but Langston had promised her to move mountains to obtain reimbursement if she recovered the painting. She knew it was a Faustian bargain, but she wanted to recover that masterpiece. She didn't know what van Coevorden's situation was.

"*Condessa* Sartini, we have your room already made up," said the clerk, handing her the key. "I only need a credit card, please."

I'll kill him! "It's Esther Brookstone. You can call me Esther. That's the name in my passport. One of my ex-husbands was the count, so I earned that title, I suppose." She handed him her gold card with the largest credit limit. "I assume I can make charges to that. I do hate to carry a lot of cash, you see.

The clerk smiled and nodded. "Now I understand. That gentleman sitting over there made your reservation and called you *Condessa* Sartini."

"Yes, I know, and I hope to have a bit of fun frolicking with him as a bit of payback, if you know what I mean." The clerk's face went red. *More proof all men are swine, always jumping to conclusions! Bastiann could just be a friend.* She waved the key. "Please, no calls until nine this evening. I need some bedtime."

The clerk nodded, still blushing.

***

Brookstone had tipped another bellhop who had brought her bags and sent him on his way when there was a knock at the door.

"The door's open, Bastiann."

"I heard what you told the desk clerk. Is that supposed to be my cover? I don't like pretending I'm your traveling lover."

163

She patted a spot on the bed beside her. "Yes, so let's not pretend and make it seem as real as possible. It's been awhile."

"You're incorrigible."

"The right word is horny, to be practical. I was thinking of you last night, in fact, in the most incorrigible way, I'll admit. It will help me sleep better. And you must be bored, sitting in that lobby pretending you can read Norwegian."

He smiled. "I can a bit. It's easier than German with its devilishly long sentences."

"Perhaps, but right now I need to exploit some of your other talents."

***

After Brookstone was sated and asleep, van Coevorden lay naked in bed and continued to analyze his attachment to her. Theirs was a strange relationship. There was commitment but distance. He suspected he was more committed than she was, but he respected her wishes to maintain a long-distance amorous relationship without marriage. *Is it because she's had too many marriages? Am I not mature enough for her? Or, is she afraid to lose another husband?*

As far as he knew, all Brookstone's marriages had been successful. *Maybe too successful?* He smiled. *Maybe she wore out her husbands? She is pretty demanding, after all, and they still were both in excellent shape without major health problems.* He knew he could continue the present kind of relationship because to do otherwise would be mentally painful. *We're both bons vivants. At our age, as long as it remains bon and vivant, what does it matter?*

He heard her gentle snores and felt her exhaling as she slept with her head on his chest. He blew at her brown curls and smiled. He had feared for her life when she went into that warehouse in Stuttgart. *What's Joachim's plan now? He understood how an auction might be attractive to the art thief, but why Oslo?*

Joachim now seemed irrelevant. *We might as well enjoy ourselves while waiting for that bastard's call.*

He decided he smelled as ripe as a room in an Amsterdam brothel. He'd never been a client of one, but he had been at a murder scene in such a room. Replacing his chest with a plush down pillow, he wriggled from under her and headed for the shower.

He would have to request a recommendation for a good restaurant from the concierge. He didn't trust his memory. He hadn't been in Oslo for some time. His most recent trips to Scandinavia had been to Malmo and Stockholm.

It shouldn't be a problem. Our tastes are so similar.

Chapter Thirty
Oslo

Brookstone and van Coevorden walked arm in arm to the Jaipur Indian Restaurant. He knew she liked Indian food, especially curries, so it was a good choice. In spite of gall stones, he did too. The restaurant was two-thirds full and just right for a date night, although night didn't apply because the sun was still well above the horizon.

"I feel much better after our amorous exercise and little nap," she said after the waiter seated them.

"I'm a little bit sore," he said with a smile. "I put some Vaseline on that bite. You're a tigress, my love. Or should I say cougar like the Yanks do?"

"Tigress is the more appropriate metaphor for this restaurant, I suppose," she said with a smile while waving her delicately boned hand. "India doesn't have any cougars, as far as I know." She studied him for a moment. "I do get carried away sometimes in the passion of the moment, I'll admit. I wouldn't have survived in the Victorian era, I'm afraid, beginning with all those deplorable clothes. One needed servants if only to lace corsets and button those awful shoes." She turned sideways, extending her leg to show her foot. "Do you like my new shoes, by the way?"

"I noticed. Did you buy them for this trip?"

"No, for Stuttgart, but we didn't have a chance to get frisky there, so I didn't go for the seductive look. I needed to play the role of rich countess for Joachim, though."

"Some would say you already seduced me long ago."

"Some would be correct, at least about the first time, but it's always a continuing saga, especially if that damn Joachim doesn't call. I'm a little afraid, Bastiann. He might be looking for revenge if he connects me to your little raid."

"You can still bail and let me handle this the rest of the way."

"Suppose he saw you? That would be dangerous for you too."

"He would have needed spotters outside the warehouse, but they would have only seen Geiszler's SWAT and forensic teams, not me. And I was never inside. That's Interpol's style."

"I don't know if you look like a lover, but you don't look like an Interpol cop either. I guess we're OK. I can't figure this menu out. Where are my glasses?" She rummaged around in her purse. "There. I now look like somebody's grandmother, but I can read the bloody menu. Ah, no wonder. Dishes are in Hindi and their description is in a much smaller font. I think a nice cabernet would go well with every entrée here. Some red, at least. What do you think?"

***

During dinner, Brookstone told him about the castle.

"How are you going to manage repairing and maintaining that?" said van Coevorden.

"You're supposed to congratulate me for joining the landed gentry. Maybe I'm due a seat in the House of Lords? 'Honorable Prime Minister, I present the honorable lady, *Contessa* Sartini, from Edinburgh.'"

He laughed. "For all you know, you're a distant blood relative of Rob Roy, the outlaw."

"That would be an honor, Bastiann. He was the Scottish Robin Hood."

"I suppose I have London's 'official' version of the story." He used his index fingers to put the quotes around "official." "Sorry. At any rate, the castle sounds like the proverbial White Elephant. What's it look like?"

She thought a moment. "That's why I went to Oslo through Edinburgh. I met a friend there who knows the area. It has potential, but you'll have to see it. The grounds look nice on my laptop, but you know how misleading real estate pictures are."

"And agents. I'm surprised, taking something sight unseen like that. The romance of it all must appeal to you."

"I do have my romantic side, don't I? Maybe we can visit the castle together."

Van Coevorden thought a moment. "Scotland is cold and foggy."

"And what's that hovering over Amsterdam's canals on a brisk fall morning?"

"Ambiance," he said with a smile. "And I'd think London has enough fog for you."

"But it's hard to find a residence there where you have to do your business in a privy."

"You're kidding! You might as well go camping and use a tree."

"That doesn't work well for a lady, you know. In the privy, you can sit at least."

"If you dare. Esther, are you out of your mind?"

"The privy had a rustic *je ne sais quoi*. And I'm respecting my relative's memory."

"You never met him!"

"A problem, I'll admit." She revisited the dream in a flash, though. "But I'd like to know a bit more about his ancestry and mine. How we're connected and about other Scots who might be related. If not Rob Roy, maybe I'm related to Lady Macbeth. Or one of the witches. Double, double, toil and trouble, hop into my pot, Monsieur Bastiann, and see it bubble."

"You'd never eat me, would you?"

"Not cooked. I eat you raw. You're my *sushi*. Hold the Wasabi."

***

After dinner, they returned to the hotel room, stripped, threw on hotel robes, and ordered dessert. Just before midnight, Joachim called.

"Madam, you must have been a party girl in your youth. Who's your lover?"

"Let's say he's a close friend." She smiled. The art thief didn't know about Bastiann's real identity. "I take advantage of holidays when I can. But I'm sure you're not operating a dating service, so why am I here?" She saw van Coevorden mouth "Joachim?" and she nodded. "If you want to meet tonight, I need a bit of time and directions."

"Tomorrow's fine. Another Mercedes in front of your hotel. Bring your gigolo along."

"He's not my gigolo. That's a bit insulting, you know."

"Whatever. Tomorrow morning, nine a.m."

"Will I be seeing the painting again before the bidding?"

"You and other clients, the players who are still remaining in the game."

"I haven't made any more bids," she said.

"Neither have they. As I said on the mobile, we've decided to have a real auction. The winner will own the painting. How she or he gets the painting out of the country won't be our problem, by the way. The painting's hot, even though German authorities think they have the real one. We attracted a few more bidders via the free advertising they provided. I expect the winning offer to be high. If successful, I plan to sell other paintings this way. I think it's fun for the buyers too. Are you prepared?"

"I have my limits. I'm not a Swiss bank, you know."

"I wish you luck then." There was a click and the dial tone sounded.

She told van Coevorden what Joachim had said.

"Sounds like we'll have a good night's sleep at least," he said.

"Unless my stallion is willing to perform again. It might be our last tryst, you know." He frowned. "Don't think twice about that. No lights, no cameras, and lots of action, please."

***

After a good frolic, the Dutchman slept and Brookstone lay awake. Alberto Sartini had been her most passionate lover, and her Oxford professor the least. In the short-fused-temper category, Alberto was the worst culprit and Alfred the best, his patience that of a saint. Van Coevorden's patience was on a par with Alfred's and his passion was close to Alberto's. The two of them were a good team. *Will he be a good companion in my golden years?*

She remembered Alberto's advice given to her on his deathbed. "Dearest Esther, my love, you know how I think. I regret not being able to spend more time with you, but you have to move on and find someone else to spend your final days with. You deserve a loving companion all the days of your life. That's what I wish for you."

At that moment, his hand went limp and she heard the death sigh. At that moment, she'd hoped he was wrong, that there was some afterlife where she could join him later. What had he always said? *Live every day as if there are no tomorrows.* Advice easier to follow than admit that when the end came, it was a final curtain call—her role in the play of

170

mortal existence only to be remembered by those left behind, not some diaphanous existence among the angels or demons. *Who has the right take?*

Maybe it was time to work on the Dutchman. There weren't many other prospects. Friends no longer annoyed her with their matchmaking efforts. Some of those friends had already died, in fact. And an older woman cruising the posh bars of London looking for men was a pathetic sight. That's something Underwood might do maybe, but not her.

Yes, Bastiann would be a good catch. They understood each other as much as two human beings could understand each other. *But can we live together?* A key question. But she'd only know the answer if she tried.

And it will be so much fun trying!

Chapter Thirty-One
Oslo

An Oslo motorist might have noticed the odd tourist couple waiting in front of the Grand Hotel and smiled. Brookstone, dressed in a blue power suit and low heels, sported dark glasses but would often raise them to examine passing cars. Van Coevorden, in a light summer suit with vest and cravat tie, wore a Panama hat and kept his Polaroids on. She didn't wear Underwood's wireless this time, a nod to van Coevorden's company and his insistence it was too risky.

He had awakened to an empty bed, but heard Brookstone return while he was showering.

"You went for a jog?" he said, stepping out of the bathroom while still toweling off.

"Fresh shrimp," she said, shedding her running outfit. "The boats come in early and cook some of the catch on their way to the docks. You can buy them and sit on the wharf and enjoy your seafood breakfast, tossing the tails to the seagulls."

"Sounds romantic. Why didn't you invite me?"

"You needed the rest, Bastiann. And I know you're not particularly fond of shrimp."

"I'll do a good scampi, but point well taken. This means I'd better call room service for my breakfast while you shower, right?"

"I'll shower, but call for two breakfasts. I'm still famished. I should have purchased two bags. They were smaller than I remembered. Inflation via packaging."

The morning had gone downhill from there as the hour for Joachim's arrival approached.

***

Van Coevorden had called in some favors with Oslo's PD. Two detectives would tail the Mercedes and be ready to provide backup if needed. The Interpol agent figured Brookstone and he would be dead by the time either the detectives or other backup arrived, but the arrangement provided some comfort all the same. Comfort didn't imply security, though. He twirled his handlebar mustache yet again, eager to get on with it.

"You can twist it all the way off, you know," said Brookstone. "It tickles a lot in my lady parts."

"I thought you liked that."

"I do, but it gets me up to speed too fast. Today you look like old Poirot much more than usual, you know. Did you dress for a trip on the Nile? Nights are cold here in the summer at one-thousand-foot altitude. There are still some glaciers around even."

"I won't repeat how others say you look, but you're a modern version of that other Christie character. I can't imagine her doing what you did last night, though."

"I don't fancy the comparison. I might be old, but I have fun. Her only game was solving mysteries. I have many others, including my official business here."

"I know that very well. But I shouldn't be the one who's sore."

"We were a bit passionate, I suppose. Appropriate for a last roll in the hay, don't you think?"

"Let's not be overly pessimistic. Joachim should only become nasty if the auction winner doesn't pay him."

"Famous last words. Logic and reason don't apply to Nazi psychos. Besides, I suspect Joachim isn't the enforcer on this team. There has to be multiple people involved even for this one painting. We have a band of thieves here, at the very least, even if they aren't some neo-Nazi conspiracy."

"And they have an agenda, and we don't know what it is. I'm thinking there's much more to this than selling some stolen paintings. I'm less optimistic than you are. Is that our ride?"

The black Mercedes sedan stopped in front of them. The chauffeur came around the back and opened the rear door for them. Joachim was sitting on the opposite side.

"You two are our first passengers today," he said as they entered, first van Coevorden and then Brookstone, the order due to her longer legs. Joachim leaned across the Interpol agent to speak to Brookstone. "To pass the time while you wait for the others, we will offer refreshments. Considering the purpose of the auction, caviar canapes and champagne are in order, compliments of our little group, of course."

"Morning refreshments?" said Brookstone. "I'd settle for tea and toast with marmalade."

"It's a special occasion, but I think your wishes can be met. We aim to please, madam."

The Mercedes headed out of town.

***

Brookstone recognized the route. It was the winding, highway equivalent to the Oslo-Bergen train ride. She had taken a spur off the latter from Myrdal to Flåm once, a harrowing 55 minute, 12-mile ride, plunging 2800 feet into Aurlands Fjord, the world's deepest and second-longest. The Mercedes pulled off the highway before Myrdal, though, onto a gravel one-lane road winding up even higher between the pines. At a pullout, the Mercedes stopped and velvet bags were put over their heads.

They lost her at first after three more sharp turns, but then she counted, realizing she could backtrack if needed. Of course, their host's idea was to confuse them. She wondered if the Oslo police had followed all those turns. Van Coevorden and she might be on their own. She repressed a shudder. *Am I too old for this?*

The Mercedes stopped, the bags were removed, and they stepped out in front of a beautiful Swiss-style ski chalet hidden in the pines. She saw some shady patches of snow, and the bright sun and crisp, pine-scented air aided by pine mulch in the gardens made for a heady mix. *Not a bad place to spend your summers, but a lonely place to die. I wonder how much a chalet like this costs.*

The building itself was late 19th century or early 20th, easily a hundred years old. But it was in good shape. One climbed four steps to the lanai and main entrance with its two massive wood doors complete with brass hardware, including lions'-heads doorknockers. The lanai featured wicker chairs with tables between them and spanned the width of the front. The house had three stories if you counted the last level nestled under the apex of the A-framed roof. She also saw windows at ground level in the foundation that stretched to four feet high in places, those not covered by evergreen bushes, evidence for a basement.

"Let me show you to the great room where refreshments are available," said Joachim.

"Out of curiosity, how many times are you going to make that trip?" said van Coevorden.

"We have other vehicles. Don't worry, old man, everyone will arrive safe and sound. It's no concern of yours. And your wait will be as comfortable as we can make it."

Brookstone noted again how desolate the location was before they followed Joachim inside. Once more the nagging thought: *Will we ever leave here?* She knew Bastiann was having the same qualms. *He's a born pessimist.* She guessed that his working closer to the European underbelly generally disassociated him from her genteel artistic world, and that would make anyone a pessimist. *I'll have to counter his attitude with optimism.*

"Hans will tend to your needs. Hans, this is Esther Brookstone, *Condessa* Sartini, from London and vicinity, and her friend, Mr. Rudolf de Groot from Amsterdam." Brookstone waved a hand and van Coevorden nodded. De Groot was one of his many aliases in the field, and Brookstone knew he wished she had one. She had come this far without it, though. *Did James Bond ever use an alias? Even if he did, that "shaken, not stirred" should always have been a dead giveaway!* The last Bond she'd seen had a rugged charm, but she still favored the original, Sean Connery. *He might feel right at home here!* "Please look after them, Hans, while we go fetch our other guests."

She estimated Hans might be six-and-a-half feet tall. His rigid posture made him look even taller. Van Coevorden concentrated on canapes and champagne; the butler provided her with tea, small pieces of toast, and orange marmalade. He then left them alone for the most part.

"I suspect we're under surveillance, Countess," van Coevorden said in a low voice.

"I suspect you're right, Rudolf," Brookstone said. She wound her way around a grand piano and approached an expressionist painting. "A decent copy of Munch's *The Scream*.

They call it the Mona Lisa for our time. It's depressing, you know. It predates both wars, but I consider it a prescient portrayal of all that German craziness, especially from the Nazis. How many screams like this one were heard in those concentration camps, I wonder?"

"Not to mention those from millions injured and dying on battlefields," he said. "But now we have terrorists who behead anyone who disagrees with them, and they carry out mass killings too."

"Oh, please, the French did that with Madame Guillotine. Think of the Armenian and Rwandan genocides. And think of all the Native Americans the Yanks whacked in their westward expansion. No nationality has a monopoly on doing violence to others, or even to their own citizens. Atrocities in Northern Ireland were over the top too, yet most Irish people I know are compassionate and charming folk. How's the caviar?"

"A bit salty but otherwise acceptable. Probably preferable to and much more expensive than your Norwegian shrimp." He saw her scowl and smiled. "The champagne is cheap, though. Maybe the fault lies in the suppliers. Shall we sit?" He pointed to a love seat with a floral pattern situated in such a way that those sitting had full view of the piano's keyboard. She followed his cue. "Do you suppose anyone plays the piano? I could see if it's in tune."

"Please don't bother. We don't want to drive bidders away, do we now?"

He smiled and nodded. "I'm curious to see who they are."

Chapter Thirty-Two
Near Oslo

There were eight bidders, arriving by ones and twos. Introductions were made but Brookstone only tried to remember first names. It was likely the names were all false, so why bother? Van Coevorden was an asset. She could pretend to be the haughty countess while he mixed with the group.

A bit after eleven when the last arrivals had finished their refreshments, Joachim entered and suggested they all find seats. Hans brought in a display easel and the painting "An Angel with Titus' Features" was placed on it. She thought the affair was looking like one of those cruise ship auctions. She had noted the copy in the warehouse was good, but it didn't match the original. It was received with oohs and aahs from auction attendees, and those exclamations also seemed real. In the cruise ship, passengers often attended the auctions only for the drinks and hors d'oeuvres. Here the bidders had almost neglected them. *They are rich and ready to buy a black market painting.* She knew which class of "art lovers" she preferred...

***

Brookstone had shut down a group selling stolen paintings and copies passed off as originals on cruise ships. The auctions were common enough and most were legit, if often a bit tacky.

But members of that one particular group of auctioneers had hoodwinked everyone, including the cruise lines' owners. The cruise lines had wanted things kept quiet for that reason. She'd never been certain whether all victimized passengers had been reimbursed, but the criminals were now serving time. Not enough, from her point of view.

The ringleaders had been ruthless. Two Interpol agents had died. One passenger who had volunteered to help was shot and was still recovering. *Maybe my art world isn't so genteel?* She had approached the woman in the waiting room for passengers bound for the Greek Isles. She showed the woman a photo.

"That's my painting!" Cindy O'Reilly had said. "My father bought it for me."

Brookstone nodded. "I'm Inspector Esther Brookstone from Scotland Yard." She flashed her warrant card. "He bought it on another cruise. You sent it for appraisal two weeks ago. I'm afraid it's a fake. The appraisers called us. Could you provide some more details about its acquisition?" Cindy embellished the tale told in the report made after the interview with Sotheby's. "That sounds like the crowd we're after. Did they provide provenance?"

"You mean papers? Yes, I don't have them with me, though."

"Those are probably fake too. They must be."

"If you're with the authorities, why don't you put a stop to this? Innocent people are being duped. Most passengers aren't art experts."

Brookstone smiled. A lament she often heard in her work in the Unit. "We have to be reactive, not proactive. You were smart to ask Sotheby's to appraise the painting. They called me because we're working on a big case associated with the cruise lines. Would you like to help us put an end to this travesty?"

Cindy thought a moment. "Of course. But how can I?"

Esther explained.

***

Brookstone had been following her boss's suggestion, but she ended up regretting going along with it. She had put ending the case successfully over putting human lives in danger.

She visited Cindy in the hospital.

"I heard we were successful," the woman said, smiling at Brookstone. She was still in the ICU, her head wrapped in bandages.

Esther frowned. "I'm sorry I involved you. I must say this case was a bit different. You were very helpful, but I put you in danger. I shall not do that again, to anyone." She patted Cindy on the shoulder. "How are you today? You were in an induced coma for a while."

"To reduce swelling, they told me. I didn't remember a lot until now, but thank you for saving my life. That was brave of you."

"Brave? Maybe foolish. My goal was to send those fellows to jail. Things got out of hand. I'm sorry. Like I said, I should have kept you out of it. You're the one who was brave. Please forgive me."

"Just my sense of adventure trumping caution. That's not your fault."

Brookstone smiled at the memory. *Yes, I might be in this for the adventure and throwing caution to the wind. I'm sure Bastiann would agree with that. But is it true? And, am I putting him in danger? Of course I am!* But van Coevorden wasn't the innocent Cindy had been.

***

On another easel, Joachim placed a poster board listing participants' names and their first bids. "You'll see we're offering complete transparency here, ladies and gentlemen.

180

Each one of you will know how the others bid. With your second and successive bids today, you not only have to increase your previous bids, you need to go beyond everyone's already placed or you're out. This is a true auction with many possible rounds." He paused and let his gaze wander around the group for effect. *A ghoulish showman*, thought Brookstone, *but not nearly as sophisticated as the cruise ship auctioneer.* "So, let's begin. I will pass around this fish bowl full of tickets. Draw a number to find your order in the bidding." Brookstone drew number three. "Do we have a new bid from number one?" said Joachim after they finished drawing numbers. "Yes, Mr. Kimura."

In the first round, the bidders were conservative, so she made it to the second. In the second, Kimura and two others dropped out. The bids kept increasing until she and an Arab-looking fellow named Nejem were the only ones left. The remainder became wide-eyed spectators. *They're probably all wondering who we are but enjoying the spectacle of the macho Arab bidding against the European countess.* She smiled and moistened her lips. *Time to end the show.*

She was an amateur psychologist. Many police were, especially the successful ones. *And maybe more practical and successful than the psychs who interview us after a shooting?* The one after Cindy's had been a complete idiot.

She understood Nejem and knew he was a sexist prick who wasn't about to be outbid by a woman. She ended her bidding.

"I bow to the sheik."

"I represent an emir, madam," said Nejem.

"Sheik, emir, what's the difference? He has far too much money. And it's Countess Sartini, good sir. For your information, you just made your boss pay millions of euros he didn't have to pay. Joachim hired me to drive up the bidding, you fool."

Nejem jumped to his feet. "That is an outrage!"

"And not true," said Joachim, shouting as well. "What do you think you're doing, Countess?"

Van Coevorden tried to mitigate the men's anger, but he also followed her cue. "It wasn't nice to expose Joachim that way, my dear. He and his people did well by us. The deed is done."

"Who am I to believe?" said Nejem, glaring at Joachim. "You, sir, are nothing but a common thief. I knew it all along. And who is this woman?"

"One who's in trouble," said Joachim. "Think about it. Why would she admit to being part of a conspiracy?"

"Because you didn't pay me enough, considering what Mr. Nejem has offered for the painting," said Brookstone with a smile. "Come, Rudolf, I think we should wait outside. The others can join us while Mr. Nejem and Joachim settle their differences."

The other bidders smiled and joined Brookstone and van Coevorden as they filed from the great room. She had them figured out too.

Minutes later, Nejem stomped from the chalet, but he waited apart from the main group of bidders.

"Think we can catch a ride with him back to Oslo?" said van Coevorden in a whisper.

"Not likely," she said. "At best, we might have to walk many kilometers and take a train. I wonder how often it runs."

"I was hoping you had a more detailed plan," he said.

"I'm making it up as we go. But by Nejem's expression, the auction failed and Joachim and friends didn't sell the painting. That was what I wanted. If Nejem had taken it back to his emir, we would never have seen it again." She winked at her Dutchman. "I couldn't let that happen."

Chapter Thirty-Three
Near Oslo

"I think it's time for a nap." Brookstone had stretched out on an old couch in the chalet's basement. They were now Joachim's prisoners. "I don't think the police are coming. I need to recharge my batteries in case we need to make a dash for it."

"I don't think that will be a problem," said van Coevorden. "Joachim will likely kill us and dump our bodies into the fjord."

"I told you last night it might be our last one together," she said with a sad smile.

"OK, so you're the Oracle of the Yard. Let's at least do what we can toward making that prophecy false."

Joachim had sent the other bidders, including Nejem, back to Oslo, all having refused to participate in any further negotiations because of the distrust Brookstone had generated. The Interpol agent was pacing.

She supposed she had less to worry about than he did. She was almost twenty years older. He probably hadn't reached the point where he had made any detailed plans to face the Grim Reaper. *Would he be surprised I've already written my obituary and bought my funeral plot?*

Unlike her husband the count, she wasn't sure about the afterlife. She'd had enough surgeries to conclude, though, that it could only be a sweet oblivion, a final R.I.P. from life's pain and suffering, especially from having to tolerate innumerable idiots. *Dylan Thomas said it all, didn't he?*

In a short poem arguably the best ever written, that wonderful Welsh poet had advised, "Do not go gentle into that good night...rage, rage against the dying of the light." Probably the best two philosophical lines ever written. First, "that good night" only described the sweet oblivion offered by Death, her thoughts exactly.

Second, the poet was urging that one still had to do battle with the Grim Reaper. *We are living creatures blessed to have some time on this planet; not to fight Death is betraying all existence.* She didn't know about the rage part, though. She preferred to use her wit, logic, and skills to cheat Death. No way was she going to let some scurrilous Nazis take her out.

***

"You're only stirring up dust and mold spores," Brookstone said to van Coevorden. "Relax. Joachim hasn't decided our fates yet. We're still alive. If you insist on doing something, take my penlight and find a way to escape."

She rummaged in her handbag and found the small flashlight in a side pocket. He now started to survey their prison, an impossible task before in the dim light filtering through the windows into the basement.

"I can't believe you did that without consulting me," he said, moving old furniture and boxes to explore stone walls. "Joachim was mad enough to kill us on the spot."

"But he couldn't. He had to deal with Nejem's ire and the others' distrust. Men are so malleable, you know." She wiggled her little finger at him. "I could convince my husbands to do anything, even in bed. They received their reward there, of course."

"And me?"

"You're a bit less malleable and more stubborn. But you still do what I want and still love me, right?"

"That's not going to do you any good if Joachim seeks the ultimate revenge. We think we're dealing with neo-Nazis, remember? 'Nazi' equals 'psycho,' semantically speaking, in my dictionary."

"True Nazis maybe, but these are version 3.0 or higher," she said, "and maybe a beta version not fully tested and operational? But they're still men and therefore malleable."

"Oh please, spare me your pseudo-Freudian psycho-babble. We're in trouble." He stopped his survey next to a back window, running a finger between old stone. "Here's a way out, but I need something strong and sharp to remove some old mortar."

"Your wish is my command, my stallion." She stood, raised a cushion, and probed where it had been. Ripping apart a thin, frayed covering, she revealed sofa springs. "The secret is to keep twisting until it breaks off. That way we'll have both a strong wire and a ready-made sharp point. You could help, you know."

They soon had several versions of her tool, and he began to dig out loose mortar around four stone blocks. He had calculated that an opening obtained by their removal would be above ground level because of their position next to the window.

"Old construction is always a bother," he said. "It's always in need of repair, you know. Otherwise it erodes, especially in variable, extreme weather."

"Ownership makes it more tolerable. Like my castle, for example."

He answered with a grunt. After four spring remnants and several broken fingernails, he asked her to help him remove the loose, fifty-pound stones.

"My gym workout for the day." After they were done, she poked her head out. "Aha. Back of the house. I thought so. Good work, Bastiann. We'll go into the woods and then circle around to the entrance road. All the turns into this property were right turns. We'll reverse those to the left going out. I do wish I'd worn sneakers, but they didn't go with hors d'oeuvres and champagne."

***

Neither one was dressed for a hike through the woods and along a gravel road. Even van Coevorden started limping, while Brookstone stopped from time to time to rub her leg muscles.

"I wonder if there are bears around," she said, looking at the woods one of those times.

"They'd be brown bears," said van Coevorden, spotting the return to the road after making the wide circle around the chalet. "There aren't many left, I'd wager. I've never heard about any tourist warnings. Seabirds are more common. This country has the longest coastline in the world."

"Oh, great. Even a gull can be nasty, especially when it comes to a lady's coif."

"Have you had a bit too much with roughing it, my dear? Don't you hike a lot in Scotland when you're there? And you're the one who wants to live in a castle where the plumbing reduces to a privy."

"Living in Scotland might be a lark. I'm not there often enough. Don't you know a true Scot wears nothing under a kilt? I always wondered about bonny Prince Charlie's traditional garb."

"You're being obscene. Maybe nerves? I won't wear a kilt, not even for you."

She became silent. They had made it through two turns when he stopped short and pushed her off to the side of the road. "Sentries," he said, "and a van." His voice was a whisper.

"How could they know we escaped?" she said, making a sour face. She shook off his grip on her arm and peered around a tree.

"Maybe Joachim received orders about what to do with us and visited the basement only to discover we'd fled? And these ruffians have mobiles." He peeked around the other side of the tree. "It's also possible they are always here to protect the chalet. We had bags on our head, remember? They could have waved at us when we went by."

"Do they look like Nazis?"

"You mean German? No, they look more like big Irish fellows. Red hair, red beards, and arms above their elbows as thick as my thighs."

"I always said you need to work out more. They could be ex-IRA members using the skills they've learned in Belfast to act as mercenaries for the Nazis. Can we go around them by going through the woods again?"

"Too much chance of getting lost," he said. "Skirting around the house was easy, but you're likely to turn an ankle with the shale and rock here. Me too, for that matter. Remember, glaciers carved the fjords and left a lot of moraine behind."

"I don't need a lesson on ancient geology. Given our physical conditions, that van will come in handy. Let's try some subterfuge. I'll walk straight toward them along the road and show some leg, and you accompany me in a crouch hidden alongside the road in that ditch. There are two sentries. If we can't take them, we need to turn in our warrant cards."

"They have guns," he said. "We don't. Our forced retirement might be imminent, Esther."

"Just work with me, dear Bastiann."

She handed him a branch, found one for herself, and began to strip off smaller branches and twigs. He followed her lead. In minutes, they had rough and heavy walking sticks that could also serve as weapons.

They both knew some martial arts. The sentries probably did too, or at least brawling tactics good for pub battles, but that wouldn't be their first choice with guns at hand, an advantage for their two unarmed adversaries.

***

"Are you redheads friends with Prince Harry by any chance?" said Brookstone as she approached the sentries. She didn't have to pretend she was limping. Tweedledee looked at Tweedledum who shrugged. "What's the matter? I need a gentleman's hand and all I get are dumb expressions. Help an old woman a wee bit, will you?"

Tweedledee approached her, pointing his automatic more at the ground than at her. *Not very talkative. Maybe I should try my Gaelic?* She took a step forward, staggered, and when he reached for her, she sent the gun flying with her makeshift walking stick. The backswing against the side of his head rendered him unconscious.

Van Coevorden handled Tweedledum, who had been surprised by Brookstone's attack and distracted enough to slow his reactions. The stick in the gut left him breathless. A harmless shot flew into the trees, scattering a few birds, as the agent crushed his opponent's windpipe with the end of the stick.

"One dead, one unconscious," she said after testing for carotid pulses. "Not bad." She took off the live one's belt and bound him like a cowboy might bind a steer. "We'll pull them both off the road."

"It's unfortunate he fired his gun," he said. "They most likely heard it all the way to the chalet. Let's hurry."

They dragged the sentries into the forest. He found the key fob to the van and then covered both of them with dried leaves and other refuse from the forest floor.

"The live one will be found soon enough," he said. "Joachim won't be giving him a speech about a job well done, I'm sure."

"Let's hope it's only a verbal reprimand and not a bullet between the eyes," she said. "I do hate violence, but Joachim might not be too forgiving."

They commandeered the van and sped off down the gravel road. He drove. In other circumstances, she might have enjoyed Norway's summer scenery, but she was worried about Joachim's pursuit. London seemed a long distance away.

They soon pulled into the lot near the Myrdal station, went inside, and bought train and ferry tickets to Oslo. Joachim might catch up to them otherwise before they reached there. They figured Joachim and friends would be looking for the van in any case, so they had parked it between two large SUVs. After doing so, they deflated all the tires, pulled out wires, and threw the keys in a dumpster. Joachim's men wouldn't be using it soon even if they managed to find it.

Van Coevorden had also found two more pistols inside the van. They were now well armed and ready for a fight if needs be.

The plan was to take the train to Flåm and then the ferry to Oslo. That plan didn't work out, though.

Chapter Thirty-Four
Myrdal

"We're being watched," said Brookstone, sipping an excellent ale in the station's little cafeteria. The two had just finished an acceptable brie sandwich. She had been admiring two uniformed police, strapping fellows with broad shoulders, gentler versions than the Irishmen and clean shaven, when she saw the man enter and look around. The police seemed to recognize him. "A bit scruffy, dressed in an old raincoat, talking on a mobile. Do you have a gun handy? Mine is in my purse buried under other necessities. Careful. He's coming our way. Don't make a scene."

She regretted the silly remark. Van Coevorden probably wondered, and rightly so, how he could be in a firefight and not make a scene. He patted his coat pocket, turned to confront the enemy, but then smiled.

"Lars, you old dog, it's good to see you again. Were you involved as backup in our little caper?"

The man called Lars smiled too. He was a bit puffy, a typical Norwegian with red cheeks and bulbous nose who could have passed for a jolly North Sea shrimper if he had been dressed differently. Brookstone had seen his clones on the shrimp boat. He offered a hand.

"We have arrested some of them. When we lost you in the Mercedes, we called HQ to see if they could determine where you might have ended up. Using sat images, we thought the chalet was an appropriate site for an auction, so we went there to check it out."

"Did you recover the painting?" she said. "I'm Esther Brookstone, by the way, Inspector. Bastiann can't introduce me like a gentleman should."

"Lars Losnedahl," the Norwegian said, offering his hand to her too. "My pleasure, madam. And no. There was a helipad. We think the painting hitched a ride on a chopper. We believe two men and a woman were on it as passengers."

"No way to trace it?" said van Coevorden.

"No markings. You can find choppers like that all over Europe. I'm sorry. On a more positive note, we'll be interrogating those persons we caught. We'd like you two to be there to observe."

"Sure thing. Can we hitch a ride back to Oslo with you?"

"Of course. I was sent to look for you. I have one of our own helicopters waiting for us in a nearby park."

"Oh, great," she said. "What I always wanted to do, turn into a ball of fire and sink into a deep fjord. Helicopters are always crashing somewhere these days."

"I assure you it won't happen," said Losnedahl as they started the short trek down the street away from the little train station. "You did a nice job with the van drivers, by the way. The brothers are ex-IRA and were wanted by British and Irish authorities for years, muscle who had used patriotism as an excuse to commit their murder and mayhem. We'll be interrogating the live one too. Hopefully we'll learn more about these art thieves."

"Hmm. I'm not hopeful." She glanced at van Coevorden, who nodded his agreement.

***

The Irishman weathered the Norwegians' interrogation well. He only admitted to working for Joachim. Brookstone figured the old fellow had ample experience with interrogations in Belfast during the Troubles. She agreed with Losnedahl's assessment of his character.

Joachim became a mute too and would say nothing without his barrister. That would take some time because he had to find one now in Oslo.

The butler Hans was more forthcoming. He informed Losnedahl there had been two men and a woman watching the auction via a CCTV hookup. He claimed not to know who they were, but thought they might be German like Joachim. He confirmed they had taken the painting and left in a helicopter.

"You served them refreshments, right?" said Losnedahl. Hans nodded. "Can you describe them?"

"Yes, sir. They had some of the same canapes and champagne as the bidders, for example. I didn't pay much attention to their appearance, though. They were critical of Mr. Joachim's choices for refreshments. Our chef found that insulting. I don't blame him. He had to stay within Joachim's budget, a severe limitation to my way of thinking."

"And no names were ever mentioned?"

"One man was the woman's husband. He called her Karen a few times. They all seemed to know each other well."

"When was the first time you saw them?"

"The night before the auction when I served them dinner. They arrived in the helicopter late that afternoon."

"The helicopter must have had a pilot."

"And co-pilot. They spoke German."

"Any idea about the helicopter's origin?"

"I heard the name Flensburg. I believe that's in Germany."

"You're right. It has a large Danish population, though. Is it possible the pilots were speaking Danish and not German?"

"I only know Norwegian and English, sir. I haven't spoken any German for many years. I suppose it's possible they spoke Danish. Mr. Joachim speaks to us in English."

"How long have you been a butler, Hans?"

"I was trained to carry on my family's tradition by my father and grandfather."

"That doesn't answer my question."

"I started working when I was eighteen."

Losnedahl sighed. "And how long have you worked for Joachim?"

"I've been on the chalet's staff for eleven years. When the original owners died, Mr. Joachim, representing new owners, bought the place and kept most of us on. It's possible some of the three are the new owners. They've been there before and are always very secretive."

Losnedahl pondered the situation a moment. "You're free to go, Hans," he said. "We might have more questions later, so don't go into hiding."

"Do I have to stay in Oslo?" Hans said, standing.

"You can return to your job."

"Who will pay the staff now? Should we be looking for new work?"

"Good question. I have no idea. Your Mr. Joachim won't be making much money in prison. Yes, I'd say you and the others should be looking for work, unless he decides to sell the chalet and the new owner keeps you on."

Hans frowned and left the interrogation room.

***

"He's an innocent victim," said van Coevorden when Losnedahl came around to the other side of the one-way window to chat.

"Maybe. But the chalet's original owners died under suspicious circumstances. And his grandfather worked for *Obergruppenführer* Wilhelm Redless during the occupation."

"Many Norwegians worked for the Nazis," said Brookstone. "I think the man's apolitical. He'll work for anyone who needs a butler. We still have that type in England. Why, Buckingham Palace is full of apolitical servants who have had successful careers serving pompous asses and arrogant nobility. God save the Queen!" She hummed a bit of the anthem.

"Redless wasn't nobility and was more than a pompous ass," said van Coevorden with a frown.

"You're biased about Hans because he's gay," she said.

"What! I am not. I have many gay friends. And how do you know he's gay?"

"Not one flirty wink with the women at the auction, for one thing—I'll admit that's often a sign of a good butler because ladies don't want their gentlemen criticizing the help—but the mannerisms indicate it too. I'm an amateur psychologist, remember. We enjoyed success at the auction because of that. Of course, I might be wrong. I was about my count originally, mistaking an aristocratic demeanor for homosexuality. I should have known better. But I was trying to flirt with Hans. No reaction at all."

Van Coevorden ignored the psychology lesson, returning to one of her phrases. "Success? I guess that's relative."

"Because they escaped in the helicopter? They didn't sell the painting, did they? We can still recover it. If it left with Nejem, no one would ever see it again."

"Which reminds me," said Losnedahl, "let's see if we can identify the other bidders. You can broadcast an Interpol BOLO or Red Notice on them, Bastiann, preferably the latter. They need to be found and prosecuted."

"Small potatoes," said Brookstone, "but let's do it. I only remember the names Kimura and Nejem. Bastiann will do better. They could all be fake, of course. Mine might have been the only real name among the group. I don't expect any of them to have facial shots on file, though. They'd hire others to commit their crimes, I'm sure."

Chapter Thirty-Five
Near Oslo

From his tiny room, Hans heard the SUV straining up the mountain curves below his beloved chalet. No matter who the owners were, he had always considered it his. He took pride in its upkeep but was fair when cajoling the rest of the staff to do their jobs. He knew that owners had received compliments about his professionalism. He'd never felt subservient, only faithful to his duty. His job was to make sure both owners and guests were as comfortable as possible when visiting the chalet.

He was certain that the Oslo police didn't understand his dedication. How could they? They thought he was an anachronism. Only the English woman seemed to understand him. He had no idea who she was, but he liked her. *Sometimes I meet people at the chalet I can respect. The current owners not so much. Were they among the three?*

He put on his long-tailed coat and went downstairs to greet the new guests arriving at his chalet. It was the proper thing to do. He had no idea who they were, but he opened the door for them with a slight bow, as was his custom. The woman and man brushed by him and went straight to the dining room where Hans had served Dunst and the Lietzkes. Hans followed.

The woman took a seat at the head of the long table, her companion at her side. She glared at Hans. "Go call the rest of the help. We need to discuss the chalet's future."

Eleven people trickled in one by one. Hans was the last to arrive.

"Be seated, please," said the man.

"Here. At this table?" Hans looked around the group, his colleagues as astonished as he was. One young chambermaid giggled.

"Sit!" said the woman. The giggler sat. Hans took the chair next to her. The others followed suit, glancing at each other. The imperious woman studied them one by one and smiled. "We are putting the chalet on the market. You will all be paid until we turn it over to new owners. Anyone who wants to leave may do so. There will be no severance pay, though. Perhaps the new owners will offer bonuses for staying on."

Hans nodded. Joachim had done that when the chalet had last changed owners.

"There is one condition," said the man.

Always conditions, thought Hans.

***

The woman looked around the group again, assessing their reactions. They had not caused trouble before, not seeming to care who owned the chalet or who the guests were. They were mostly invisible, as all good servants should be. Her eyes fixed on Hans, though. *The man is an automaton, but automatons can malfunction. The Reich requires absolute fidelity.* It was a hard lesson for some to learn. It was their duty to make sure the help learned it. Joachim understood, but he still might be silenced because he knew too much. Time would tell.

"No one may speak about what has occurred here during the time after the property was last sold. Do you understand that condition?"

"Do you have papers for us to sign?" Hans said. "That's the usual procedure, you know."

The woman eyed him.

"No papers. This will be an oral agreement. It's enforceable too. Anyone who talks to police will die. Do I make myself clear?"

Hans nodded automatically. The woman nodded to her companion. He took out a gun and shot Hans. The young chambermaid screamed and the others jumped. The butler slumped in his chair, his face and starched white shirt spattered with blood and brain material.

She pointed at the young chambermaid who had been sitting next to Hans, her white apron also speckled with slate gray and bright red spots. "That occurred because Hans spoke to the Oslo police. The same fate awaits anyone who does that. Clean up the mess. And I don't want to see any blood stains when you're finished."

***

The man and woman walked around the chalet. They knew the help were watching.

Her alias was Ruth Mayer; his Jacob Eisenstein. They had different pasts: the woman's roots were in East Germany, the man's in France, but descended from a soldier in the occupying forces during the Vichy government. The Fourth Reich had brought them together.

"We have put the fear of the Reich in them," said the man with a smile. He had a legal pad and was noting things they needed to do to prepare for the chalet's sale as they walked about.

198

"This property is worth more than that damned painting," said the woman, "considering we received nothing for it. *Frau* Lietzke's indulgences are now a thing of the past. They weren't even here that much."

"She is our leader," he said.

"Even Hitler made mistakes. *Herr* Dunst is right. Besides, we have more immediate plans. We need to return to Oslo."

"I think the help will behave. The real estate broker will think they're the best staff he's ever seen." He raised eyebrows. "I'd like to have a recording of what Hans said to the Oslo police."

"He could only describe what he saw, and that's not important now." They finished their survey at the front entrance. "There are places on the way to Oslo that are perfect for dumping his body. Stay here while I go threaten the others one more time, just for good measure. They're young, not one of them near Hans's age. They have no memory of the Nazis in Norway. I'll need to remind them once again about what we can do. Obedience must be absolute."

***

On the road to Oslo, the Nazi pair stopped and Jacob dumped Hans in a ravine, pushing the body over the edge and not bothering to see where it fell. He then took the opportunity to find a tree. Nature called.

"Why didn't you go at the house," Ruth said when he returned to the vehicle. "We're on a tight schedule."

"If I can't take a pee on my own schedule, Dunst's can be damned."

"You can say that to me. Don't try it with him." She started the SUV and turned on the radio. "Call and check that flight info."

As they rode along, Jacob glanced at her. "Why did you have me kill Hans? I liked the old boy."

"That's partly the reason. And he talked too much. I also wanted to test your dedication to the cause. We can't afford to put our emotions above our goals. Change the subject. It's done. Our future is what's important."

"Our future? You mean, you and me?" He smiled.

"Don't be an ass. I'd die before I fucked you."

"Because you don't like men, right?"

"Yes, but more because you hesitated with Hans."

"You're a strange bitch, you know. Like a bad, psychotic robot."

"It's called discipline. If we're going to win, we must have discipline."

"And good plans. Are you sure ours are good?"

"We had to adapt them to circumstances. Time will tell if they're good enough. I think destiny is on our side."

Ruth and Jacob soon arrived at the airport where they would wait for the others.

Chapter Thirty-Six
Oslo

"Maid service."

Van Coevorden sent a questioning glance Brookstone's way. Both of them were exhausted. They had ordered room service for a light dinner with the goal of getting a good night's sleep soon after. They had just sat down to appetizers.

"A change of towels and bathroom necessities might be in order," she said with a wink. "One never knows."

He shrugged and went to the door. He saw a pile of fresh towels through the peephole. He opened it to find not a hotel worker but a woman with a Glock. A man with another Glock put the towels back on the maid's cart and followed her in, and the woman shut the door.

"When my brother brings the car around, you two are coming with us," said the woman.

"*Herr* and *Frau* Lietzke," said van Coevorden. "I recognize you from your photos. Karen Lietzke. Karen. I should have made the connection. I'm sorry to see you're still peddling stolen art. I've learned a bit since I left you that little message. I thought you and *Herr* Dunst were half-siblings. But you're just the bastard daughter."

She smashed the gun barrel against the side of his face. "You pitiful excuse of a little gnome. The *Führer* tried to eliminate inferior scum like you. You're probably a damn Jew."

"Are you OK, Bastiann?" said Brookstone, kneeling at his side.

The Interpol agent wiped away blood and glared at the woman. "The interrogations will continue tomorrow," he said. "They're expecting us."

He was lying. They were tired because they had put in a grueling day in order to finish the business with the Oslo police.

"They will be disappointed then. We're off to Austria. We'd like to invite you two to accompany us."

"Linz, I suspect," said Brookstone. She had helped van Coevorden to the table. They were now sitting. She palmed a steak knife and slid it into the sleeve of her robe and then took a sip of coffee. "I'm certain you people don't compose music as beautiful as Mozart's symphony written in that place. The *Führer's* new art museum is likely a World War Two bunker near there, I suppose, nothing at all like he planned. How many artworks do you have, by the way?"

Walther Lietzke looked at his wife, surprise on his face.

"Ignore her," said the wife, confiscating the pair's mobiles. "She's guessing. Gerhard will torture them, discover everything they know, and then kill them. If he doesn't, I will. We're wasting time."

"Do I have time to change?" said Brookstone. "I'd like to be in sneakers when I break your necks. They're much more comfortable than these slippers for running, but I could likely still outrun you two even in them."

"*Halt die Klappe!*" said *Herr* Lietzke. "You're going just as you are."

***

"This could work out well," Brookstone whispered to van Coevorden.

They were sitting in the rear of a private jet. Engine noise kept the others from hearing their conversation, but the three neo-Nazis in front didn't seem to care that they talked. The two of them were bound hands and feet with zip ties. *Frau* Lietzke had discovered the knife and slapped Brookstone. Her cheek was still red.

"Why do you say that?" he said.

"Wherever they're taking us, I guarantee you that's where the painting is now. It might even be on this plane."

"But I bet they're angry about our spoiling that auction," he said. "I shouldn't have opened that door."

"You expected a maid and got a Nazi bitch. It's 'The Lady and the Tiger' with only one door, and the hotel employee would have been the lady in this case, although calling that bitch a tiger is an insult to that noble beast. Don't worry. Everything will be OK, my love."

He rubbed his cheek. "I wish I could share your optimism. I'm worried."

"If they wanted to kill us, Bastiann, they would have done so in Oslo. Plenty of forests around there, and there's always that deep fjord. With some stones to weigh us down, we would have been food for the bottom-feeding fish."

"Your cover's gone," he said, "so it's not about the bidding."

"But they still might want my money? Don't worry. You're always worrying before you need to do so. I wonder if the flight attendants would serve us some of that nice wine."

"They have shoulder holsters, Esther. I think they're more than flight attendants."

"Yes, and they're fine Aryan examples of manhood who could be Nazi poster boys—blond and blue-eyed and extremely fit. Did you know the poster boy for the Wehrmacht was told to resign? He was half-Jew." She chuckled. "Aryan Supremacy was Hitler's wet dream, and the stereotypes were often so comical. There was a marvelous musical play called *The Producers* expressing my sentiments about the Nazis. Have you seen it?"

He nodded. "No matter how comical their stereotypes, those Nazi psychos still murdered millions. And I'm still suspicious of Hans."

"Leave it alone. It's the VIPs we want, dead or alive. Hans doesn't play a major role in this melodrama."

"Let's hope the drama doesn't become a tragedy for us."

Chapter Thirty-Seven
En Route

Up front in the plane, Karen Lietzke examined Brookstone and van Coevorden's mobiles. She was surprised when the Interpol agent's announced a message's arrival with a soft beep. She went to the back of the plane.

"You, Dutchman, I need your thumb print!" She showed him his mobile. "We censor our prisoners' messages." Her smirk indicated that she thought that was humorous.

"Don't do it, Bastiann," said Brookstone.

"Shut up, old woman. I only need a thumb print. To have it, I can remove his thumb if I need too. We have a really good wire cutter up front we use for zip ties. *Herr* van Coevorden, what is your choice?"

He shrugged and managed to press his thumb to the ID patch even with hands tied. He wasn't about to encourage her to go fetch the wire cutter. She nodded and returned to the front where she took her seat again and began scrolling through the phone's contents. She frowned when she reached the following new message:

"Likely your Nazi art dealers use some part of proceeds to buy arms. Lietzke is the name to watch for, a husband and wife team. I'll be incommunicado working with the *Carabinieri* for a while. Good luck. —Hal."

She frowned. *Typical machismo putting Walther first.* She showed the message to her husband, though.

***

"They are watching us," said Dunst. "Keep your voices down."

"There's too much engine noise," said Walther Lietzke. "We need to hear ourselves, Gerhard. This message is worrisome."

"We should toss them off the plane right now," said Karen Lietzke. "They know too much."

"The Interpol fellow didn't receive this message," said Walther Lietzke. "Maybe they don't know a lot, and they just have made a lot of guesses."

Dunst had his chin resting on a little steeple made from his hands. "These two are resourceful, you'll have to admit." He thought a bit more. "I wanted them alive so I could determine what they know about our operation. I'm beyond that now. For the moment, let me just say I think their resourcefulness could be useful. It's better to put their lives in danger than our own personnel's. When we arrive, I'll talk to them."

"Why are you being so mysterious?" said *Frau* Lietzke. "They're no use to us that I can see. Only troublemakers."

"I second that," said *Herr* Lietzke.

"Shut up, Walther," said his wife. "Gerhardt, what are you planning?"

"I need to hone the details of my plan. You'll both know soon enough."

Chapter Thirty-Eight
Near Linz

Before the plane landed, Brookstone and van Coevorden's feet were untied and velvet bags placed over their heads by the two flight attendants. After a long ride—Brookstone guessed over highways plus a gravel road—their hands were untied and the bags disappeared. They faced a huge bunker in the woods with its heavy metal door.

One flight attendant keyed in a combination and opened the door, motioning them inside where it was much cooler. By the hinges' squeal, she knew the place was old. The Lietzkes and Dunst took one corridor, the flight attendants motioned them along another. They were left in a small, dark room with a sofa, a few bookcases filled with some books, and a desk.

"Someone's away-from-home office," she said, studying the books with hands behind her back in a professorial pose. "I dare say my guess was good. This bunker might date back to World War Two. Possibly some Nazi VIP's bomb shelter?"

Van Coevorden, who was stretched out on the sofa, studied her. "You're likely correct. Lucky guess, that. They want us for something more than questioning and revenge killings, or they'd already be well into the first. We probably landed at a small airfield and drove to one of their HQs. Are you pacing or pretending to look erudite?"

She was looking at book titles. "Medical texts, many on infectious diseases. I bet we're in one of Gerhard Dunst's secret lairs. That's a clue to what was stolen by ISIS, by the way. Now I am getting worried too. We could be guinea pigs in a bioweapons test, a sadistic form of revenge, I'd say."

A door hissed open. "Countess Sartini, you are a paranoid old hag," said Dunst as he stepped inside. "Or, should I say Esther Brookstone, of the Metropolitan London Police, also known as Scotland Yard. It took us a while to figure that out, even longer than determining de Groot here is Interpol agent Bastiann van Coevorden. When amateurs go undercover, they'll be discovered eventually, but we were a bit too late." He sighed. "We'll have to see if we can make up for that."

"So, who's the one who hopes to be the next *Führer*?" said Brookstone. "Are the neo-Nazis shattering the glass ceiling and obeying *Frau* Lietzke now? That seems appropriate for two men who are such imbecilic apes."

Dunst took a seat behind the desk. "I'll ignore your taunts and insults. We are indeed a new generation. This time we don't intend to fool around. We'll start cleansing Europe by first destroying the pathetic remains of the British Empire. We will then take care of the Jews and immigrants and purify the continent." He waved his hands. "But those are still long-range plans. We have a problem. Sit, madam, and I'll tell you a story."

Brookstone sat next to van Coevorden. "Patience isn't one of my virtues. I already know the ending. ISIS stole your bioweapons."

Dunst smiled. "That's a lucky guess. We reported nothing stolen."

"Of course not. That would have created panic. But why else would the Germans send the *SEK*? You were developing weapons for the German government. Or, maybe even NATO."

"Indeed, we have a contract with NATO to determine the efficacy of certain biological agents," said Dunst. "Also to determine if there are antidotes for them. We used that research to further our own agenda, of course."

"I can guess what ISIS wants with those weapons. The destruction of Israel is probably the top priority with the destruction of London or some other major metropolitan center in the West right behind. 'Maximize the terror' being the mantra. If you were certain it was London, you could let them do your dirty work for you, make new batches of your bioweapons, and go about your business while they go about theirs. But you don't know that, do you?"

"I might be stating the obvious, but world domination is pointless if there's nothing left to dominate. The Bolsheviks learned that eventually, and the U.S. counted on that in the Cold War to maintain the détente. Who wants to sweep up nuclear ashes after World War Three?" He made a steeple with his hands and rested his chin on the pinnacle. "Except for destroying England to substantiate our threat against the rest of the world and enjoy a bit of revenge too long in the making, the mere threat of a massive bioweapons attack should be enough to establish the Fourth Reich. We will not use ISIS to do our dirty work."

Brookstone fell silent with that. Van Coevorden squirmed. Dunst seemed lost in thought.

***

"ISIS destroyed your records, right?" van Coevorden said after a bit.

Dunst shrugged. "Not destroyed. They stole them, and we have no samples to reverse engineer and duplicate. A strategic error on our part, I'll admit. The whole problem, you see, is stability. It's a tricky one. Scientists can synthesize a bacteria based on a few hundred genes. The genetic material of viruses is more complicated. They need their own genetic makeup but also need to match their target's. We need those records back."

"And money," said Brookstone. "Whatever infestations you've planned, you need large quantities to show you can make good on your threat. You need to buy basic materials—lots of them. That's where the paintings come in. How many have you sold so far?"

"Lots, and almost enough. We don't just depend on the sale of paintings, though. Far from it. Walther and I are industrialists with many irons in the fire. With profits from our industries and dividends from our investments, proceeds from the sale of the paintings are only needed to top off the budget. The financial part will not be the problem. And, unlike you, Countess, we're patient. We've been working toward our goals for many years. We need those records, though. You are going to find them for us."

At that moment, *Frau* Lietzke entered. "Walther, as always, is a useless ass. He's having problems with reservations. I'm surprised this bitch agreed." She looked at the pair and then at her half-brother. "You haven't told her?"

"I was getting to it, Karen. Go away and let me do my job."

Brookstone studied Karen Lietzke. She reminded Brookstone of a stern schoolteacher she'd had in public school who was into corporal punishment. Brookstone had escaped the year with only a stab in the head with a pencil; others had not fared as well. Most girls had trembled at the sight of her. Especially her old friend Natalie.

Karen Lietzke was a plain woman who exacerbated her plainness by wearing no makeup. Old fashioned steel-rimmed glasses were accompanied by cords allowing her to hang them from her neck. Bony cheeks and that long neck made one think of an emaciated goose. *I'm a runway model compared to this witch! But maybe it's only show?*

Brookstone had known women who had used that look to make it in what they considered to be a man's world. She had no qualms about being a strong, smart female, but men were too much fun to put them off. *And it's more fun to seduce a man than rape him,* not that she would ever do the latter. Having a willing partner was a *sine qua non.* She wondered what *Frau* Lietzke's relationship with her husband was like.

"What haven't you told us, *Herr* Dunst?" she said. "Besides pandering to your half-sister, just what is your job?"

"Gerhard or Walther don't pander," said Lietzke. "They do what I say. Isn't that right, Gerhard?" She glared at her half-brother. He nodded.

"Of course. We couldn't have come this far without you."

And there you have it. Brookstone smiled and winked at van Coevorden. *The Fourth Reich will be run by a she-wolf. Talk about women's lib! Or women in politics!* She could imagine Hitler spinning in his grave.

Chapter Thirty-Nine
Oslo

Lars Losnedahl faced his squad. Two men and a women. He generally thought them to be capable. Now he wasn't so sure.

"Because you've been incompetent, I'll be seen as incompetent," he said

Their faces were like those of the gargoyles at the Nidaros Cathedral in Trondheim. He had assigned all three to keep an eye on Bastiann and his friend until they left Oslo. They had failed.

"We had no idea what they looked like," said the woman. "No one coming into the hotel looked suspicious."

The red in his face was slowly returning to its normal pink. "OK. Let's spread out. We have some grunt work to do. Jørgen, check the CCTV of the hotel. Maybe we'll get lucky. Karla and Matteus, you're with me. We'll check the guest list and interview anyone there if we can. Someone must have seen something."

After more than four hours, all they had were three figures entering the staircase at the back of the hotel, one woman and two men.

"They must be the ones old Hans mentioned," said Losnedahl. "They never left the country."

"Their helicopter is probably parked at a local airfield somewhere," said Matteus.

"It could sit down anywhere," said Karla.

"Keep the good news coming. Bastiann is Interpol. We'll have to inform them." The ringtone of his mobile interrupted his morose thoughts. He answered it, listened, frowned, and turned to the three. "Let's go for another ride to the countryside. There's a body in a tree. The locals want to know if it has anything to do with our case."

"Nice of them to inform us," said Karla.

"There are competent cops. They just don't work for me." He nodded to Matteus. "You're driving, lad."

***

By the time Losnedahl and his team arrived at the spot about two-thirds of the way to the chalet, the locals had pulled the body down from the tree and snaked it up the steep incline using a tow line. He zipped open the body bag.

"It's the butler, old Hans. I guess he's not involved in this mystery about who kidnapped Bastiann and his friend." He looked at the third eye and was sad. No matter a person's past, that wasn't a good retirement present.

"Yeah, the butler didn't do it," said Matteus.

Both Losnedahl and Jørgen glared at him and Karla made a sour face.

Losnedahl turned to the local crime scene investigator who was packing his kit. "Find anything?"

"They might have killed him here," the man said. "Our victim took a pee on a tree. I have samples."

"Or the killer did. It's possible he was killed at the chalet and the body was ditched here."

The techie raised eyebrows. "Long story. Another case. Work the samples and send me copies of the results." He turned to his crew. "We're going back to the chalet, folks. I want to interview all the help there again."

"If it happened there, it might be a warning to the help to keep their mouths shut," said Matteus.

Losnedahl smiled at him. "First intelligent words out of your mouth today. Let's move it, lad."

As he walked toward the SUV, he was wondering about Bastiann. He was a good cop; he was a better friend. Losnedahl felt bad about failing him.

***

One of the young chambermaids broke her silence. Stuttering and sobbing, she explained how the man and woman had murdered old Hans. Losnedahl called for that techie, but he didn't expect much from an examination of the murder scene. The help had done too good of a job cleaning it up.

"We're up to five now," said Jørgen as he started the police vehicle.

"Yes, and I'm not liking this at all. This is much more than a conspiracy to sell stolen artworks. Bastiann's friend was right. There's more to this than meets the eye. These people are serious and dangerous. God help Bastiann and the old lady." *And I will too, if I can.*

"Not so old and more than a friend, it seems," said Karla from the back seat. "They were sleeping together at the hotel at least."

"What? Who told you that?"

"Forensics." She waved her mobile. "Report came in. You'll have it on yours too."

Losnedahl smiled. He had liked that twinkle in Bastiann's friend's eye. *Apparently Bastiann does too!*

Chapter Forty
Near Linz

Lietzke left to put a fire under her husband. Van Coevorden was still thinking about what Dunst might say.

"I don't know what you expect from us," the Interpol agent said, "but you expect something. Otherwise we'd be dead."

"He wants us to go after ISIS and retrieve what they took," said Brookstone.

"We don't know anything about ISIS," he said, "except for what we read in the media and in reports."

"Good guess again, but it's not only ISIS," said Dunst. "They've learned about 'the enemy of my enemies is my friend' business model and many countries' foreign policy mantra, including Great Britain and the U.S. Do you have any idea where in the world they might find expert scientists and technicians willing to process massive quantities of bioweapons?"

"Iran could do that, but they're Shi'ites," said Brookstone. "ISIS, who are Sunnis, would prefer to exterminate them than trust them. And al Qaeda doesn't have the infrastructure or personnel. So, eliminate the Middle East. That leaves only one possibility."

"Drug traffickers," said van Coevorden.

"Good. You two go to the head of the class. In Colombia and Peru, specifically. How's your Spanish?"

Brookstone nodded. "Chen and Castilblanco told me about their escapades fighting that cartel in Juarez. This is even bigger." She studied Dunst. "You can't possibly believe we're capable of going to Colombia or Peru to retrieve your damn records. Why don't you outbid ISIS? The drug lords would probably accept the highest offer."

"I see you're still in an auctioneering mode," said Dunst with a smile. "Leave that behind. Your auctioneering days are over, Countess. Besides, what you suggest would mean we'd need even more funds. And we'd still have to recover our records. Time is of the essence now."

Because we're on to you, thought Brookstone. *Too many people know what I was attempting.*

"I still don't know why you think we can help," said van Coevorden. "We don't even know Spanish that well."

"But you've proven you can work undercover. Who would suspect two journalists who are old codgers? I do prefer the young ones, by the way. It's nice that the media continues to employ TV personalities far beyond their prime, I suppose, but I'd rather have a handsome young man or beautiful woman reporting the news and doing my talk shows. I'll make a note of that for our future broadcasts. Youth sells these days."

Brookstone frowned. *A veiled criticism of her age?* That was enough motivation to keep her going in the Yard in spite of the encouragement to retire.

"Esther will go as a writer for a British tabloid, and Bastiann, you will go as her camera man. We will have Plans B, C, and so on ready, but I think using you is the best one, so that's Plan A."

"You must have a good idea where those records are," said Brookstone.

"Indeed. We know exactly where they are. We obtained GPS coordinates by means I won't divulge, and we now know what exists at those coordinates. You'll receive a complete briefing."

"And if we refuse?" said van Coevorden.

"I will be happy to create a painful death scenario for you." The smile became Machiavellian. "Or leave it to Karen. She can be creative as well."

"I'm in on one condition," Brookstone said, winking at van Coevorden.

"I don't see how you're in a position to make conditions, Mrs. Brookstone, but go ahead. I might find yours amusing."

"I want that painting. It belongs to the public and the art world, not a bunch of psychos."

"Pay for it, then."

"I can only offer my original bid."

Dunst thought a moment. "You have my word. If you retrieve our records, you can have the painting for that original bid. Is that acceptable?"

She shrugged. "If it's the best deal I can obtain, yes. Shall we draw up a contract?"

"No need. My word is gold. It's settled then. The Ruth I spoke to you about and a colleague will be accompanying you, and all four of you will be under additional surveillance."

"I bet her name's not Ruth," said van Coevorden.

"For you two, that's still her name."

***

On the plane to Lima, van Coevorden was in the window seat, Brookstone in the middle, and Ruth Mayer in the aisle seat. They were all traveling with fake documents, although their companion used the same name, which Brookstone thought was fake to begin with. She and van Coevorden were posing as employees of a British tabloid, an online ezine.

Mayer had dark curls and brown eyes and was thin and gaunt, hardly the Brunnhilde-type. This Fourth Reich, dominated by ugly witches as it seemed to be, would have to forego the Aryan ideal. No golden-haired and blue-eyed Nazis would ever pop from Mayer's womb. *Had Frau Lietzke ever been a mother?* She was another harridan.

Mayer had an expression that made one think she was always sucking on a lemon. *Is she a psychotic killer?* Brookstone had a difficult time reading her.

"I think Ruthie likes me," Brookstone said to van Coevorden. "Do you think she swings the other way?"

Mayer glared at her. "Make only small talk. Any discussion beyond that and you will die."

"I don't think your boss would like that, dear," said Brookstone. "He's counting on us, you know. Can you catch the flight attendant the next time through and ask him for a vodka martini, shaken not stirred. I'm feeling a bit like James Bond."

"They don't have a full bar. Your choice is beer or wine, I'm sure."

"We should be flying first class then. Don't you hate being trapped here with all the common people?"

"You're an elitist."

"And you're a killer. I prefer to be an elitist."

"Stop badgering her," said van Coevorden. He leaned across Brookstone to address Mayer. "She's lying. She's no elitist. She votes Labour." He smiled.

"Love, let me have a little fun. This woman's face is like stone. She's far too serious."

"I'm putting on my noise-cancelling headphones," said Mayer.

Steven M. Moore

Part Four

I dislike feeling at home when I am abroad.
—George Bernard Shaw

Chapter Forty-One
Lima

Ernesto Lopez stepped from his limo and followed his bodyguard into the old house on the outskirts of Lima. The cartel leader grimaced as he ambled through the residence. A typical colonial house, the owners had neglected its upkeep, both outside and inside. The man waiting in the living room was better dressed than Lopez, though, who was always more comfortable in his expensive *guayaberas* and slacks than in anything more formal. But he was in much better shape than the Arab. *It doesn't matter what he or I wear. He's fat and old.* He realized the foreigner wasn't that old, though; the obesity only made him look old. *What yanquis call a fat cat.*

"You have come a long way," said Lopez, offering a hand.

The man stared at it. *Don't they shake?* He remembered something about how they employ toilet paper. *Strange cultures. Brits drive on the wrong side; Muslims use the wrong hand. No wonder the world is a mess.* He smiled. *Or, the bastard just doesn't want to shake hands with me!*

Except for the three-piece suit, the terrorists' banker, Youssef bin Sayed, could pass for a sultan from the Middle Ages. He was a bit like a swarthy Churchill in his later years—receding hairline, bulldog jowls, and piercing black eyes buried in folds of fat. There was no beard. The golden chain of a pocket watch dangled across the vest matching his tropical white suit. With the tasseled loafers, he could pass for a costumed actor who played a corrupt lawyer and had escaped from the set of the TV show *Miami Vice* in its heyday. *So could I. He doesn't look like a terrorist; I do. How ironic life can be sometimes.*

"OK, I get it, I'm an infidel. Sometimes you have to dismount from your fanatical high horse, my friend, and talk business with the infidels, especially if you want to buy what I'm offering. I met your associates in Germany. They seemed to be a lot more practical. Don't you work for them?"

"We all work together, but my job is to make sure they receive what they paid for. They work hard for it, after all. I told them we can find others who will do this same job for less."

"After I met them, I suppose. That's called buyer's remorse." He shrugged. "You're welcome to try, of course. It will take time. No skin off my nose. You can take your business and shove it where the sun doesn't shine as far as I'm concerned."

Bin Sayed bristled. "You're an uncouth savage."

"Right back at you. My group doesn't cut people's heads off with a dull scimitar. That's more than uncouth—it's obscene. I have degrees from the U.S. and Britain. Do you want to compare pedigrees?"

"Idle threats. You want our raw product."

"Bullshit. I don't need it. Don't you think I can buy product from someone else? You own one little corner of Afghanistan in agreement with the Taliban and you think you control all the poppy fields. That's arrogant and stupid. But I'm willing to do business with you if you're ready to come to terms."

"I'm ready to walk out of here instead."

"Now...that's a problem. When I said you're welcome to try, I forgot to say you need to do it outside my personal playground. The only way you'll leave this house is in a body bag provided by the Lima police when they find what's left of you. If they do. And if they have one big enough. Your men have been neutralized. You're in my country now, you fool." Lopez sat on a worn sofa, crossed his legs, and smiled at the Arab. "I don't even know why you bothered to come to Lima. A transfer to my account in the Cayman Islands would have been sufficient to seal the deal. And we could have picked up the goodies you stole from Germany anywhere you liked."

The banker nodded. "I knew that. I wanted to see what kind of man you are. You're a ruthless SOB."

"Just like your leader. Just like you. So what?" He pointed to the laptop on the table at the end of the sofa. "I assume this house has Wi-Fi. Otherwise, you're wasting my time. If there's no transfer of funds, the deal's off. Simple as that. If you're lucky, I'll pay for your funeral. I'm sorry. I'm a businessman."

"It's not good to build a business relationship on threats."

"Oh, please. Why did you have your thugs surround this decrepit hacienda then?"

The banker frowned, sat next to Lopez, and put the computer on his lap. "I'll need the account number."

***

"The bastard still didn't shake my hand," Lopez said to his personal bodyguard after the terrorist left. "Tell Tito to take a few men and tail him. Keep the others on ice. If he even looks suspicious, make *ceviche* out of him and his men. I'm going to have Felipe check and make sure the funds are there and then transfer them to Panama. We might be in business. It's never a bad idea to have another source. You never know when the rest of the damn Taliban or that corrupt Afghani government will become unreliable."

Lopez spent more minutes walking through the house. It had potential. *Maybe sell it as a safe house to the Lima police? Or the CIA?* That would be a hoot. He chuckled even while he relieved himself in a bathroom that had seen better days. Drips from the sweaty tank high on the wall had left a line of rust stains. He pulled the chain and had to step back as water rushed into the bowl. *I wonder how old this place is. And who the hell owns it? Maybe fatso had them killed just for this meeting?*

He considered himself an ethical man who was forced by an unethical world to do unethical things to make money. He came from an aristocratic Lima family, one that had made sure over the centuries their blood was purely Spanish with no Native American or Japanese contaminants. For Peruvian elites, he was a businessman with many successes in shipping and trading. His fleet of merchant ships, most registered in Peru, Ecuador, and Colombia, was the largest on South America's west coast; he also owned various fishing boats, a profitable business in Peru. All those legitimate businesses, while successful, were cover for the most lucrative business of all, drugs.

His business had taken a hit, though, when cocaine had been replaced in the U.S. by the new drug of choice, cheap heroin. He had competed by undercutting the prices of the latter drug, creating a price war among suppliers. That in turn had led to sidelines like smuggling, human trafficking, and arms sales. He understood capitalism, though, and had steered his pirate ship with skill through treacherous commercial seas, changing course as needed.

He was the consummate middleman. Raw drugs came to the cartel, they processed them, and they shipped to dealers. His clients were often Mexican cartels, but he went around them when he could, becoming buyer of raw product, processor, and seller. Not so much for the U.S., but elsewhere. Drug addicts could be found from Patagonia to Lapland and from China to Europe. One of his best clients was a Macao triad. For the sidelines, they were becoming more profitable every day.

***

"You're back early," said the girl. "Do you want to celebrate?"

What's her name? He drew a blank for a moment. Felipe had found her. His mother's aunt's granddaughter or something. *Malena is her name.* The innocent look was an act. She was a slut. Her huge tits threatened to spill over the bodice of one of the expensive nightgowns he had given her. All women—at least ones he was willing to play sex games with— were sluts. Knowing how to please men was a prerequisite.

In his college days, he had been amazed how slutty the coeds were. Some threw themselves into his dorm bed, willing to spend the entire night with the handsome Latino student. Others spread their legs almost anywhere with only a bit of encouragement. A trip to a supper club at Princeton had often ended afterward in sex. They all had been the same as this woman, only this one was much younger and more stupid. The coeds had been more devious and extremely needy.

"It's only business," he said. He could now see the fifteen-year-old's perky breasts through it, nipples standing at attention. "You're sexy, you know."

She smiled. "And I can make you come in many ways."

He crushed her to him. "Don't be too cocky, *palomita*. When you cease to please me, I might feed you to the pigs."

Her expression was now a pout accompanied by a trembling lip. *Oh, she's good.*

"I've angered you in some way?"

"No. You're a much more pleasant devil to get in bed with. I didn't like the bastard I had to meet. And I still don't, even with his money."

Lopez didn't trust the terrorists' banker. *That fucking group is filled with some real bloodthirsty bastards who don't have a shred of culture beyond their fanatic desire to return to a 6th century caliphate.* He couldn't understand how they managed to survive.

Malena would have to work hard to make him forget Bin Sayed's malevolence. After he made the transfer, he probably should have shot him. *What a pig! Now that would be a good insult for a raghead!*

***

Later Lopez went to visit his guest scientists. He found the two in the small sitting area upstairs watching TV.

"Practicing your Spanish?" he said in English.

"It's a German channel," said the woman. "We don't know your language."

"We do not want to know your language ever," said the man, his words almost a growl.

The woman looked like Eva Braun near the end of the war; the man looked like Himmler. Lopez had studied world history enough to make the comparisons. *They're essential to my plans, so I must treat them nice.* He decided to ignore the implied distaste for his beloved *castellano. The Germans aren't the only Europeans who are brilliant in the arts and sciences, but they're hard to take sometimes.*

"I hope you have found your temporary lodgings comfortable. We will be providing a full wardrobe, by the way, before we move on to my labs. Even formal evening dress. I love to have guests at my dinner table. It's so boring to dine alone, and Malena isn't a brilliant conversationalist."

The woman shrugged; the man frowned. Lopez decided the woman had been pretty once, but she had let herself go. Her bun looked like something from the 19th century. The man had probably always been an ugly gargoyle.

Rembrandt's Angel

"I demand to know how long we will be here," said the man. "You have broken many international laws by kidnapping us."

"I'm not guilty of that. Like you, I'm just the hired help. And, if you do your jobs, you will soon return to your country. And, if you don't, they'll never find your bodies. Please, return to your TV show."

He went down the stairs smiling. *Scientists think they're so superior, but they're just tools in the hands of more intelligent men.*

Chapter Forty-Two
Lima

Brookstone dozed on most of the eleven-hour trip between Frankfurt and Houston on Lufthansa and tried to watch a movie on the six-and-a-half-hour trip between Houston and Lima. During the nearly two-hour layover in Houston, Mayer shadowed her, and a passenger from the first leg shadowed van Coevorden.

He used a pen to scratch a name, number, and short message on the inside of his stall door in the bathroom, though, and left another message written on bathroom tissue in the security check-in bin where his shoes had sat. Both started with skulls and crossbones. He assumed she would also invent something clever, but he had no idea who she would try to contact. *If anyone.* He hadn't had a chance to talk with her, but she seemed to want to go through with this only to save that damn painting. *I don't have a good feeling about this trip.*

When they boarded the Houston-to-Lima flight, he found his shadow was now in the aisle seat and Mayer had taken his seat in the rear of the plane. He reached across Brookstone's lap and offered a hand.

"Welcome. I'm Heinrich Dircks," he said in German. "And who might you be?"

The man stared at the offered hand. "I'm Jacob Eisenstein."

"Pleased to meet you, Jacob. Are you a friend of Ruth's?"

"You'll be busy during the next days. Try to rest. You'll need it, old man."

Old man? If I were sitting next to him, I'd stab him in the eye with the pen.

He spent some time wondering which message his NYPD detective friend would receive first. Maybe neither attempt would be successful, of course, and, even so, would the big cop understand his message? He'd been a bit obscure in case it was discovered by the shadow.

Jacob looked like the Lutheran preacher in the town where van Coevorden grew up. He wasn't much taller than the Interpol agent, but you might not see him if you looked at him sideways. Sunken eyes and cheeks and pasty white skin gave the impression of a skeleton's head with some pie dough spread on. *Alas, poor Yorick! I knew him, Horatio.*

When they checked in at the Hilton Lima Miraflores Hotel, Ruth and Jacob took seats in the lobby and pretended to read local papers. Brookstone and van Coevorden took adjoining rooms again.

"I wonder where our shadows will sleep," he said to Brookstone in Italian.

"I have a king-size bed, but it would be crowded with four," she said with a smile. "Besides, it would be risky for you to sleep with Jacob. Ruth is lesbian and he might be gay."

"I guess *Herr* Dunst and his Nazi friends have become a bit more modern," he said, returning her smile. "First Hans, now Ruth and Jacob. That's a sharp contrast with the old days." He patted her hand. "We need to talk, though, so we need to have some time away from them."

She nodded her agreement. "Maybe at dinner."

He had wanted to try talking in one of their rooms, assuming their two shadows would be elsewhere. But maybe she was right. The two shadows could bug their rooms, and the restaurant would have background noise to hide their conversation. He would have to wait.

***

Five-star hotels often tout their own restaurants, and sometimes locals even believe the hype, but Brookstone always preferred to go out. They weren't allowed that culinary adventure, though. Their shadows sat at a separate table half the dining room away from them. There was enough background chatter that she and van Coevorden were comfortable talking about their plight.

"I left two messages that our friend Castilblanco might receive. He has enough connections. He should be able to do something."

"I did the same for Dietfried Hofer and Kurt Geiszler," she said. "I figured Germans started this whole mess, so they can help end it. I'd think you'd have tried Interpol."

"And you, Langston or Jeremy Brand. Interpol considers me on vacation, remember. They've been trying to make me take more time off."

"Same here, although Langston knew I was pursuing the case. I asked that nice Norwegian inspector to keep Langston informed so he doesn't worry."

"You'd think he'd worry when he learns we disappeared from the Grand Hotel."

"If he learns about it. We finished with the Oslo authorities, remember?"

He nodded and took a sip of wine. He frowned at the quality. "OK, let's not mull over past mistakes. I'm glad you tried to make contact. I thought you were going to throw caution to the wind to recover the painting."

"Dunst accepted my deal."

"Oh please, why would you trust that bastard?" He knew she could tell he was upset with her. *Why doesn't she listen to me?*

"I've been inventing as I go my whole career. And before. I've been successful at it." She smiled. "Besides, someone has to balance your pessimism."

"It's not pessimism. It's being cautious and practical. You're going to be responsible for the murder of many of your compatriots, lose all your money, and you still won't have the painting. All your husbands are likely turning over in their graves."

"You're cute when you're angry, Bastiann. It gets me all hot and bothered. Keep it up and dessert will be upstairs in my room." She now winked and licked her lips.

"How can you even think about that in the situation we're in?"

"We're still alive, love. And the two of us are smarter than all these Nazis combined." She smiled across the room at Ruth and Jacob. "At least I hope so." She grinned. "I neglected to mention I have a surprise for them."

"What did you do, Esther?"

"I think I'll have the rack of lamb tonight. This remoulade is interesting, isn't it?"

***

Brookstone and van Coevorden were starting on their main courses when Peruvian authorities arrived. They searched Ruth and Jacob, found their small pistols, and hauled them off.

"How did they get those guns?" said van Coevorden.

"They didn't have them aboard the planes," said Brookstone. "Their threats were real, though, because they most likely could have killed either one of us with their bare hands."

"I assumed that was the case. So, the guns were in their checked luggage? Wasn't that scanned?"

"It helps to be observant. In the customs inspection, I noticed the inside dimensions of their two suitcases were different from the outside ones. They're not smugglers, so the hidden space had to be for weapons and ammo. Those are ceramic guns made with a 3D printer, Bastiann. My Bernini bust was made by one. Quite the technique. Otherwise, they'd have needed heavy lead shielding. I suppose they had firing mechanisms and ordinance stowed somewhere else under little sheets of lead." She raised her wine glass and toasted him. "I dropped a little note written on a napkin with lipstick to the immigration agent after customs saying we overheard them arranging a drug deal. Looks like Peruvians have no problem going after foreigners in the drug trade, even Colombians and Mexicans."

"Although I bet some locals might accept a hefty bribe and let the miscreants go," he said with a smile. He toasted her in return. "Good thinking. How long will they be off our back, do you think?"

"Probably long enough to do our jobs unfettered as we pretend we're after an interview with the drug kingpin. We need to discover where they're processing bioweapons for the terrorists. I didn't want those two around to interfere. Any idea what those bioweapons might be, by the way? What are we looking for?"

"They could be anything given genetic engineering successes nowadays. I don't think they'll be conventional WMDs like sarin gas or anthrax. They could make that in Germany. Maybe even Raqqa."

"A cartel would have the necessary materials and lab space, but why would they have a bioengineer or virologists?"

"They wouldn't. I don't think records were the only items ISIS stole."

"Brilliant! Of course! That ISIS crowd is a bunch of ignorant thugs. They're technological savages who are much worse than the average person in Europe or the U.S. who are just users of technology. I sensed something wrong with Dunst's story. You concluded ISIS needed someone who can understand those stolen records. Sorry I'm a bit slow, Bastiann."

He smiled. "Just not pessimistic enough. You dig into the weeds; I see the entire lawn."

"Oh please. That metaphor is silly. I hate to work in gardens. That's why I own a flat."

Chapter Forty-Three
New York City

NYPD homicide detective Rolando Castilblanco was at his desk wondering what was wrong with the department's intranet. *I hate computers*, he mused. He had wanted to access the criminal record of a suspect on a case, but the machine had taken lessons from the hare or tortoise, depending on which one you believed really lost the race. His desk phone rang. He recognized the number.

"Hi, Ashley. How's it going?"

"This isn't a social call," said friend and DHS agent Ashley Scott. "A TSA agent's message has worked its way up to me. And lucky you, you're involved."

Castilblanco frowned. *This day just keeps getting better.* His partner was off having lunch with his wife; the two women were probably discussing their spouses. Then the intranet fiasco. Now this.

"Where did this message originate?"

"Houston. You have a friend passing through Texas."

The frown deepened. The last time he was in Texas, it hadn't been pleasant. He still remembered the drug lord and his pets. His friend Hal Leonard had almost died from gunshot wounds. Scott was on that task force but stayed out of the action.

"OK. Give me the bad news."

"It was reputedly written on bathroom tissue. After a skull and crossbones and this number, it said: 'Call Castilblanco. Neo-Nazi attacks imminent in Europe. Warn all concerned. BvC.' If it helps, the v is lower case."

"It does. I'm not sure what to do with this." Bastiann van Coevorden was his other Interpol connection besides Hal Leonard and also a close friend. "What day did they find this message?"

"It was left in one of those containers used for belongings at the TSA security check-in." She gave him the date. "I second your observation: what should I do with this? I'd have to pass it up the ladder farther if you think it's legit and we need to warn our European counterparts. In the process, the urgency usually gets watered down. Who's the sender, by the way?"

Castilblanco explained. "Can you check and see if he really passed through Houston?"

"Hold on." The cop heard the muted sound of a person pounding on an old keyboard. He hoped her intranet was faster than his. "No. He didn't fly through there unless he was flying under an assumed name."

"I wouldn't put much attention to the message then. It might be a prank, and Bastiann might not be involved at all. But go ahead and escalate it. Let the people with the high-paying jobs make the decision about calling European authorities."

"OK. That's on you, though. I think it sounds pretty desperate. It was on toilet paper, after all."

The computer network awoke after he talked to the DHS agent. By the time the cop went home, he had forgotten about the whole thing.

***

It was 2 a.m. when Castilblanco awoke in a sweat with Ashley Scott's words rattling around in his head. "I think it sounds pretty desperate. It was on toilet paper, after all." *What was I thinking?* Only he would know what BvC meant!

"What's the matter?" said his wife, propping herself up on an elbow.

"I might have really screwed up," he said.

"It wouldn't be the first time," she said. She rolled over and ignored him.

He barefooted it into the living room of their tiny Brooklyn apartment and picked up the phone. It took him an hour to get through.

"Congratulations and good morning, detective. You are very lucky. You made it through several layers of staff. Even though your name is revered here, you should still buy a Powerball ticket today—that luck might continue. What can I do for you?"

"An immense favor, your highness. You can make people listen a lot easier than I can."

"Go on. What's wrong?"

Castilblanco scratched his belly. *How to put it to his regal buddy?* He didn't want to waste his time. *Oh hell, tell him all your paranoid thoughts.*

They were on the phone for half an hour. The detective checked on the kids and went back to bed feeling better, knowing that across the Atlantic, a man in a castle would begin his workday making calls to European security people.

Chapter Forty-Four
Lima

Brookstone looked around the parlor, appreciating the décor. "Furniture is from the late 1500s or early 1600s," she said to van Coevorden.

They were driven to a sprawling, luxurious colonial mansion she guessed was on the outskirts of Lima, although it was hard to gauge distance from the duration of their ride, some of it over 16th century cobblestones. The Nazis' zip ties and velvet bags had been replaced by a drug cartel's rough cords and flour sacks. The sacks had now been removed, but they were still tied.

"There's a nice breeze," he said. "It's interesting how these old villas were constructed to take advantage of natural air conditioning. I love the tile pattern. It's Spanish. Maybe the original tiles?"

"They might be from Italy by way of Spain," she said, "but probably originals. The Spanish were well settled here long before English colonists even reached North America. It's amazing what the obsession with gold could do to motivate the blaggards. They managed to destroy an entire Native American civilization in the process of searching for *El Dorado*."

"Multiple ones if we count the Aztecs and others, as well as the Incas. And the Catholic Church helped things along."

"Spoken like a true Lutheran."

"I'm agnostic, partly because I think religions mess up the world a lot, even now, if we consider the Middle East, with Christians, Jews, and various Muslim sects, for example."

"I suppose you're right. You know, I'm getting bored with the wait."

***

As if they had heard Brookstone's complaint, a man entered and stood before them. He had Asiatic features—many Peruvians had Japanese heritage that combined well with Incan. He sported a thin black mustache to match his black, oily hair, and was dressed in a three-piece business suit.

He cut her cords first. "Mrs. Witherspoon and Mr. Dircks, *bienvenidos*. My name is Jorge. We have collected your camera equipment, Mr. Dircks, along with both your luggage pieces. We also took the liberty of checking you out of the hotel."

"That sounds like we're your guests, and we'll be allowed to do our story," she said.

"That, or we will hold you for ransom. Maybe both. In any case, you will be useful, never fear. Please don't make my life difficult. I convinced *El Jefe* this was a good idea." He reached over and caressed her cheek. "You must have been quite the hot number thirty years ago."

"I wouldn't even put out for you then," she said. She saw the flash of anger in his face. "That didn't come out well. You're just not my type."

Jorge cocked his head, smiled, and then gave a little bow. "A headstrong woman, I see. You remind me of that Cat Stevens song. It must be uncomfortable for you to work with such a boss, Mr. Dircks."

Van Coevorden smiled at her. "You don't know the half of it."

"What Cat Stevens song was he referring to?" Brookstone said after Jorge departed.

"One of Steven Demetre Georgiu AKA Cat Stevens AKA Yusuf Islam's biggest hits," he said. "'Hard Headed Woman.'"

He looked around the room and decided the videocams were well hidden.

***

They didn't stay at the colonial mansion long. They both heard the whump-whump-whump from a helicopter. Their bags and equipment were loaded, and they were forced onto the chopper.

"Here we go again," Brookstone said. The whisper was wasted. No one could hear her, not even van Coevorden.

She was uncomfortable the entire two-and-a-half hours of the ride. She attributed part of her discomfort to the chopper's unusual speed, which meant it would be even worse for them if they crashed. Considering the terrain they were flying over, she didn't fancy that. She sat back and tried to relax, though. *At least this infernal machine has good AC.*

The chopper landed on a flat river bank in an area surrounded on three sides by corrugated aluminum warehouses. The bags came off again, and they saw the second leg of the trip from a medium-size hydrofoil. They hadn't even had time to stretch from the helicopter ride before they were off on their river tour.

The landscape was filled with jungle flora and fauna. She saw New World monkeys swinging underneath the forest canopy, some making a game of trying to maintain pace with the boat. Flocks of parrots and other birds with vibrant colors took to the sky as the boat's passing disturbed their steamy tranquility. Only in a few places could she tilt back her head and see bright blue sky filled with only a few puffy clouds. The rain forest had swallowed the sky, for the most part, forming a tunnel over most of the river. Of course, humidity was so oppressive it didn't matter that it wasn't raining—they were soon soaked, even though they were dressed in light clothing.

"At least this is a quieter ride," she said to him, "if not by much."

"I would have liked to see more of the surroundings on that flight too. We flew in a new Eurocopter, the fastest chopper in the world. A vista disappears before you can even focus."

"I thought that infernal machine looked strange. Does it derive all that speed from the extra motor?"

"Precisely. Cutting edge technology based on an obvious and simple solution: if you want twice the speed, use two motors. It's amazing what millions of euros in drug money will buy you. I suspect we're on the Amazon River, by the way, somewhere beyond Iquitos. That dock and old warehouses on the river bank we left are likely associated with the drug operation."

"But not the HQ?" she said.

"Likely just storage, not the production center, which must be better hidden. There also might be more than one. And I'm sure *El Jefe* is at the one where they not only process drugs but will do the terrorists' dirty work." He watched as a large bug was left behind in the boat's slipstream. "I wonder what the mosquitoes will be like once we stop. They'd probably be with us all the way to the Atlantic Coast. Leftover Zika carriers might be a problem."

"Just don't fall overboard. I think I saw a water snake." She indicated a separate group that didn't associate with their guide Jorge or those manning the boat. They were dressed simply in white cotton shirts, pants, and sandals and lounged among supply containers and luggage. "I wonder if the drug cartel exploits the *campesinos*."

"From my Interpol briefings, *campesinos* and other poor souls don't have much choice in the matter. And they make more money working for the bastards than they could otherwise."

"Damn blaggards, exploiting the poor blokes."

"They make use of cheap labor pools, from Southeast Asia to Afghanistan and here. Capitalism at its worse. Lives have little value in the drug trade."

After about two hours, the boat slowed, and they turned into a narrow tributary. They headed upstream a bit and then pulled into a small inlet formed by a much smaller river and hidden by tree canopy. Men were waiting at the dock, ready to assist in the mooring.

"They must have a pretty good communication system," he said.

Their guide helped her off the boat, leaving him to fend for himself and his camera equipment.

"Follow me. *El Jefe* is waiting." He looked back at van Coevorden. "I assume you'll need time to organize your equipment, Mr. Dircks?"

Van Coevorden grunted. "Are we free to ask any questions we like?" said Brookstone.

"Yes, but I'm not sure they will all be answered. You'll understand, I'm sure, that there are many things about our operation we want to keep secret."

"Something like the American's Skunkworks and Area 51 and everything MI-6 does," she said. "I understand. We'll ask, and *El Jefe* will decide whether he answers. That's fair enough."

"We want the world to see our operation in a positive light. We're one of the biggest employers in the region, after all. Everyone benefits."

***

Brookstone and van Coevorden followed Jorge through the house and into another study, a much simpler abode than the one in Lima, but comfortably furnished.

"Please wait here. Mrs. Witherspoon, you can sit and relax. I can have a maid bring you some refreshment, if you like. Mr. Dircks, I suggest you ready your equipment. *El Jefe* is a busy man."

"What about my refreshment?" said van Coevorden after Jorge departed. "He must think I'm your slave."

"You're my sex slave, love," Brookstone said with a laugh. "You might be careful what you wish for. Drinking any tropical fresh-squeezed juices might lead to unpleasant consequences. He never asked what I wanted, by the way."

But the maid came to ask them both. Brookstone opted for coffee—after all, they were near Colombia—and van Coevorden requested a cola with ice, thinking about his innards.

"I assume the ice is OK."

"One never knows. The bugs can sometimes tolerate freezing." She looked around. "I think you'd better set up your equipment as Jorge said. *El Jefe* can't be kept waiting, you know."

They were the ones kept waiting. A handsome man who looked a bit like a beefier Antonio Banderas entered the study a half hour later.

"I'm Ernesto Felipe Lopez Diaz. Welcome to one of our factory sites, Mrs. Witherspoon and Mr. Dircks. Jorge has spoken highly of you. I must apologize. I had some urgent business to attend to before I could relax with you folks—it couldn't wait."

"Your English is excellent, Mr. Lopez," she said.

"So is my Spanish. My Peruvian family goes all the way back to the *conquistadores*, to the time of Cervantes, as they like to say. I studied in Princeton and then in Oxford, so I'm afraid my

English is a mishmash between East Coast American and the Queen's English. I'm equally fond of both countries."

"As Eliza Doolittle proved, one can always learn to speak correctly, no matter his origins."

Lopez frowned. "If you're suggesting they speak a dialect at Oxford, that's being a bit too London-centric."

"Hardly. Eliza was from London. I was only making small talk, something Eliza did so well after Higgins was through training her. My readers will be interested in your background, but your ancestry could be Inca for all I care. We Brits pay too much attention to 'good breeding.'" She used her index fingers to form the quotes. "The Yanks handle diversity much better, one of their few positive traits, I dare say."

"That's a bit more than small talk," he said. "And opinionated. Shall we start? I'm a busy man."

Brookstone winked at van Coevorden.

***

El Jefe gave them a little over an hour. Brookstone asked the questions. Lopez answered some candidly and refused to answer others. She thought he was like a rooster preening before the hens. He would even stand and pace with his hands behind his back as he pontificated like an Oxford emeritus professor. Indeed, just like Alfred, her late husband, on occasion. When they finished, he shook their hands.

"That went well. Let me state your questions were fair and unbiased. I won't censor your article, by the way, but I suppose you'll slant everything to paint me as an ogre, though."

"I deal with facts," she said. "That's good journalism. Lord knows what my editors will do. One more picture for posterity. I'd love to have that Obregon and Botero in the picture's background. I was recommending Obregon to a friend not long ago. Are those cases climate controlled?"

"Precisely, because they're originals. The area is humid. Please join me, madam." She went and stood by him. "The Beauty and the Beast," he said with a laugh.

"I'm flattered. I'm only an old reporter who should retire."

After van Coevorden took yet another picture, Lopez shook her hand again. "Please feel free to wander about the grounds, Mrs. Witherspoon. No cameras, please, Mr. Dircks. There are areas where you won't be allowed, of course, more for your own safety, but I'll tell my men to give you two plenty of warning about that. Don't go near the river either. Local flora and fauna can be annoying and sometimes dangerous."

"Will we see each other again?" said van Coevorden.

"Not likely, little man. My presence is required in Colombia during the next few days. I'm so sorry."

"When will they take us back to Lima?"

"Either tomorrow or the next day. The boat makes several trips per week to bring provisions from Iquitos, so you can hitch a ride. For now, enjoy yourselves. Arrange your notes and write your story. Please send a copy to this address." He handed a business card to Brookstone with only a Miami PO Box number on it.

Chapter Forty-Five
On the Amazon

"He's a narcissistic sociopath," said van Coevorden.

"Of course he is," said Brookstone. "They all are. This wine is excellent, by the way. Much better than what we had at the hotel." She nodded to the bottle of white wine sitting in the ice bucket. "I'll have to remember the provenance. The Yanks have some good wines. It's good the French have some competition. Mitigates their arrogance a bit."

"You know Californian vintners saved the French wine industry, right?"

"Of course. But they also made selling wine a huge business, using up the world's cork supply. It's not quite the same sniffing the aroma of a metal cap, you know."

She waited for him to mull that over, expecting his usual repartee, but he only tweaked his handsome handlebar mustache. "How are we going to find the records?" he said instead.

She was surprised he hadn't defended his French heritage. *My Bastiann, ever the diplomat.* But there were other ways to get a rise out of him.

"Thanks to your brilliance, it should be easy. Find the scientist or scientists kidnapped from Germany and we'll find the records. Keep your ear tuned for German."

"What about Arabic?"

"ISIS cut-throats onsite, you mean? Possibly, but I doubt it. I suspect Lopez or a henchman met with them in Europe, maybe Germany. There might have been some bartering and not only an exchange of money. ISIS has made inroads into Afghanistan. That poor country is still like an ice cream shop— twenty-one flavors of terrorist groups. ISIS gets some money from oil, but they likely control some heroin supplies too. It's a tangled nest of snakes. Fortunately we don't have to sort it all out, only find the records."

"I'd like to destroy any WMDs they've made too."

"Maybe too soon. They're likely still trying to organize. At least I hope that's the case. I'd be watching what comes in via boats and where it goes in the compound. That will be our clue." She took another sip of wine but became annoyed when the condensation from the glass dripped into her cleavage. "How uncivilized. They need better AC here. We're in a rain forest, after all."

***

Watching where loads from incoming boats went paid off. They zeroed in on a large building where walls and roof were corrugated aluminum, a new structure although similar to the warehouses. There were no windows.

"I wish I had my ninja clothes," said Brookstone as she and van Coevorden dressed at three in the morning to pay a visit to what they now called the WMD lab. "It's good there's no moon tonight. We're a bit conspicuous. We'll have to pretend we had insomnia from jet lag if we're caught."

"I wish I had a gun," he said.

"One gun against all these thugs? What good would it do?" She laughed. "If you're shot, please come back and haunt me. I always wanted to make love to a ghost. I bet ectoplasm heightens orgasms."

"Please, be serious. This is dangerous business. 'For your own safety,' the man said, but I'm giving that a double meaning. These men can be violent."

"I realize that. 'Can be' is giving them too much credit. I'm old, so it doesn't matter so much. You're younger and could have many more years to enjoy life. But I'll take care of you, Bastiann."

"Ah, so romantic. Why don't I feel better?"

"Because you're a pessimist." She finished tying her sneakers. "You know, we can't just march out of here. We need to be stealthy. Shall we use the window?"

He pulled back the curtain to the room's only window. "It's only a foot drop from the little balcony, but please don't break an ankle."

"My goodness, no. That would ruin everything, wouldn't it?"

They managed the drop to ground level and melted into the dark.

***

"Not much action around here this morning," Brookstone said in a whisper. They were hiding in shadows at one corner of the target building. "Hard to hear anything over the AC, but there are no lights. I'm ready to try the front door." She turned the corner and moved along the long front, the side they had seen from their window. He followed. She put her ear to the WMD lab's door and listened again. "Still only AC and no voices. The laboratory is closed for the night."

"The locked door would suggest that," said van Coevorden in a lower-pitched whisper. "You'll notice there's a keypad. We forgot to ask Lopez for the combination."

She examined the numeric device set above the doorknob. "Let me try some obvious sequences." She first tried 7-9-3-1 then 7-1-3-9, clockwise and counter-clockwise. Then she tried 7-3-9-1 and 9-1-7-3. There was a click with the last sequence.

"Not too smart, but considering non-friendlies aren't likely to be strolling around this compound, they probably don't worry too much about security." They went inside and shut the door. "I wonder where the light switch is. Ah, found it!"

"Wait!" He took off his T-shirt and put it along the door's bottom, covering the gap between door and ground. "OK. Now."

She looked at his bare chest and smiled. "Clever fellow. Good thing I keep you around. Your chest hair is getting gray, though. I never noticed that before."

"You're too busy doing other things when my chest is naked," he said. He looked around. "Definitely a lab. Any idea where to start?"

"Let's take a general survey to obtain our bearings. Keep an eye out for filing cabinets. Or unfriendly cartel members."

***

Workbenches were mostly empty. In one large room, they saw opened crates containing lab equipment and computers. They only found two locked filing cabinets in a two-person office. They sat at either end of an old brown leather couch facing two desks. The desks didn't look used.

"Serious work hasn't begun yet," said van Coevorden in a low voice.

They were interrupted by the front door slamming shut and girlish giggles.

"Hide," Brookstone said in a whisper. They returned to the large room and crouched behind some server banks. The air was freezing in that room. "It must be ten degrees in here."

"They keep it cool for the equipment, I suppose," he said, "but they're not operational yet, as you suggested. Only Inca ghosts still inhabit this place."

"I thought the Incas were a mountainous people."

He shrugged. They watched as one of the guards and a woman went into the office they had just vacated. The woman was the giggler. They could see all the action through a window between the lab where they were and the office.

"No finesse, but I'm getting the itch just watching them," said Brookstone.

"Oh, please. Who do you think the woman is? Lopez's wife maybe?"

"I doubt it. He seems to be the kind of man who wouldn't tolerate any funny business from his wife—a possessive macho if I ever saw one."

"That's a bit of a stereotype. I'm surprised at you. You were married to an Italian."

"I'm not saying I don't like possessive machos. I like to be possessed. What are we going to do?"

"Wait. They might be in a hurry."

"A quickie." She thought of the missed opportunity with Giorgio. "How boring. But you're probably right. The guard was carrying his rifle. He probably should be on duty. But I still want to know who the woman is."

"Maybe a lab technician. Or a German scientist? Who cares?"

***

True to their expectation, the pair soon finished and left. They moved back into the office.

"They didn't clean up much," said Brookstone, eying the couch. "Smells like a wet dog rolling in unwashed gym socks."

"The AC isn't as effective in here," said van Coevorden. He was examining the cabinet. "Simple key locks, and not up to European security standards. But I don't have a lock pick."

"Normally I'd say break them open," she said, "but we don't want to leave a trail." She searched some desk drawers packed with unopened office supplies and found a new box of paper clips. Bending one around, she started to work on the lock. "I once recovered some artwork stolen by a burglar. Not a bad fellow. Good looking too. When he left prison, we had dinner a few times. He showed me some tricks of the trade. This shouldn't be difficult."

It took her five minutes to open one filing cabinet. "Go through the contents while I work on the other one."

"Stop," he said after a few minutes, waving a file folder. "Computer printouts in German. Let's take a look at them."

They concluded after another few minutes they had found Dunst's missing experimental records.

"At least we know the type of WMD," he said. "They bioengineered a new version of the Marburg virus. I don't understand details, but this is scary. They must have a biocontainment room somewhere. I didn't see one."

"Maybe not yet that far along," she said. "There's enough empty space here to build one. Weren't the Soviets working on Marburg as a WMD?"

"For all you know, we or the Yanks are too. Maybe all of us still are."

"I suppose it's appropriate Dunst and friends chose this. The virus was first discovered in Marburg, Germany. Or, should I say identified?"

"Semantics. I wish I could photograph these sheets."

She pointed to a copier. "We could use that, but I'd also like to falsify the original information."

"Make the copies." He sat at the workstation on one of the desks. A printer/scanner was connected to it. "If the OCR is any good, we can make an electronic file and muck around with it. What's our time limit?"

"I wouldn't stay out of the room for more than an hour," she said.

"So, let's say I have twenty minutes. I can do it if I can figure out the password."

"Try 'password123'," she said, starting to copy.

It worked. He smiled at her. She shrugged.

***

"Think we changed enough?" Brookstone said as they made their way back to the compound's main house. She had copies and originals hidden inside her slacks. The folder with the papers containing sheets of falsified data had been returned to the filing cabinets.

"My knowledge of biochemistry is limited," said van Coevorden. "Not my best subject in college, to be sure. But changing some quantities, doubling here, halving there, as well as centrifuge times and so forth, will make it impossible for them to duplicate experiments. Of course, there's always a chance a kidnapped scientist has an eidetic memory."

"If she or he isn't pure evil, they won't make corrections. This is serious and time-sensitive enough I want to brief MI-6 ASAP. We need to make contact. Maybe when—"

"*Alto!*" A guard stepped around the corner of the main house. "*Que hacen afuera de la casa?*"

Given she could see even in the dim light she was staring into the barrel of an AR-15, she decided to invent a reason for being outside the house. The guard's clothes looked more wrinkled than one might expect even for the tropical climate. She hadn't obtained a good look at the woman's lover in the lab, but this one had the same build as far as she could tell.

"It was a bit hot in our room after all the sex," she said in her halting Spanish. "We opened the window, saw it was cooler, and decided to take a romantic walk."

She saw flashing white teeth from a wide smile. *Good guess, Esther!* The gun barrel was lowered. "*Perdoneme, mi señora.*

Vayan a su cuarto de la misma manera y nadie necesita saber." By appealing to the guard's romantic side, amply displayed in his tryst in the lab, their only punishment would be having to enter their room the same way they came out.

"A bit close," said van Coevorden once they were back in the room. He rubbed a groin muscle he had strained. The taller Brookstone had climbed onto the little balcony more easily than he had.

"Latinos love romance, bless their sexy souls. My count was a fine example of that."

"And what about Dutchmen?" he said, knowing Alberto Sartini was Italian.

"You do just fine, love. Determined pragmatism works well too. Help me remove these slacks so I can stow away the experimental records in a safe place, and we'll have a go at it. We might as well have some fun while waiting to greet the dawn."

Chapter Forty-Six
On the Amazon

Late the next morning after the hydrofoil departed with the reporter and her photographer, activity at the cartel's hideout returned to normal. In the new lab, Gretchen Koch was smiling as she tried to adapt her desk to her personal style. The cartel leader Ernesto Lopez had turned out to be much more civilized than those ISIS devils, even more so than Gerhard Dunst and his cronies. She was reliving her encounter with the guard in the early morning. *This job has some interesting fringe benefits too.*

The bioengineering and virology expert had specialized in altering viruses at Darmstadt and had taken Dunst up on his offer because she knew it was far more than she could ever receive in academia. When the terrorists had kidnapped her, she realized that had probably been a mistake.

She had to have her desk just so before she could even think about setting up the new lab, including the placement of new equipment in just the right spots and transfer of the used that was still serviceable from the old lab. Sharing time between the old and the new facilities was already a bore. She couldn't wait to have the new lab completely functional.

She dropped a box of pens when she heard the bombs start to fall. Raul, her guard, burst into the lab and grabbed her.

"We're being attacked by drones. You have to get out."

She always wondered what terrorists felt when hell rained down from the sky from the silent drones above. Now she knew.

***

Many died in the attack and most buildings were destroyed, including the new lab. No one knew who had launched it. Smoke filled the air.

After the bombing stopped, Gretchen went to the old lab to survey the damage. She knew flaming debris was still scattered around the main compound, but the old lab being retrofitted to serve as additional storage space for the modified virus was well hidden and some distance away from the main compound. Raul had said the slight damage was caused by an errant bomb that had landed a few meters from the back wall. *We're still in business.*

"We were lucky," he said, approaching her. "We're all going to hide here. We expect the soldiers to come soon to investigate."

"It will take time before we can resume production," she said. "How long will they stay here?"

"If they're convinced the whole compound is destroyed, they won't remain long. We're leaving the bodies where they are to increase that perception. *El Jefe* is shutting everything down and shipping the product elsewhere."

"What will become of me? Of us?"

Raul smiled. "I told him you know a lot about chemistry too."

"He wants me to make drugs?"

"Designer drugs. You will head up a new team." He put his arm around her. "I'll be one of your bodyguards."

She nodded. *It could be worse.*

Chapter Forty-Seven
Lima

The boat had left them in Iquitos early in the afternoon. After discussing the issue, Brookstone and van Coevorden paid for plane tickets in an old single-engine prop plane that might have belonged to the Red Baron. The motor sputtered and coughed upon takeoff but was soon flying over the jungle, retracing their helicopter ride at a slower pace. They arrived in Lima as the sun was setting.

"A hotel is in order," she said, "but not the one where we stayed before. If possible, it would be nice to avoid the evil Nazi twins, Ruth and Jacob."

"Yes, they might no longer be our fans with that little trick you pulled," he said.

A taxi took them to a less expensive hotel.

"Let's hope this one-star place doesn't have fleas," she said.

"Bedbugs would be worse."

They hauled their luggage inside and made their way to the desk. The receptionist was a wrinkled old woman with striking Native American features, definitely not of Spanish descent. She assessed the two strangers.

"I only have a room with two singles," she said.

"They won't need it," said a familiar woman's voice. "The reporter and her photographer have a room reserved at our hotel."

"Hello, dear," said Esther, glancing at Ruth. "Nice to see you again."

"Jacob will get your luggage. Follow me."

"How did you find us?" said van Coevorden, once they were tucked into the dusty Mercedes. She wondered how much it cost in Peru.

Jacob was maneuvering the vehicle through the chaotic, narrow streets. Ruth, in the passenger's seat, turned to them.

"After we were released by the Lima police, we brought in some help to keep an eye on the hotels. That was a clever ruse, by the way, but we're not incompetent, you know, although we're operating in a foreign country."

"We had the same problem," said Brookstone. "But Dunst and I have a deal. We were going to look for you."

Ruth shrugged. "It doesn't matter. Was your mission successful?"

***

All was forgiven when Brookstone and van Coevorden handed over the experimental records they had taken. The two shadows made no mention of Dunst's missing scientist or scientists. Brookstone and van Coevorden saw why in the news that evening. Mysterious explosions had occurred near Iquitos and farther down the Amazon, leveling familiar warehouses—satellite images were shown.

"That's too much coincidence," she said to him. They were sipping drinks and lying naked in bed. "No wonder Ruth and Jacob weren't too upset. They must have tracked us somehow."

He went over to the closet to examine his old suitcase. "I'd be willing to bet we have a GPS locator in here somewhere. In your luggage too. They checked the bags in Frankfurt, remember. So much for their hiring help to find us. They didn't need to."

"Devious," she said, taking another sip of her martini. "I think we need to buy some new suitcases."

They didn't have to worry about new luggage, though. On closer inspection, van Coevorden found the GPS locators powered by small lithium ion batteries. Instead of destroying them, Brookstone slipped hers in her purse and he put his in his pants pocket. They were counting on Ruth and Jacob not noting the small differences in distance between a plane's luggage compartment and where they sat in the plane. Once in Germany, leaving the locators in an appropriate place might aid their escape.

"Good thing that hunk Ernesto was in Colombia, don't you think? He'll just be terribly pissed instead of terribly dead. He survived the Nazis wrath by using one of his nine lives. *El Jefe es el Gato*. And a handsome one at that."

"Maybe related to the Cheshire Cat as far as Dunst is concerned? What will ISIS think?"

"Depends on how much they paid Lopez. I guess Dunst had backup scientists and didn't mind losing one or two to exact revenge on *El Jefe*. He attacked soon after we left. Nice of him to wait. I wonder how many cartel members, house staff, and workers died in that little carpet bombing. Poor bastards. Dunst's problem was recovering the experimental records. Once he had them, it was time for payback." She studied van Coevorden who still held the suitcase. "Put that down, love, and come hither. They're going to show some live flyover images from Iquitos now. After that, we can turn off the TV set and concentrate on more important things."

"Like how to warn MI-5 and MI-6 about Dunst's plan?"

"That, and escaping our shadows, if you insist on not having any fun beforehand. They'll be doubly cautious now. But I think we have to return to Germany with them. I still want to recover that painting, so there's no way around it."

"Recover the painting, or die trying," he said, stretching beside her.

Small fires still burned in Lopez's compound, but now some soldiers could be seen milling around. Peruvian authorities claimed the events represented a success story for their war on drugs. The two lovers knew better.

***

Ernesto Felipe Lopez Diaz eyed Youssef bin Sayed sitting diagonally from him. They were watching the same newscast in his suite in Bogotá's Hotel Tequendama.

"That's too bad. I assume you don't have any property insurance," said the banker. "Maybe your life insurance is in better shape."

Lopez glanced at the two terrorists sitting at the small dining table. "You're worried about losing all that? I don't need insurance. I make my own." The two put their hands inside their coat. "We have enough virus stored to meet your needs. True, the new lab would have doubled production and maybe made a higher quality product, meaning more stable yet more lethal, but you can still do plenty of damage."

"And where might this product be?"

"On its way to Sardinia. I already made the call. You can do whatever you like with it. Our business is done." He handed the slip of paper to his guest. "Now, tell your bodyguards to stand down, or they'll be dead along with you."

Bin Sayed nodded but looked around. He told the two men at the table to relax in Arabic after reading the slip of paper. "I'll assume you just made a bluff and not a valid threat. No matter. As you say, our business is finished."

Lopez stood. "I am an honest businessman. I always keep my side of a bargain." He brushed a piece of lint off the shoulder of the banker's expensive suit. "Just an FYI, old fellow: I never bluff." He waved a hand. Three of his men from the adjoining hotel room entered with AR-15s still trained on the three terrorists. "My life insurance, you see."

***

The return trip to Germany seemed longer. Brookstone was tired but couldn't doze on either leg, the first not going through the U.S. this time. She was also worried, and her worry wasn't about dealing with Dunst and recovering the painting.

At least they didn't kill us when they received copies of the records. She thought that meant Dunst was going to keep his word about the painting.

No, she was worried about her relationship with van Coevorden.

How does that song go in My Fair Lady? I've become accustomed to his face. Especially now. She had spent more time with the Interpol agent than ever before.

She knew what was happening. She had experienced it with her husbands. The old female-male chemistry of the species, no matter the lovers' ages, had turned into something leading to a more permanent pairing. It was a law of nature. The fictional Henry Higgins failed to escape the clutches of Eliza Doolittle, at least in the movie. She couldn't remember the details in *Pygmalion.*

Her worry was that it took two to tango. Van Coevorden was in some ways like Higgins, a confirmed bachelor, a bon vivant, and not known for long romantic commitments. One excuse he made was that he was in a dangerous occupation. *But we both are.*

She thought of that NYPD detective Castilblanco. His wife was a crime reporter, so, in a sense, they were both involved with the underbelly of New York City. Moreover, Pam Stuart often did exposés. But even a little vacation in Europe had turned dangerous for them both, as well as some more recent events. Yet the pair enjoyed a commitment that only grew stronger with the years. *And look at Chen, Castilblanco's partner, and her husband, Kulmala, who was an ATF agent. Isn't that the same type of relationship I have with van Coevorden?*

She hadn't had enough time with her many husbands to enjoy a complete commitment. Employing an oenological metaphor, their relationships had been more like a wonderful young Beaujolais than a well-aged Bordeaux. Her relationship with van Coevorden was maturing nicely, far beyond Beaujolais, but they still hadn't tried living together.

She realized that might not be possible. They both were dedicated to their careers, although she suspected hers might soon be over.

On the second leg of their journey, she gave up trying to predict her future with van Coevorden and focused on the coming confrontation with Dunst. Both the Interpol agent and Ruth were too engrossed in movies. Brookstone had already seen the old classic *13 Hours*, though, and hadn't wanted to see that tragic true story about official ineptitude unfold again.

***

"I assume the originals were destroyed in the explosion and following conflagration," Dunst said, waving the reports. His expression was noncommittal.

Brookstone smiled at van Coevorden. The neo-Nazi had just confirmed they had destroyed Ernesto Lopez's compound. *Who else?* The Peruvian government hadn't had anything to do with the carpet bombings. *Does he even care about the scientists?*

"It wouldn't have mattered," she said. "The originals were computer printouts. Bastiann scanned them, altered the data, and printed them again. Even your scientist would take forever to recover the original data and continue with the project's developmental stage."

Now Dunst smiled. "Very creative. I commend the two of you. I could have saved some carpet bombs, although that exercise was a good proof of principle. Your tactic would have been an amusing trick to play on the cartel and ISIS. We have no use for either one, by the way. They are both groups of thugs not fit to exist in a new Reich."

"Yes, you wouldn't want to dilute that Visigoth blood of yours," van Coevorden said.

She saw the flash of anger and put an elbow into his ribs. "Let's not sink into a political quagmire," she said. "I believe we have a deal, *Herr* Dunst. You owe me a painting."

He nodded. "There are only a few left. You two halted the sale of the Rembrandt, but we continued with our offerings. A deal is a deal, but I made no commitment about time of delivery. I'm afraid we have to hold you until our little business with England is finished. Better for you, madam—soon you might be the last Englishwoman alive. We're well on our way to completing our plan. I plead for your understanding. Ruth and Jacob will show you to your rooms."

***

"I was afraid this would happen," said Brookstone after their two shadows left them.

The rooms were adjoining and shared a bathroom. Except for the locked entrance doors making them into prison cells, the rooms were as comfortable as those in a five-star hotel. Van Coevorden stretched out to take a nap.

Sometime later, she called to him.

"Could you ring Jacob, love? I need some ice." She opened the door a crack and handed the bucket to him. She had noticed it when she entered the loo after Ruth and Jacob left.

"I don't know why you expected otherwise," he said, recalling her comment before his little nap. "And, with all our travels, I don't think people we tried to contact have any idea about where we are. That's assuming our messages even arrived, of course."

"I wouldn't count on that, but maybe your pessimism is rubbing off on me. Do you suppose that's our dear old butler?"

Jacob entered and listened to van Coevorden's request. *Good, he's ignoring me because he thinks women are weak, especially non-Aryan women, therefore not dangerous.*

"Jacob, old traveling companion, I hate to be such a bother, but I think I have something in my eye. Can you see what it is?" He glanced at her and then at van Coevorden. "Bastiann needs glasses and is too proud to admit it. I need someone who can actually see."

Jacob shrugged and came near, bending toward her face. With all her force, she buried what was left of one side of the plastic ice tongs into his right eye. She had sharpened it to a fine point on the grout and rustic tiles in the WC.

He howled but became silent when she grabbed a lamp and clubbed him with its base. He fell to the floor and lay still.

"Remind me not to get on your bad side," said van Coevorden with a smile. He took two of his ties and bound the faux-Jew thug. One of his handkerchiefs and Brookstone's nylons served as a gag. "I hope the rest of your plan works as well as this first part. It would have been nice to know you had one."

"I don't have the rest developed yet, but let's move. We have no idea about where we are or how to leave this estate, so I need time to figure things out."

"Let me grab the suitcases," he said.

"We don't have time to pack!"

"We'll put the locators back in them," he said with a smile. "We'll combine our ideas, as far as they go."

Steven M. Moore

Part Five

In a battle all you need to make you fight is a little hot blood
and the knowledge that it's more dangerous to lose than win.
—George Bernard Shaw

Chapter Forty-Eight
Stuttgart

It wasn't hard to elude Dunst's other thugs. Brookstone and van Coevorden tossed the empty suitcases into a drainage ditch several miles from the house. Soon afterwards, they found what looked like a major highway and hitched a ride in a box lorry. She invented the story their auto had broken down, and he couldn't fix it. He didn't seem amused. *But he isn't handy with tools.*

The driver accepted the story; he was on B10 headed for Stuttgart. Once there, they left the locators on the lorry, which was bound for Prague, and went to the police. After telling their tale to astonished inspectors, wheels were put into motion to stop Dunst and the Lietzkes. MI-5, MI-6, and Scotland Yard were informed. Geiszler was called. Agencies in charge of recovering artwork stolen by Nazis were added to the mix.

While it was impossible Dunst's people had already produced their variant of the Marburg virus in sufficient quantities to attack England, the British government would now be prepared just in case there was some attack, and the whole E.U. would be looking for Dunst and his accomplices. Brookstone's only regret was she now had no chance to save the painting.

***

"You two have been busy," said Kurt Geiszler. "Let me see." He consulted his iPhone. "Destroying a drug cartel's compound in Peru, thwarting an ISIS plan to wage biological warfare in the Middle East, and warning the government in the U.K. about an imminent bioweapons attack by neo-Nazis." He frowned. "Any other plans for getting into trouble I should know about?"

Brookstone laughed at his serious expression. "Why, yes there are. I'd still like to save that painting."

"Forget about it. A security detail will accompany you to your hotel. I want you two to stay put there until we clean up your mess. Dunst has already proven he will take revenge on those who cross him. We'll find him and his friends, never fear. But that painting is irrelevant now."

"Not for me," she said.

A motorcade took them to a local hotel. Two guards were posted at the doors to their rooms and three more in the hotel's lobby, all watchful for the evil neo-Nazi trio. She thought it unlikely they would make an appearance, though, because everyone was looking for them. Besides, Dunst probably would send a bunch of thugs to do his dirty work, and they could easily overpower the five guards. She felt a bit exposed.

"*Herr* Dunst's country manor accommodations were far superior," she said, testing the ordinary double bed. "I can't roll away from you if you snore."

"That goes both ways, Mrs. B. I take it you've given up on the painting as Geiszler suggested?"

"I'm hoping the appropriate German authorities will do their jobs with that after we see Dunst and the Lietzkes in jail. I'm certain we've stopped his revenge plan against Britain. And there will be no continued development of that Marburg variant."

"For now. He has the records, but he has no more time. Ironic that ISIS and their lackeys in the cartel helped save London, don't you think?"

She thought a moment and soon started to tap the hard mattress with her left fingers.

"Bastiann, suppose they already had a biocontainment facility somewhere at Lopez's compound hidden away from the WMD lab? We didn't see one, but that doesn't mean it wasn't there. It would be logical to keep it separate, in fact. They would need some Marburg to start with, right? Sort of like keeping starter yeast around for baking bread. There's a good chance the scientist or scientists even developed some of the deadly variant cultures already. Dunst's carpet bombs might not have come close to that facility, and test runs and the scientist are still there."

"Wouldn't Peruvian soldiers have found them?"

"They could just stay put if the facility was hidden well enough. Lopez might already be back there, and ISIS might have some of what they paid for while we were wasting time with Dunst and company back here in Germany."

"I wish you'd thought of that scenario earlier," he said, throwing open the door. He crooked a finger at the surprised guard. "We might have a major problem!"

***

Authorities now involved in the case included the CIA, FBI, DEA, and DHS from the U.S. MI-6 also expanded their activities to include Peru, joining forces with Peruvian authorities and the DEA and CIA; all involved increased surveillance efforts on ISIS sympathizers and known neo-Nazi groups. Many were apprehended and questioned by representatives from European counterterrorism efforts, from Rome to London.

Brookstone and van Coevorden were also questioned. She thought that time was wasted trying to poke holes in her theory. Geiszler was their last visitor.

"I know you meant well," he said, "but I'm thinking the probability ISIS or the neo-Nazis have bioweapons in sufficient quantity already available is near zero."

"Because Dunst bombed the compounds?" she said. "I'm thinking Lopez would want to keep the biocontainment facility as far away from the WMD lab and his other structures as possible."

Geiszler nodded. "*Ja.* I understand your theory. But you both said the WMD lab wasn't operational yet. That implies they weren't producing product yet."

Van Coevorden shrugged. "I'm sure that's occurred to the other agencies. And mightn't an older facility have been operational before the new lab? The authorities know everything we know. Apparently they're not willing to take chances. I wouldn't be willing to do that either. You can make your own choice."

Geiszler nodded again. "I'm worried that it's only a distraction when we should be tracking down Dunst and the Lietzkes, but better to be safe than sorry, I'll agree. Anything else, my super-spies?" They shook their heads. "I bid you *auf wiedersehen*, then. Try to get some sleep."

"Is your pessimism winning me over here?" Brookstone said to van Coevorden after Geiszler left. "Am I justified in my perception that all these people are stumbling over each other and will accomplish absolutely nothing, while something serious is about to happen? Brussels déjà vu, as it were."

"We are the theater goers who yelled 'Fire!'" he said. "The stampede toward the exits to flee the function is best handled by waiting a bit and calmly walking out. Otherwise, one can be trampled."

"An appropriate metaphor," she said. "Let's continue with that line of thought. Let authorities worry about a bioterrorism attack, which might just be a manifestation of my paranoia. We should worry about the neo-Nazi trio just like Geiszler said. Where would our evildoers go?"

"We neglected to describe the bunker. It must be in the suburbs of Linz, I suppose. That's where I'd go."

She smiled. "We are quite the team. I might recover that painting yet. Follow me!"

***

Their guards' function was to protect them, but that would also normally make it difficult to leave the hotel. They made the excuse of looking for midnight snacks. Because there were no vending machines on their floor, they had to descend at least one, but both guards suggested the machines off the lobby had more variety. Because their companions were there, they saw no problem with that. No one expected them to flee the scene.

They found a twenty-four hour hire-a-car agency nearby—there were many hotels in the vicinity—so soon they were heading toward Linz. It was about a five-hour drive from Stuttgart via A8 and A1. Traffic was light in Augsburg and Salzburg, but Munich was starting to awake, so they lost some time there.

"We shouldn't even try to find that airfield," she said, negotiating a curve, a maneuver causing her passenger to grab for a strap. "I'm heading for *Frau* Lietzke's art gallery. If the old fascist isn't there, we'll toss the place to try to find the location of that bunker. If she is, we'll make her take us to it."

"Don't take this as a criticism, but we don't have guns and she likely does. And, in Oslo, she looked like she knew how to use one."

"If I have the jump on her, that doesn't matter."

"Excuse me? She's a Valkyrie who most likely dances to Wagner. She's *Die Führerin*, after all, and no physical weakling like Hitler. We'd need all the guards at the hotel to take her. Maybe even more."

"Let me give you a Bible lesson. Ever hear about David and Goliath?"

"We don't have a sling and stones either. And I thought you were an atheist."

"Trending that way. My ex, Count Sartini, was convincing. No matter. We make our own heavens and hells right here on Earth. And that's all irrelevant. We'll buy a bottle of cheap wine."

"Why cheap?" He saw her expression in the Opel sedan's rearview mirror. "Oh!"

Chapter Forty-Nine
Stuttgart

"They were just going for a snack."

Geiszler glared at one of the guards who had been on detail at the hotel. He bit his tongue and let his anger subside, though. In their defense, they had been told to protect Brookstone and van Coevorden, not to keep them prisoners in the hotel. They had no reason to suspect that the two would be off to do more mischief. *I should have known better!*

"OK. Let's regroup and try to find them before the bad guys do."

He assigned his men their tasks and returned to his temporary office. He had just sat down with a mug of coffee to finish mellowing out when the desk phone rang.

"*Ja?*" His voice came out like a bear's growl.

"Helga here. Is this a bad time, Kurt? I'm wondering about my exclusive. It seems like a lot is happening. Have you gone to the major media?"

"Major media has captured the story, as you well know— there's a lot available—but don't worry. I've said 'no comment' to more reporters than I can count. They're parasites, you know, present company excluded."

"Glad to hear the last. Keep me in mind for an exclusive."

"I will, I will. I need to ring off now. I'm very busy."

"I thought it was all over with and you were in cleanup mode."

He frowned. "So did I, damn it. Keep in touch, but I'll call you as soon as I can talk."

"Don't forget that promise."

He hung up the phone. Just another thing to do: decide how much of this story could be told to Helga. He had to give her more than what the rest of the media was getting. She deserved her exclusive. *I'll make sure she calls me an "anonymous source," though.*

***

Geiszler entered the interview room. The hire-a-car attendant sat across the table looking like he might wet his pants. Geiszler took a chair opposite him and scanned the notes from his colleague.

"Hassan, you can settle down. I know you're here on a work permit, and this isn't about immigration." They had already checked that work permit, of course. He pushed the photos of Brookstone and van Coevorden across to the nervous man. "My colleague said you recognized these two."

Hassan nodded. He had relaxed a bit, but his fingers still drummed softly on the metal tabletop. "I didn't know they were fugitives. Believe me."

"How could you know? You gave us the make and model of the hire-car. Can you provide any more information about them?"

Hassan thought a moment. "It was late. I was sleepy. They seemed to be in a hurry."

"Any idea where they were headed?"

He thought some more. "South maybe? They turned left out of the garage. I saw the headlights, then the taillights."

What was south? Geiszler remembered Brookstone's involvement in the case had started in Munich. There was that warehouse too. They would have to check those sites again, but he had a nagging feeling the pair was heading elsewhere. He sighed. *Are they heading for trouble yet again?* It wasn't enough that trouble found them. They had to go looking for it!

Chapter Fifty

Linz

Van Coevorden waved at the bookseller, who was arranging books in a few rickety old bookcases in front of his store, and entered the gallery from the front dressed in a hoodie. He saw *Frau* Lietzke toward the rear using a jeweler's loupe to examine a painting on a worktable. She was near enough to the backdoor, so he sent the pre-written text message to Brookstone and rang the bell on the counter.

"I'll be with you in a moment," Lietzke said in German. He hit the bell on the front desk several more times. "*Ja, Ja,* patience is a virtue, you know."

She took two steps toward the front. Brookstone was already inside, and he had created enough diversion so that Lietzke didn't even sense Brookstone's presence. Fortunately the wine bottle didn't break. Lietzke fell to the ground, twitched twice, and remained still.

"She might have a concussion," he said, finding the weak pulse in her neck.

She held up a book after looking at its title. "An interesting reading choice." She scanned the section of the novel where Lietzke had left her bookmark and began reading aloud to him.

"Stop!"

"And you think I'm lascivious. We should take this along. We can read it as a bedtime story whenever this little adventure is over. Consider it a literary education too, because we'll see what the new erotica authors are producing."

"You're incorrigible."

"No, this author is. I'm an amateur in comparison. And one's never too old to learn a few new tricks, my dear."

He sighed. "About that concussion?"

"Too bad. We'll tie up Annie Oakley and put her inside the Opel. The backseat might be a little tight—she's Odin's spawn, after all—but she deserves some discomfort. Tie her up while I look for her gun stash."

"Annie Oakley?"

"I know my trivia, love. Of course, maybe the good *Frau* can't shoot that well, but I'm guessing the opposite." She grabbed a screwdriver off the worktable but found she didn't need it. The middle drawer of the front desk was unlocked and contained a Glock and Beretta. "Proves my point." She thought a moment. "Oberndorf's near Stuttgart. You'd think she'd have some H&Ks. But we'll make do. One gun for you and one for me, plus ammo. How convenient! Let's hoist this Wagnerian heroine and put her into the car. Here. Slap some duct tape on those pale lips. I don't want her to start singing *Liebestod* in front of the bookseller."

***

Brookstone saw the bookseller watching them from the window of his shop when they pulled away from the curb. She smiled and waved at him. They drove to a nearby multilevel garage near Schillerpark. She put a finger to her lips when she saw that the attendant, who seemed Middle Eastern, was looking at Lietzke, who was nearly covered with a blanket they had found at the gallery—only pale legs were showing.

"My poor, stupid niece is sleeping off a hangover," said Brookstone in a low voice. "We've driven from Salzburg and are a bit beat ourselves. We'll take naps too, if you don't mind."

"That's a new one," he said, but he understood hotels were expensive luxuries for travelers needing only a short and safe nap. "But, as long as you pay for the time the car's here, what do I care?"

"Good fellow." She drove up two levels and parked between a Mercedes and a Porsche. "We're the only middle class car here, Bastiann. Maybe Austrians are all rich? Wake her up."

"How? She might be in a coma. You know that a full bottle of wine has some weight to it, even if it's cheap wine."

"Especially if it's cheap. I only tapped her over the ear, and she's wearing a wig that should have cushioned most of the blow. I thought I would have to hit her twice, in fact. Slap her on the cheek a couple of times to wake her. Or, here, use this."

"It's our coffee thermos."

"The coffee's tepid now, but it's wet. Whatever. Do something creative. I'm eager to find that bunker."

Lietzke regained consciousness with the splash of coffee, but she remained pale when she saw her own Beretta pointed at her nose. The fear didn't last long, though. "You! And the other meddler! You have some nerve. You will die for this."

"We all die sometime, *Frau* Lietzke," said Brookstone, waving the gun, amused the woman's eyes crossed following the barrel. She showed Lietzke her other hand containing a pair of pliers she had also pilfered from the gallery. "But you won't die yet if you tell us where the bunker is. You might lose some teeth first, though, depending on your resistance to my charms. Or, should I go after those nice long fingernails? No, they're not natural, are they? Maybe the privates? Replacing the saucy erotica in your cute little book with some S&M?"

"You wouldn't! You're not capable of that. You're an art lover, like me."

"Oh, please. I'm sure you're capable of torturing me, no matter what artistic sensibilities you might have once had, but right now I have the upper hand. Come now. A little information will help your cause. An address would be nice. This Opel has a GPS unit."

"The only address is for the farmhouse on the same plot of land. The entrance to the bunker is off a gravel road going into the woods from the rear of the house."

"So, let's have the address of the farmhouse, *bitte*."

***

Brookstone peered over the window sill and saw two thugs playing cards. She returned to her crouch. She showed van Coevorden two fingers. He motioned toward the rear, eyebrow raised, and she nodded. He moved off. She soon received "Ready" as a text message to her mobile.

She put the phone away and knocked on the door. The sound of her four loud knocks reverberated through the nearly empty dwelling. The door was flung open. One of the men faced her.

"I'm wondering if one of you gentlemen could help—"

There was a thud as his companion in back of him hit the floor. When the first thug spun to see what was going on, she hit him behind the ear with the Beretta's handle.

"Like a London bobby, love, we can function without guns."

"I'm not sure I'd have the courage to depend only on a nightstick," he said.

"They often wear vests because criminals have guns, but there's pride and tradition among the Metropolitan Police. Americans could learn a thing or two. They're so gun happy over there, even the police. It's like the Old West. City streets are like that fight at the OK Corral."

He said nothing. Scotland Yard always was a bit too prideful for his taste. He began to tie the two after she frisked them.

They weren't Nazi-poster quality. The stubble on their chins was as long as that on their heads. The swarthy complexions, wide faces, and square chins were non-Aryan features. Dunst and company must have personnel problems if they had to scrape the bottom of the barrel to come up with these foot soldiers.

"Where do we put them?" she said.

"There's usually storage space under the stairs. Remember Harry Potter? It should be empty. This place hasn't been inhabited for years, except for these two."

"I'm not keen on leaving Lietzke there."

"She likely wouldn't fit under the stairs with them. She's a big woman and they're large oafs. She's OK in the Opel and will be more comfortable there."

"It's not her comfort I'm worrying about! Someone could discover the car and free her. I'd prefer them to find it empty when we park near that bunker."

"'We'll leave her in a closet here then. I'll ram one of those chairs against the doorknob to make her more secure. And we'll pull the Opel off the road before arriving at the bunker."

Chapter Fifty-One
Near Linz

It wasn't hard to find the bunker using *Frau* Lietzke's description. They stopped short on the gravel approach road when they saw two Mercedes sedans ahead, one blue and the other black. The bunker's mound, which they recognized, was behind the cars, complete with its heavy door.

"*Herren Dunst und Lietzke*, I presume," said Brookstone, driving the Opel into the woods.

"I'm guessing there are more here than those two," said van Coevorden as they walked out of the woods back to the road and toward the bunker. "They'll have some lieutenants."

"*Oberleutenants*, you mean. I have three clips. How many do you have?"

"Four. Depending on how many bad guys there are, we might not have enough."

"Better to have some firepower than none." She studied the bunker entrance. *We're not getting in there easily.* Ideas flew through her head. She discarded most of them and then sighed. "Here's my plan."

As she outlined her strategy, he first smiled and then his grin widened.

Both cars had alarms set, their red on-lights flashing on dashboards. Given the location's remoteness, they figured car doors weren't locked, but the alarm had set automatically. They elected the blue Mercedes with a flip of a coin. Stripping to their waists, they opened the rear door on the driver's side, leaving it unlatched, tossed their clothes in front, lowered the window, and began amorous activity in the back, the alarm now bleating.

"Slower," said Brookstone. "You're getting me hot. This is supposed to be a theater production, not a porn show. But pour it on when someone comes out."

The thug who exited the bunker and approached the car carried what looked like an H&K G36—serious firepower. She recognized it easily as she nibbled on van Coevorden's earlobe. The oaf could be a clone of the two in the farmhouse.

"What are you doing here?" he said, leaning through the window.

Brookstone, underneath van Coevorden, used her longer legs to kick the door open, sending both thug and gun flying. Van Coevorden jumped from the car and put their victim under with a chokehold.

She went over to pick up the assault rifle, hefting it with appreciation. "Finally, a real weapon. German army issue, don't you think?" She put the butt of the gun on the ground and saluted him.

"While you cut a much sexier figure than Rambo," he said, "I think we'd better dress, Esther. Our mentally challenged victim has a vest on. I wonder if that will fit you. I'm too barrel-chested, I'm afraid."

They dressed, and she held up the armored vest. "This won't fit me, but turning it around, we can put this Nazi in a straitjacket, where he should have been since he was born."

He nodded. "More mercenary than Nazi I'm afraid, like that Irish pair and the pair in the farmhouse. I'm pretty sure Dunst and company don't have thousands of Teutonic soldiers sitting around waiting to parade along Ku'Damm in Berlin. Let's hurry. Soon they'll start wondering what happened. And we have a problem. He shut the door."

"Check him for key fobs," she said. "Now that we have some firepower, I'm modifying the plan."

Their prisoner had them for both cars. They put him in the backseat of the black Mercedes and locked the doors. Van Coevorden pocketed the fobs.

"You mentioned Rambo, but who does Mad Max?" she said. "Heads or tails?"

He won. "I don't like this game. What am I winning?"

"I drive, you ride shotgun. Better said, H&K. I'm ramming that door. We'll see if all those commercials are true about how safe this car is in a collision. Please remain alive to register a complaint with Mercedes if I fail, but old women drive into buildings all the time, and the buildings suffer the worst for it. Give me your Glock." She took the wheel and put the gun between her legs. "I always wanted to be one of the Sex Pistols." He smiled and took the passenger side. "I'm not sure this is a good idea, but it's the best I have right now."

"What if the painting isn't here?"

She glared at him. "Don't even think that!"

***

Brookstone backed the blue Mercedes far enough away from the bunker's entrance to obtain room to accelerate to a good speed. She put the vehicle in first gear. With one foot on the clutch, another on the accelerator, she revved the motor into high RPMs, and then released the clutch with a smooth stroke. Gravel and dust went flying as wheels spun a bit. The many horses then took over and she shifted through the gears. The car swerved a bit at first, but she straightened her accelerating battering ram. It hit the entranceway at almost sixty mph, sending door, cinder blocks, earth, and wood flying forward and sideways. The engine acted like a heavy, protective barrier. Air bags did the rest.

They came to a stop unscathed except for a few nicks from flying chips of safety glass. That differed from the fate of two mercenaries who had probably been coming to check on their companion at the moment of the crash. One of their H&K's was damaged. Van Coevorden tossed the other to her. "Put your peashooters away, kid. Bonnie and Clyde now have some real firepower!"

They moved forward, turned a corner in the tunnel, and were met with a bee's swarm of bullets. Both had already hit the ground and started to fire back, creating a curtain of flying lead. There were screams of pain, and then all was silent.

"They're moving back to regroup," she said. "How far do you think this bunker goes into the hill?"

"And down. Who knows? I doubt they obtained building permits, so you won't find any plans on record. Your guess is as good as mine, but I heard a lift. If that's the only way to flush them out, we'll want to think twice about going after them. I'm not crazy about exiting a lift to face automatic weapons. We might not be so lucky this time."

"Wait here," she said. When she returned, she showed him the grenades. "I thought at least one of this dark fairy tale's ogres might have some. The well-equipped mercenary and all that. Not very smart, considering we crashed through the door, but no one said mercenaries are that bright. If they were, they'd be in some other occupation where they might live longer, at least as long as a pedestrian in London."

"So you agree they aren't Nazis?" he said.

"Who cares? What we need to figure out is how to put a timer on these cute little pineapples so they'll explode when the lift's door opens."

"That's easy. No timer required. I'll arrange that the pins fall out when that happens. But how will we protect ourselves? Not even a vest would do any good."

"Hmm. You're right. I didn't think of that. Do I have to do all the planning here?"

"Out of deference to your feminine ego, I'll assume that question is rhetorical." He thought for a moment. "It's possible there's a service hatch in the lift's ceiling."

"Brilliant. How do we climb up there?"

"Another problem. I'm short, and you likely don't have any arm strength."

"I work out, but you're right. I haven't been able to do a chin-up in years. Natalie and I used to skip the required physical education classes. We weren't the only ones."

He looked around at the ruins. "There are chairs, a desk, and a filing cabinet. Probably for security guards, maybe the three we already dispatched."

"Yes, every museum with valuable paintings must have a guard station to be respectable. We'll use that filing cabinet. It's high enough. We can't move that heavy desk and the chairs are too low and unstable to be useful. We can toss contents of the cabinet, but, even so, how do we lift it, my little Dutchman? Where's Schwarzenegger when you need him? Isn't he one of the good Austrians?"

"I'll take that as rhetorical too. We'll slide the cabinet into the lift. We can push on it. Rather, I can. You cover me."

Chapter Fifty-Two
Near Linz

Brookstone used the cabinet drawers as steps and waited for van Coevorden on the lift's ceiling while he performed the delicate task of setting the grenades. Her groan interrupted him.

"I hate spiders. I know the little fellows do good things like trap and eat obnoxious insects, but they make all these damn webs." She brushed her hair. "And it smells like an auto mechanic's shop up here."

"Just old grease and oil, I'm sure. Maybe the spiders live on that too. Now, quiet. I'm concentrating. The last time I did something like this was in the service."

"I bet you had a military haircut and no handlebar mustache then. And fewer pounds."

"I'm not overweight, Esther. I'm compact."

"Like that dwarf with the battleax in *Lord of the Rings* film."

"Please. I'm much taller. Silence!"

One-track mind. I'm trying to calm him down! She felt something crawling on her neck and brushed it away.

"I hope I can manage to climb up there," he said, "but we're ready. There are three floors below. Where should I send the lift?"

"To the floor where it came from, of course. That's where the Nazis are."

"But maybe not where the painting is?"

"If we take them all, we can find the painting later."

"I'm testing you. I wanted to see if you had come to your senses. You finally lost your obsession with the painting."

"I did not! I only know Dunst and his collaborators won't let us leave with it until we put them out of commission."

"Like I said, you came to your senses. Here goes."

She watched him punch the correct buttons. The lift wasn't speedy, but he needed all that time to join her. They closed the hatch as the lift came to a halt.

They heard the door open and then gunfire, but the explosion of the grenades followed. Silence then prevailed.

"I just had a bad thought," he said to her. "The explosions might have moved the filing cabinet. It might not be in the middle of the lift under the hatch anymore."

She opened the hatch and looked below. "Always the pessimist. But you're right. It hit the back of the lift." The sides of the lift were buckled. *Circular blast, Esther.* The explosive shock wave hitting the mercenaries must have been even stronger against the walls and cabinet. She thought a moment more. "If you can sustain me for a short time, I can drop to the floor and slide the cabinet over."

"Let's do it." Even though she wasn't that heavy, he knew he was losing his grip as soon as she dropped below the edge of the opening. "Esther, I have to let go!"

"Do it. I'm OK."

"Don't break or twist an ankle."

She dropped onto the lift's floor and felt a slight twinge in her right ankle, the one she had injured back in Oslo. "Oh, bother! I'll be a bit gimpy now. But don't worry. We're playing for the World Cup here. I'll tough it out. Give me the guns and ammo first, and then I'll move the cabinet."

***

Brookstone and van Coevorden peered from the lift at the smoke and dust-filled corridor. There were at least five dismembered bodies, assorted body parts, and a lot of debris. They picked their way through the carnage.

"Maybe one grenade would have been enough," she said, looking back. "I think the lift's out of service now. But the blast might not have been enough to take them out otherwise."

"All thugs," he said, inspecting bodies. "Dunst must be holed up somewhere safer, letting these fellows fight his battles."

"Fellows and a bird," she said. "This one's a fem-Nazi in the true sense. You'll remember our friend Ruth, but you're excused for not recognizing her. There's not much left of her face, but I remember her swastika tattoos from the plane rides when she was dozing."

"What a waste," he said. "She seemed much more capable than our friend Jacob. I guess with *Frau* Lietzke at the helm, women were bound to play an important role in this conspiracy."

"Equal opportunity in the Fourth Reich. At least for mercenaries who will die for the cause. I want to put their weapons out of commission. Any ideas?"

"Same models we have. We take all their clips and leave the guns empty. Does that make you worry less?"

"Yes. The extra clips could be useful too. Hurry. We might still have the element of surprise."

"You're kidding, right?"

They pocketed the clips and moved on.

He had no ball of thread, but he still thought of Theseus searching the maze for the Minotaur. Most of the bunker's cool and humid halls and rooms were empty. They found more guns and ammunition in one large room.

"Are we lost?" he said some time later.

"I think we've been in this area before. But it all looks the same. And they'd never have the paintings here. It's too humid and moldy." She wiped her hand across the wall. It came away wet, leaving a dark smear on the concrete. "They must be in a climate-controlled vault somewhere. We only have to find Dunst and Lietzke, and most likely we'll find the paintings."

"Correct. They'll be in that same vault."

She nodded. "It would be a panic room for them, but also a treasure vault for the paintings. If they're even here, of course."

"I just want to find those two Nazis and have this over with."

***

Van Coevorden started marking corridor corners with an X and an arrow using the butt of his gun. That helped them cover the labyrinth more efficiently.

"There's another floor below and two more above," he said when they later came upon a previously marked X.

"Along that way," Brookstone said, indicating the arrow's opposite direction. "It has to be on this level. Why have mercenaries guarding it so well otherwise?"

"To deceive us maybe?"

"Oh, please. They're not that smart. This corridor is new. What do you think Nazis stored here during the war?"

He pointed to old barrels in racks they had discovered in another large room they explored off the corridor. "French wine is my guess. At least this room was used for a wine cellar."

He pounded on a barrel. It sounded hollow.

"The sots drank it all," she said. "I could do with a nice French burgundy myself right now." She swung up to sit on top of an upright barrel and swung her legs. "I'm getting tired, Bastiann. We'll have to find them soon or I won't be able to pull the trigger."

"Understood. That corridor continues. Rest a bit and then we'll move on."

Chapter Fifty-Three
Near Linz

"This is all your fault," said Lietzke.

Dunst and he were watching the Scotland Yard inspector and Interpol agent's progress through the bunker's maze of corridors on a CCTV monitor.

"Walther, you're a whining little maggot. This is no one's fault. They've outmaneuvered us at every turn. You just saw an old woman and her gigolo dispatch hired mercenaries who should have had no problem killing them. If we had these two in our movement, we'd already own Europe again."

"Save your speeches to motivate the youth corps," Lietzke said. "How do you propose to get us out of here?"

Dunst walked to the bar, poured himself a cognac, and held the bottle so Lietzke could see it. The latter shook his head in the negative. *How could the man be so relaxed in these circumstances?*

He'd never liked his wife's half-brother—Dunst's arrogance and narcissism went far beyond what was needed to be a leader of the masses. And his evil genius paled in comparison to his wife's. The two siblings' plans were now only failed dreams for world domination.

Dunst jerked a hand toward the bank vault door between them and their foes. "How do you think they'll be able to reach us in here? We have enough food, water, and liquor to last for months."

"That's easy. They'll bring in backup. This vault isn't indestructible, you know."

"It's built to withstand a bunker-buster, assuming the present German Air Force were even competent enough to target it correctly. I'm not worried. My only misgiving is I'm sealed in here with you. I'd kill you, but your rotting corpse would stink up the place."

Lietzke mulled that over. "It's always been about you, hasn't it? You're only using our movement for your own gains. I'm not sure what your agenda is now, but I'm certain establishing a Fourth Reich is only a means to some self-serving end. Karen had you figured out, but she insisted on using you for lack of a better alternative."

"Yes, she used me in many ways. I went along with it. You're just jealous because Karen was smart enough to pick me over you, you stupid ass. She'll be an excellent *Führerin*, an iconic leader for the masses while I work behind the scenes. It's always better to be Machiavelli advising and serving princes while enjoying the spoils of their power."

Lietzke made fists. He'd always suspected.

"Isn't it amazing what they can do with the worst grapes," Dunst said, sniffing his cognac. "Hitler was dumb to invade the Soviet Union. If he'd been satisfied with France and the rest of continental Europe, we'd now own the vineyards producing this marvelous elixir, don't you think?" Lietzke saw Dunst wink at him in the bar's mirror.

Fists became more clenched. "I'm not a cognac aficionado. The French wines are good, though."

***

Rembrandt's Angel

Dunst watched Lietzke in the bar's mirror. *What an idiot! Not a shining example of Teutonic ingenuity.* Walther was the one who Karen had truly used—his money, his paranoia, his xenophobic hatred, especially for Jews. There weren't enough like him who they could rally around them anymore. Germans had betrayed their heritage. They had needed to resort to mercenaries for many things, soldier-prostitutes who sold themselves for money, not a cause.

In spite of their patience and long-term planning, he now realized that it hadn't been enough—they had rushed things. One needed to scour all of Germany to find like-minded persons with enough purity of soul to become faithful servants of the Reich. That took time. That mistake was on Karen.

"But their wines are possibly overrated, as are most things French. Not long ago, I enjoyed an excellent cabernet from Australia. Who would have guessed?" He turned and shot Lietzke. "But why bother arguing with a toad?" He went over to Lietzke, who was still alive and clutching his neck. Dunst shot him again in the forehead. "You know, old friend, I just remembered seeing a bag of lime in one of the storage closets. Possibly left over from the construction? I won't be stinking up the place with your corpse after all."

After putting Lietzke's body in the storage closet and covering it with handfuls of the white powder, Dunst rinsed his hands in the WC and returned to watch the progress of Brookstone and van Coevorden.

"I had many chances to kill those two," he said to the empty vault, "but I like the old witch. She has the heart of an artist. My mistake. Karen and I both made mistakes." He went to the refrigerator and removed a bag of frozen shrimp. "Not as good as fresh, but these will do. Now, where's the damn cocktail sauce?"

He was enjoying his third shrimp and still sipping cognac, when he spotted his half-sister. *Where'd she come from?*

***

Karen Lietzke had difficulty controlling her rage. She was out for blood. After rubbing her wrists raw to loosen her bonds, she crashed through the closet door, van Coevorden's chair-brace no match for that rage. She searched for the mercenaries who were supposed to be guarding the farmhouse. In her rage, she didn't think of looking under the stairs.

She had staggered from the old house and made her way to the bunker. She found a bottle of aspirin in the surviving Mercedes's map compartment. She chewed six, letting the acidic mash strengthen her resolve while mitigating her pain. The pain medication also diminished her anger somewhat, at least to the point where she thought more clearly.

Brookstone and her gigolo will pay for their meddling.

She entered the bunker, taking stock of the damage and carnage. When the lift didn't rise from below, she descended via hidden stairs, exiting many feet away from the mercenaries' bodily remains.

She found them soon enough, though. The familiar stench of death—blood, urine, and feces—didn't stop her. She paused only to examine guns, cursing when she found they had no ammunition. *That doesn't matter!* She wiped the tacky blood off her hands and looked around. She picked up a rusty steel rebar and knocked off some clinging cement. *I'll break the necks of those two!*

She figured Brookstone and van Coevorden were still exploring the bunker, or they'd be waiting at the vault door. There was no way they could enter there. Either way, they would soon pay.

She went straight to the vault and found it unguarded. *I must have avoided them.* She keyed in the combo, and the door slid open. A hirsute hand grabbed her neck and drew her inside. She was thrown to the floor, and the rebar went flying.

"It's me," she said with a growl. "Where's Walther?"

Dunst, after sealing the vault door again, turned to her. "They killed him. You led them to us, didn't you, Karen!"

"We're not the only ones who can torture," she said. "Don't be a fool! You're the one who's ruined everything."

"You don't look any worse for wear outside of that fat bump on your head. You probably caved like the coward you are. But don't worry. We'll live to fight another day for the Fourth Reich." He smiled. "We'll be honored as national heroes by marching thousands in a parade on *Ku'Damm* yet. You're still my *Führerin, Liebchen.* But, never mind. We're safe here. We can hold out for months. My only regret is that the destruction of England is postponed for the time being."

She stared at Dunst, fury etched on her face. Had he forgotten her husband had earlier learned authorities had thwarted ISIS efforts to pull off biological attacks at several London sites? Although they had outflanked the Nazis, thanks to the cartel, they had failed too. In an unrelated action, a government minister's wife had confessed to helping the Nazis plan their own attack by hiring some Bulgarians for the dispersal. The minister had a heart attack and died.

Regrets? Gerhard is a disaster!

Frau Lietzke knew why he was obsessed with the destruction of England. While she also hated the World War Two allies, he had a special loathing for Great Britain. In the early years of the war, they were the only ones who stood up to the Nazis. Their bombing missions had killed millions, including their parents. As the bastard daughter, Karen Lietzke had no love for a philandering father and the naïve and weak woman who had raised her, but she had despised the Jewish birth-mother who had been her father's mistress even more. Dunst's opinions about their parents were entirely different.

She saw him look at the rebar, thicker than normal to strengthen the bunker's inner walls after the makeover.

"What were you thinking? They have guns. And they took all the mercenaries' cartridges. I saw it all."

She shrugged. "I want revenge. Especially now. Where's Walther's body?"

His grinned. "I covered it with lime. It's in a storage closet."

"Let me see him."

"No. There's no need. He's dead. Get over it."

"He was my husband."

"And I am your lover who says you have to forget about him. You're better off without him. He's only another German patriot who died for the Reich. Come, relax a bit, and have some shrimp. Cognac or white wine?"

She took a seat in the chair where Walther Lietzke had been sitting. "I'll have some chardonnay if it's cold but no cocktail sauce for my shrimp. I don't like to disguise the delicate taste."

"A true gourmet," he said, preparing her order.

She felt something wet on her right hand, looked, and discovered it was blood. Old blood but still tacky. Eying the door, she thought a bit and then scowled. The iron rebar was close at hand.

"You killed him, you bastard!" Her howl echoed through the vault as she swung the rebar toward Dunst's head.

She sank to her knees after Dunst collapsed. Soft sobs were the only sounds now remaining in the vault.

Chapter Fifty-Four
Near Linz

"It looked a bit suspicious, but the *Frau* is known to imbibe a wee bit when business is slow." The bookseller watched as Geiszler's crew broke into Karen Lietzke's art gallery. "I thought about it a bit and concluded that I should call the authorities."

"Thank you for that," said Geiszler. "We appreciate it when our citizens help us."

The bookseller bent closer. "Will there be a reward?" The last was almost a whisper.

"For doing your duty?"

The bookseller blushed. "That was unconscionable, I suppose. How'd you end up here from Stuttgart?"

Not easily. None of Dunst's warehouses had checked out, including the one where Brookstone had viewed the painting. "By checking with local authorities along the route. A colleague also knew *Frau* Lietzke had a gallery here."

"So, my information helped?"

"Yes. And a hire-a-car attendant pointed us in the right direction."

"Hmm. I'll probably derive at least a short story from all this. I've already made the connection to the recent news. I'm thinking of some embellishments, of course."

Geiszler thought of Helga. "Stay tuned. You might not need them." He saw one of his colleagues motion to him from the entrance to the gallery. "Thank you again, *Herr* Moore. You've been a great help." He went to chat with the colleague.

"Looks like they smacked her with a wine bottle. Darius checked our records. The *Frau* had two legal gun permits. They're missing."

Geiszler looked to the heavens. *Lord, what are they up to?*

***

"You are Zaki al-Hussein?" said Geiszler, sitting next to the garage attendant. The unmarked patrol car they were in was parked next to the man's booth. He nodded, his eyes going around the car focusing one-by-one on Geiszler's colleagues who were standing at attention with their automatic weapons. Another patrol car was on the other side of the booth. "These were the two people you saw in the Opel?" He nodded. "Were they alone?"

"I told the other officer they weren't. They had a body in the back."

"Could you see the face enough to ID that person?"

Zaki continued his scan around the outside of the car. "Am I in trouble?"

"We're not immigration, Zaki. Just answer the question."

"The woman driving said the person in the back seat was her drunken niece. I couldn't see the face, only the legs. They looked like a woman's."

"How long were they here?"

"Over an hour. It was most unusual. They parked upstairs somewhere. The driver said they were all going to take a little nap. When they left, I couldn't see whether the body was still in the backseat."

"You say body. Do you think the woman in back was dead?"

"I couldn't see well enough. Maybe just unconscious?"

"OK. Back to your booth, Zaki. And thanks for helping us out."

After he left, still eyeing the automatic weapons, Geiszler spoke to a colleague standing outside the patrol vehicle.

"Get forensics here. We need to scour the upper levels to see if we find anything."

They were still into it two hours later when he received a call from dispatch.

"A woman is trying to reach you, sir," said the dispatcher.

Helga? She's becoming a nuisance! Reporters! He smiled, though. "Put her on."

"*Guten tag, Herr* Geiszler," said Esther Brookstone. "Have you missed me?"

Chapter Fifty-Five
Near Linz

Brookstone had heard the muffled screech while they were still in exploratory mode in the bunker. She cocked her head. *Where did that come from?* Van Coevorden smiled at her.

"This way," he said.

He led the way through some corridors and down five steps into an area they hadn't explored yet. They stopped in front of the vault door.

"Sounded like a woman," she said. "You don't suppose Karen Lietzke beat us here, do you? Wouldn't she have passed us?"

"Not necessarily. This place is a maze. She would know where she was going and head straight here. We didn't. If it's her, she has admirable fortitude."

Brookstone put her ear to the door. "Might be someone became too rough in a naughty Nazi ménage à trois. How are we going to get through this door to find out?"

"We're not. But they won't escape either. We now have time to wait. Let me go see if one of the hired help long gone to Valhalla had a mobile that's still functional. I think our work here is done. Whoever's behind this door might as well be in a prison cell. All we have to do is stand watch until authorities arrive." He winked at her and preened his mustache like a silent film villain. "I'm betting there's a lot of stolen art inside, plus some Nazis." He watched her start to pace. "It's still about that painting, isn't it?"

She nodded. He shook his head.

***

When Kurt Geiszler's team blew the vault door, the team's leader found Karen Lietzke's body. She had shot herself.

"Dead silence," the leader called back to Geiszler. "Literally. Fritz reports two more bodies. Three total."

"Come out, then, before you contaminate the crime scene."

Brookstone had used the functional mobile van Coevorden found on Ruth's body to call Geiszler. She hadn't known they were so close. They had been ready to wait for hours. She was happy they were prompt, though, because she was ready to collapse.

The German put on forensic gloves and booties before entering, examining the woman's body, and closing the staring eyes. He next found Dunst with a crushed skull. The rebar beside him, tipped with his matted hair and blood, was the obvious weapon. Finally, he found Walther Lietzke's body in a closet covered with lime.

"I guess that brings an end to this conspiracy," Geiszler said to Brookstone after rejoining her, van Coevorden, and the SWAT team, and calling for his forensics people. "But there are no paintings here," he said. "In particular, there's no Rembrandt's Angel."

"Someone has to keep looking for them," said Brookstone. "They must be stashed somewhere else because not everything was sold, according to Dunst."

"We don't have enough personnel to mount a European-wide search. It's clear this group operated internationally. That search would be complicated too, with multiple countries involved. What about Interpol, Bastiann?"

Van Coevorden shook his head. "Not a chance. We don't have enough personnel either. I wasn't even supposed to be working on this case." He waved a hand toward the vault. "Our work is done for now. Are we free to go?"

"We'll need your statements," said Geiszler. "I suggest you find a hotel near our HQ. Would you like some help with your superiors?"

Van Coevorden nodded.

"Mine too," said Brookstone. "If you can put a good word in, we'd appreciate it. Considering we were nearly killed, I don't see how they can complain, but mine have always been thinking about creative ways to convince me to retire."

"Maybe I should tell the Yard not to even think of it," said Geiszler with a smile. "You're too valuable to retire, although I personally recommend you don't continue at this killer pace. You can take that literally. Bastiann?"

"All I need is a statement thanking me for my contributions while I was on vacation. Esther would be better off if we had recovered some paintings, but my superiors will be fine with that kind of statement."

"I promise we'll keep the bureaucracy to a minimum here so you two can return to a normal life. Tomorrow afternoon maybe, at HQ?"

"Sure, why not?" said Van Coevorden. "We'll need a ride because our Opel is part of a huge crime scene, I suppose."

"That works. I'm off to meet with Helga Schmidt. She's a reporter. We have to pretend to keep the media in the loop, you know. Because this is wrapped up, I can give her an exclusive."

"No pictures of us, please," said Brookstone, hooking her arm into van Coevorden's. "I have enough problems attracting a good man as it is."

Rembrandt's Angel

Chapter Fifty-Six
London

The ISIS terrorist had driven the lorry toward Victoria Station along a deserted side street at two in the morning. It looked like any other lorry delivering produce to the concession stands there. With the morning trains, bleary-eyed commuters would be searching for coffee, tea, and pastries, or even more substantial breakfasts. Everything seemed normal. He was ready to meet Allah.

He turned a corner and saw the barricade formed by patrol cars. He came to a full stop and began to back up, only to find that other patrol cars had moved behind him. He stopped and wondered what to do.

The sniper's bullet tore into the side of his head, and his last thought was that he had failed in his mission.

That scenario had repeated five more times across the city. Jeremy Brand watched the action on the huge screen and sighed.

"Do we have all of them?" said his superior, Robert Ridgewood.

"As long as our intel is good. This was only one cell. We knew that capturing that one fellow and interrogating him might cause them to move their attack time forward. We were lucky to get all the sites covered."

"We have to test six lorry loads," said Ridgewood, "but I'm betting it's all the same deadly stuff. Good job."

"We had ample warning," said Brand with a shrug. *Thank you for that, Esther and Bastiann.*

"You have a call from the PM," an aide told Ridgewood.

Brand watched the rotund man with heavy jowls move to a corner of the huge command center to take the call. *We're going to be asked to keep this quiet, I'll bet. Never praise, only blame when the shit hits the fan.*

***

"Is he conscious?" Brand said to the guard.

The other MI-5 agent uncovered a small window in the heavy cell door and peeked inside. "Barely, sir. I suppose using that drug is better than physical torture."

"Easier for him but not for us. There's not much satisfaction in sticking a needle in a man's arm when you know he'd cut off your head if he had the chance." The guard nodded. "Let's see if he's coherent enough for some more questioning, shall we?" Brand entered the cell; the door was shut and locked behind him. He shook the terrorist. "Abdul, we need some more information."

The terrorist eyed him with bloodshot eyes. "Go to hell."

"I hope to avoid that, but you, sir, have your place reserved there for certain." He pulled the man up by his collar. "Now listen to me. We can put you under again and again until we learn the details about how you thugs financed and obtained the bioweapons. I want to know about your network. Do you understand?"

This time the terrorist answered by spitting in Brand's face. He backed away and wiped the spittle off with his handkerchief.

"I can see we might be wasting our time. A better solution might be to release you." The terrorist's scowl turned into a smile, but his eyebrows raised in question. "Broadcasting, of course, that your whole plot failed because you gave us details about the attack in exchange for a lighter sentence."

"You drugged me," said the terrorist. "I don't make deals with infidels."

"Do you know about computer simulations, Abdul? Maybe not. Our filmmakers can bring dead actors to life and create wild animals that look lifelike. There's no way to tell whether they were filmed or computer generated. When I say broadcast, Abdul, I'm talking about a video that shows you betraying your brothers. They won't know that it's computer-generated trickery either. They will soon take their revenge." Brand spun on his heel and reached for the door, but he looked back over his shoulder to say, "Let me know if you change your mind. Be assured my patience isn't long in these matters."

Brand rapped on the door, and the guard let him out.

***

Youssef bin Sayed, the terrorist's banker, shook his head in frustration as he watched the news reports in his hotel room. Missions had failed before, but this one represented a considerable investment. *But we always come back. They have too many soft targets.*

The plan had been a work of genius. They needed more clever ideas like using the Nazis' own bioweapons for their own purposes. Employing Western technology to end the infidel hegemony wasn't only clever, it was a gift of Allah. They owned the failure, though. They hadn't made proper use of what Allah provided.

There was a knock at the door. "Room service."

He scratched the stubble on his chin and looked at his Rolex. Bad timing. He looked at the messy bed where he had enjoyed the Parisian girl and sighed. The West had its charms.

He launched his considerable bulk from the comfortable chair, went to the door, and looked through the peephole, seeing the ID tag of the hotel's staff around the chambermaid's neck and the service cart.

"Come in and be quick. You'll have to clean around me."

Hearing her swipe her master key card, he tightened his robe and headed back toward his chair and TV. He never made it. As he lay dying on the plush rug, he felt the woman place a gun in his hand.

***

Brand followed his boss into the small conference room. The assistant head of SIS, the Secret Intelligence Service, otherwise known as MI-6, stood and reached across the table, first shaking Ridgewood's hand, then Brand's.

"We are prepared to supply the particulars about the ISIS banker, Youssef bin Sayed," said Mark Higgins, the MI-6 leader, after the three were seated.

"An encrypted teleconference would have been sufficient," said Ridgewood.

"The Foreign Secretary suggested a more personal approach," said Higgins with a smile. "He feels we might have stepped on someone's toes."

Brand had always wondered who he preferred, Ridgewood or Higgins. His own boss seemed to be more human and took vacations with his family like a normal husband and father. Higgins, on the other hand, was an ascetic person who fit his mental image of Sauron from the *Lord of the Rings*. They both had a reputation for being fair, impartial, but demanding taskmasters.

"Ours," said Brand. "We're supposed to be on the same side, you know."

The man across the table shrugged. "Sometimes time is of the essence. The Foreign Secretary and our director made the decision for swift action. The DGSI located our target in Paris, and we had an asset there ready to go."

"Let's hear the story," said Ridgewood.

When the MI-6 VIP finished, Brand glanced at his boss and then at the man across the table.

"It would have been useful to interrogate the banker," said Brand, nodding at his colleague.

"It's more useful to have him out of the way and take our time learning about their finances," said Higgins.

"That's not possible," said Ridgewood. "Someone has already taken his place, I'm sure, and that fellow will change everything. Besides, you'll need the account numbers and passwords that he probably had memorized or in an encrypted file. Did you recover a personal laptop or computer?"

The MI-6 man nodded. "We'll soon have what you ask for when we break the encryption. Having him alive wouldn't change anything."

Ridgewood frowned. "Maybe not, but bank accounts are only part of the story, I'm certain. And he probably had a lot of good intel stored in his head."

"And why make it look like suicide?" said Brand.

"Looks better than 'unknown assassin' in the French media. Besides, DGSI insisted. The angle was a bit difficult because bin Sayed was left-handed. He must have been very remorseful about the failure of their plan, don't you think?"

The MI-6 man's smirk annoyed Brand. Ridgewood stood; Brand followed suit. "It was a close call," said Brand's boss.

"And never would have happened if the Germans had done their jobs in vetting Dunst's little program."

Brand put his palms flat on the table, leaned forward, and stared into the cold eyes. "Dunst waited for his opportunity and took it. NATO handed him that opportunity. I'd think the Foreign Secretary, the PM, or some other high-level bureaucrat better damn well find out why NATO was designing a new version of Marburg."

Ridgewood grabbed his arm. "Let's go, Jeremy."

Outside, Ridgewood looked back and then halted. "I have some new lab results. That Marburg variant wasn't viable. That crafty drug lord Lopez pulled one over on those ISIS devils."

"Do you think they know?"

"Probably not. He went to Oxford, after all, so he probably has an emotional connection here. He gets an opium deal and helps take out two of the realm's threats. I want to hire him."

Brand just smiled.

Chapter Fifty-Seven
London

Reginald Fox followed his solicitor into the courtroom. Esther Brookstone was the claimant and he was the defendant in a case thrown into the small claims track because the repairs on her Jaguar sedan were less than £ 10,000. He took a seat and looked across the aisle, but she wasn't there, just her solicitor. The three stood when the judge, more an arbitrator in such cases, entered and took his place.

After some preliminaries, Brookstone's solicitor explained his client's absence. "Mrs. Brookstone, as you might know, is working with MI-5 and MI-6 and security agencies of several foreign governments to conclude a case involving international terrorism and illegal art deals. I am her legal representative today."

The judge nodded. "I've studied the case and her circumstances." He glared at Fox and his solicitor. "This might not be the trial of the century, gentlemen, but there's no one who annoys me more than a solicitor and defendant who waste the time of our county court system when the defendant is clearly in the wrong. To avoid wasting any more time, this court declares in favor of the claimant, Mrs. Esther Brookstone. As defendant, Mr. Reginald Fox will pay for all damages to Mrs. Brookstone's vehicle. There's also the matter of Mr. Fox's deck."

"Objection. The latter is not in Mrs. Brookstone's claim."

"Not specifically. It's covered as exacerbating the good woman's distress about her automobile's damage. By not asking the association to fix his deck, Mr. Fox is responsible for Mrs. Brookstone's pain and suffering from the fallen debris. You will be receiving notification of enforcement proceedings. That's all, gentlemen. Good day."

***

"What just happened in there?" Fox said to his solicitor outside the courtroom. "It's a legal travesty! Was I just run over by a lorry called the British government? Or Scotland Yard?"

"That's a myopic view," his solicitor said with a smile. "You were run over by a humongous lorry called public opinion. In hindsight it was predictable. Inspector Brookstone is an international heroine at this moment. Your timing was bad, Reginald. You didn't have a chance."

"So I have to pay up?"

"Or go to jail. The results of the enforcement proceedings will specify the options available, but those will be more or less the main two. My professional advice? Pay and make your peace with Mrs. Brookstone."

"Maybe I'll pay, but I'll never make peace with the bitch now."

The solicitor cocked his head and smiled. "Good luck with that."

Chapter Fifty-Eight
London

Langston handed Brookstone the invitation her first day back on the job. She was in a good humor because Fox had decided to pay for the ding on her car. There would be compensation corresponding to his falling deck debris too, which was a mystery. She didn't understand his change of heart, but things seemed to be going her way. *But what's this?*

"You'll note it's the Italian Embassy's stationary," said Langston. "I guess you're an international celebrity?"

"Balderdash. I suppose it's some tax debt my late husband and I neglected to pay. The Italians finally found me."

"That wouldn't come from the embassy."

She found the letter opener in her desk drawer and slit open the envelope. "You're dying to know, aren't you? Maybe it's only an advertisement for a new Italian restaurant. Like we need more of them in London."

"So, what is it?"

That question answered her question, of course. Langston often had to play a secondary role in famous cases. He was a good sport about it, but she could understand his curiosity. She knew it was hard to be a manager.

"I've been invited to a special function in Rome honoring patrons of the arts."

"For the recovery of the Bernini, I suppose. Congratulations."

He jotted down a few notes in his leather-bound agenda book. *What's that about?*

"Will I have to resign to accept this?"

He paused in his writing and smiled. "I think we can work our way around the rules a bit. Will they also pay for your escort?"

"They don't say anything about that. Do I need one?"

"That's the usual protocol." He peeked over her shoulder and frowned. "I'm sorry that it can't be me. I have a weekend planned in Edinburgh at that time with my wife. Why don't you see if your Dutchman is available?"

Yes, why don't I invite Bastiann? She thought of that last night in Berlin. The next day, van Coevorden had returned to Amsterdam, and she to London. "I'll do that. Do I have the Friday before and the Monday after?"

"Yes, OK. You deserve that."

"And while you're in Scotland, take a look at my castle. I'd value your opinion."

"That's a possibility. We're not staying in those ruins, though. No way. That's your commitment, not mine."

***

After Langston returned to his office and shut his door, he found her file. It was incomplete, of course. It contained a few items about her life previous to working at the Yard, but her contacts in the nation's security establishments implied there must be a lot missing.

In a sense, he knew what was missing was irrelevant to his decision. *Was it time for her to retire? How long can we expect people to keep working to provide security for the country's citizenry?* Those were questions someone would have to answer about him soon. Inspector Esther Brookstone had served the nation well. Didn't she deserve to go gentle into that good night?

He had been cleaning up her messes for a while. The last one with Fox was a personal favor he had done as a friend. That was easy; he knew the magistrate arbitrating the case. Esther's insistence on pursuing Dunst and his neo-Nazi cronies had been over the top, though, and bordered on insubordination. She was also lucky to be alive.

Or, was it skill? She was always creative. He didn't think she had learned that at the Yard—not all of it, at least. While some of her inventiveness was innate, she must have had previous training. *If I ever get cozy with some ghostly MI-5 or MI-6 types, maybe I can learn more about her past.* Unfortunately, Brookstone knew too many of those types; he, not one, at least not anyone he could call a true friend. *My God! Maybe she should still be running this office?* He smiled.

She deserved recognition for her work on the case of the Bernini bust, though. The Yard still had to find that mistress, but she was small fish compared to the old communist Brookstone had landed on a hunch. *I'd still like to be a fly on the wall at that reception.* He knew she would inevitably ruffle some feathers.

Chapter Fifty-Nine

Rome

Van Coevorden knew Brookstone was looking forward to the banquet with all the Italian dignitaries more than the speeches from Italian government types. He also knew pompous ceremonies were never her cup o' tea.

"You look ravishing but dreadfully serious," he said, eying her over the rim of his whiskey glass. "Be upbeat. It's not every day one receives an award from a European government's artistic bureaucracy."

"I was only doing my job. I had no idea the bust was stolen after the war and purchased by an ex-commie, no less. When you think about it, that old fellow's mistress did the art world a favor. She should be getting this award."

"Your modesty is overwhelming, Mrs. Brookstone," said a man who had turned away from a small group to confront her. "You have made it possible for future generations to enjoy the beauty Bernini created from his imagination."

"And you are?"

"Count Leopoldo Gonzaga, chairman of Rome's art history committee. I specialize in Bernini, by the way."

She poked her finger into his cummerbund. "Would you please explain to me how you can call yourself Count Gonzaga when the Italian government has denied me the right to be called Countess Sartini? They supposedly banned all references to nobility in 1946, but I should be the *condessa*."

The Count turned red. Van Coevorden smiled and shook his head. *This might be a long night!*

***

After speeches from bloviating fools listing art patrons and art discoverers—it was amazing how much dusty or moldy art people found in their basements or attics—dinner was served. Brookstone decided the only thing good about it was that it was free for honorees. She had split the trip's cost for van Coevorden with him as an enticement to come, but he had received a free dinner and cocktails too.

They were about to leave when the Interpol agent received a call.

"This might not be a good time, Bastiann," said NYPD homicide detective Rolando Castilblanco, "but I'd like to apologize."

Van Coevorden gestured to Brookstone to follow him to an isolated balcony. "Let me put you on speaker phone. We're in Rome, and Esther is here with me."

"As I was saying, I'm sorry I couldn't help more. As soon as I received your message, I acted on it. The wheels of bureaucracy moved fast in this case, but we were still too late to do any good. I'm happy everything ended well."

"When and how did you employ my message?" said van Coevorden.

"It's a long story, and I'd prefer not to discuss it to protect certain federal and European contacts. Let me only say that a royal friend who I respect a lot helped grease those bureaucratic wheels, not that any of it mattered, then or now."

"You owe me an Indian dinner," said Brookstone. "I'd prefer that to tonight's menu." She explained where they were. "Your royal friend would be right at home here among all these VIPs."

"How are you doing, Esther?"

"Not getting any younger."

"Me neither. Slowing down. Maybe I should take my pension and run. More of a question about being a victim of my own success, I guess. Chen can handle it. She's younger. Your answer was a bit evasive, by the way. You don't want to make a habit of getting into firefights with neo-Nazis, do you?"

"Are you suggesting I retire?"

"Never said that. That's up to you. I have my own situation to resolve. That's enough. I think you and Bastiann deserve some time off after your adventures, though. Any chance of that?"

They continued to chat for a while, but Brookstone was tiring.

"It's late here, Rollie," said van Coevorden. "We'll be in touch."

"Sure. Job well done, you two. Between Metzger and those other guys, you're a Fourth Reich demolition squad. Have a good evening."

"A good friend," said van Coevorden after the U.S. cop hung up.

"Yes, but I might have to go to New York to collect on the dinner he owes me. He won't be able to afford it when he retires, being on a fixed income."

***

The pair said their thankyous and goodbyes to all and found their way out of the building to the busy Roman avenue.

314

"Please flag a taxi, Bastiann. I'm ready for my bed." She squeezed his arm. "No friskiness tonight, old fellow. I've had far too much food and drink."

"I echo those sentiments," he said, stepping to the curb and waving his hand.

The traffic noise didn't hide her scream. He spun in time to see the man rush her. He was carrying a large knife.

Later he decided that her scream had been calculated to interrupt her assailant's concentration. She ducked under the knife thrust, lifting the man's right arm with her left hand while her right fist struck him in the throat.

"Is he dead?" she said as van Coevorden checked the man's condition.

"You were a little off, but good blow, my lady. You almost crushed his larynx, but he'll live." Still kneeling, he made a call. He then began to search the man. "Let me see who this is."

"Can it be a random attack?"

Van Coevorden found the assailant's wallet, opened it, and read the name.

She shook her head. "I know that name. He must be a relative of that Bernini thief."

A police car soon arrived. They had been on patrol around the building. With all the dignitaries and the constant terrorist threats across Europe, no major function was without police presence.

Brookstone didn't have her warrant card, but van Coevorden had his Interpol papers. After another hour, the speechless assailant, who was the son of the ex-communist and ex-owner of the Bernini bust, was on his way to jail, and another *Carabinieri* patrol car took them to their hotel.

"A handsome young policeman," said Brookstone as they waited for the lift in the lobby. "He had one of those awful

Roman noses, though. I can imagine him outracing you in a snoring contest. What's taking this lift so long?"

She fell asleep as soon as he tucked her in. He kissed her forehead and crossed to his own room.

Tomorrow would be a travel day.

Chapter Sixty
Hamburg

Nejem sipped his double espresso and sighed. It was only an approximation to good coffee, but it would have to do for now. He was homesick. He peered out the café's window at the huge cargo ship.

The port of Hamburg was the second largest in Europe next to Rotterdam's. He could already see many containers on the ship's deck, many bound for his country. *They'll arrive long after me.* The ship would soon set sail. In any case, his work was done for now.

There was a beep. A text message from the emir's assistant secretary—Nejem was number one—appeared on his smartphone. "Were there any problems?"

"I thought all was lost when the German federals moved in on the bunker," he typed, struggling with the small keyboard on the screen. "The paintings were stored elsewhere, Allah be praised, near the good Frau's gallery in another old warehouse they had retrofitted with climate control. Not sure we have all that weren't sold."

"But you have the Rembrandt?"

"Yes."

"Good. Have a safe flight."

***

Nejem would fly first class as was his custom. But he went outside one last time and checked the large container still on the dock. It was only one of many bound for his country. They were all filled with quality machine parts, something commonly shipped from Germany—the German factories were known worldwide for their quality control.

In this one container, though, twenty-one priceless masterpieces could be found well-padded and packed in a sealed, watertight plastic crate at its center. He smiled. *No, not priceless. We had to pay for the shipping.*

He supposed he'd read about the fate of the neo-Nazis. *Is it a psychosis that groups want to rule the world?* It made no sense to him. The good life could be had without being power hungry. And he agreed with his emir: A return to the sixth century wasn't desirable either, no matter how much power one wielded. The sooner all his Arab brothers realized that and played along with the West, the better off they'd be. *Play and invest.* Investing profits from oil by buying into Western businesses and acquiring real estate made much more sense—the oil wouldn't last forever.

He returned to the café to have another espresso and order his ride to the airport. *They do have good AC in the West, though.* In his home country, it wasn't so humid, but the AC could hardly keep up with the higher temperatures. *That's a problem. The emir's palace is fine, but my house could use a stronger unit.*

Epilogue

The possibilities are numerous once we decide to act and not react.
—George Bernard Shaw

Brookstone and van Coevorden took the whole week off, not only the Monday allotted by Langston. They went to her castle near Edinburgh, exploring the Scottish countryside as they traveled and after they arrived. On the way, they stopped to have dinner with the Edinburgh barrister George Cearrach and his sister Minerva.

"You have a lovely home here," Brookstone announced.

"Thank you," said the barrister. "Minerva and I are so happy you accepted my invitation. I'm very pleased you remembered."

Cearrach was the more serious of the siblings. His spinster sister Minerva looked like she might be the hit of the ladies' afternoon tea parties. *Or the nightly pub scenes?* She bubbled with enthusiasm and made her older brother seem dour and boring.

"And what a pleasant surprise that you brought Mr. van Coevorden along," said Minerva, fluttering her lashes at the Interpol agent. "Imagine! Internationally famous representatives from Scotland Yard and Interpol dining with us in one evening. It's so exciting. Did you ever think it possible, George?"

"No, but it's a small world. I'm afraid we've heard a bit about your escapades, and Minerva is desperate to ask you questions in order to have gossip available for her next afternoon tea." *I knew it!* thought Brookstone.

"George, they'll think badly of me." She smiled at van Coevorden. "I do have some questions, though."

He shrugged. "If we can answer them, I suppose we're game." He glanced at Brookstone with a pleading expression.

"Yes, I know. Security and all that. Did you have to kill anyone?"

George dropped his spoon, splashing the soup. "That's not a good dinner topic," he said. He tried to dab up the blotches with his napkin.

"I could put it more politely, I suppose. How dangerous were the gun battles?"

Van Coevorden looked at Brookstone again with eyebrows raised. She only smiled.

"Both of us are trained for such things, madam," he said, "so it's really nothing. Moreover, we were lucky. Many times over, in fact."

"You're so modest, Agent van Coevorden." She glanced at her brother. "Don't you feel safer with him here, George?"

The barrister looked at the ceiling and rolled his eyes.

***

"I feel so safe with you here," said Brookstone as they left Edinburgh after making purchases at a camping supply store. She patted van Coevorden on the leg. "She would have torn your knickers off if I hadn't been there."

Van Coevorden grimaced as she downshifted and took a curve at twice the speed he would have. Coming out of the curve, she pumped the accelerator. "Have to give my old beast some exercise. He was feeling neglected."

"Joke all you want," he said, "but that was what I call a comfortable home. Even that hotel bed will be infinitely more comfortable than camping out in the wild." They had purchased a kerosene stove, lanterns, camping toilets, and enough food for the week. "Visiting your castle will be like traveling back in time, I'm sure."

"Where's your sense of adventure?"

"I would like a little peace and quiet, Esther. It's been a little hectic, don't you think?"

"Just sit back and enjoy our holiday in the country. You'll soon have all the peace and quiet you need."

He leaned back in the seat and did just that, always grabbing for support when she took the curves. Esther knew the way now. They soon arrived.

She made him admit the castle's demesnes were beautiful, but she couldn't convince him about the damp, drafty, but sturdy stone house with its defensive ramparts she remembered from her tour with Ophelia.

"Remember, it has potential," she said as she did a U-turn that sent gravel flying in the rustic driveway. Ophelia's Mini Cooper was gone. *I wish her well.*

"I can see the need for a big investment of time and money. Good luck with fixing it up."

"I thought you were going to help me?"

"We never discussed that." He eyed the huge wooden front door now hanging ajar on one wrought-iron hinge holding on to one rusty bolt for dear life. "I guess I'm game if you are."

"That's the spirit."

***

They had promised to see more of each other back in Rome, so he had suggested the trip, surprising her. Ease into a more permanent relationship while touring the lowlands, he'd said. The castle was in bad shape, but there was some old furniture scattered around amidst the cobwebs and mold, serviceable once they tidied up a bit.

"You might have had squatters here at one time," said van Coevorden. "I imagined the inside to be a lot worse. Some rooms are almost habitable."

She remembered spooning the sleeping Ophelia and smiled. *Definitely habitable.* She wondered if van Coevorden suspected anything. She hadn't discussed the gender of her friend. *A lady has to have secrets she keeps from her man.*

She had been lucky to find the note in the kitchen before he did. She folded it multiple times and tucked it away in her cleavage, to read later. Her opportunity came when he visited the privy, bravely passing on his camping toilet—it was a bit low to the ground, even for him.

"Dear Mrs. B," the letter began. "You are a true dear. I said you reminded me of my mother. I could never imagine doing the things we did with my mother, though." *I hope not!* "You made me remember nights of experimentation at college. But that plays second violin to making me realize I'm wasting my life. I might not become famous or anything, but I always fancied becoming an artist. Our bedtime chat about the grand masters was uplifting in that respect. Bless you, Mrs. B. I hope you have a long life. Perhaps I will see you again. I hope so. Yours, Sylvia Bassett, your Ophelia."

***

After a few days of more cleanup and exploring the grounds, the old ruin felt more like home. She smiled at him across the old dining table one evening, the meal not as meager as the one she had partaken with Ophelia. She knew they were both hesitant about this new arrangement. It was good to start in neutral territory. *What better place than Dughallach Castle?*

Sometimes more commitment destroyed a relationship even when two people loved each other. And both knew their jobs might keep them apart. Their future was uncertain.

But Brookstone was considering retirement. She'd discussed it with no one beyond van Coevorden, except for the bureaucratic paperwork necessary to continue as inspector. Her last two cases had solidified her legacy in the Yard. *Maybe it's time to go out on a high note? Could I live in Holland? Could Bastiann live here or in London? Maybe take a trip around the world with the Dutchman?* All questions needing to be answered in good time. *But not tonight. And not in the next few days here either.*

"I like your friends in London," he said, eying her over his wineglass. "Scots are a little standoffish to me, but that barrister is a jolly old fellow. I bet his days in the firm are numbered, though. I didn't see anyone older." He took a sip and straightened his mustache. "I don't have many friends in Amsterdam, you know. And Chen and Castilblanco are too far away to be in my close social circle."

Scots cold? Ophelia was hot! And MacDougall in her dreams could have made any woman's heart melt.

"You won't mind my friends calling you Poirot behind your back?"

"Not nearly as much as you do when they call you Miss Marple." He sipped the wine and thought a moment. "You know, I'm amazed old Agatha never put them together. What a team they would have made."

"They couldn't compete with us. You'll have to admit this last case was fun. We'll have to do it again, love. No one has found those paintings. I do hate to have a cliffhanger at the end of a novel, you know."

Rembrandt's Angel

Author's Note

You have just finished reading *Rembrandt's Angel*. I hope you enjoyed it. I realize you have many book choices, so I am honored you chose this one. Please take the time to post at least a short review on Amazon or other review sites stating what you liked and disliked and why. Other readers will find that information as useful as I do.

***

Although it can be read independently, this book is a spin-off from the "Detectives Chen and Castilblanco Series." Here's a list of books from that series you might also enjoy:

The Midas Bomb
Angels Need Not Apply
Teeter-Totter between Lust and Murder
*Aristocrats and Assassins**
*The Collector***
Family Affairs
Gaia and the Goliaths
*Introduces Interpol Agent Bastiann van Coevorden
**Introduces Scotland Yard Inspector Esther Brookstone

Notes, Acknowledgments
and Disclaimers

This novel has several "origins." First, I've been collecting what-ifs for stories since about the time I wrote my first novel at thirteen or earlier. (Don't look for that novel—I tossed it in the trash bin when I went away to college. The plot wasn't too bad, something like an R- or X-rated version of the movie *City of Angels* with the angel being the female protagonist—X-rated at the time I wrote it, but most likely only R now.)

At that time, I read good sci-fi and wrote bad erotic sci-fi and fantasy (similar to some of the wildly erotic sci-fi and fantasy novels and comic books now on the market, I suppose), and I read and wrote mystery stories (sometimes both genres in combination, mimicking Asimov's detective sci-fi). I was precocious maybe, or just a young nerd, but I also enjoyed reading the relatively tame and sedate mysteries of G. K. Chesterton, Agatha Christie, and Arthur Conan Doyle, as well as H. Rider Haggard's thrillers. While I was certain I could write sci-fi, I wasn't sure about mysteries (I restudied the whole mystery genre when I wrote *Teeter-Totter between Lust and Murder*—the genre has changed a lot from Agatha's time). I also discovered more recent thrillers.

After meeting Miss Marple and Hercule Poirot in numerous Christie books, though, I considered the obvious: what if the inimitable Agatha had written a mystery that put these two wonderful characters together? My well-read sister-in-law, who first discovered Christie by reading her writings on archaeology (I too was a fan of archaeology and anthropology until I decided harder sciences were easier), recently told me many people have asked this same question. If so, this book is my answer to everyone, although Agatha might be upset with some of the goings-on between this 21st-century crime-stopping duo. But then again, why can't older people have any fun? She also might be upset by my adding thriller elements to a mystery. My only excuse for these potential sins is that she wrote in a different and simpler time when terrorism amounted to the neighbor woman chasing her husband out of the house with a rolling pin, or said husband coming home drunk and taking it out on his poor wife and kids (while such actions were never condoned and can now lead to restraining orders, time in jail, or divorce, we'd hardly call them terrorism today).

There are some more obvious and recent origins. While this novel can be read independently, both Esther Brookstone and Bastiann van Coevorden have appeared in a few novels in my "Detectives Chen and Castilblanco Series," Esther most notably in *The Collector* and Bastiann in *Aristocrats and Assassins* and other novels. The two had more than a platonic relationship even there—Brookstone was clearly pursuing her Dutchman— but they were clamoring for their own novel too, especially Esther, who can be persistent. They got my muses on their side (my muses are really banshees with Tasers), so I had to write a story where they had top billing. This is it.

The painting in the title and many of the other paintings stolen by the Nazi's for Hitler's museum have never been found. While searching for information about the Rembrandt, I only came across the black and white version. Like the Gardner museum artworks mentioned in *The Collector*, it's a shame these paintings are no longer available for public viewing. If you know anything about them, please inform authorities, the FBI in the U.S., Scotland Yard in the U.K., or your local authorities. You will be doing all the world's art lovers a great favor.

There are some philosophical passages about death and the afterlife from both Brookstone and her late husband, the count. I even took the liberty of indicating a real website. While Mrs. Brookstone might have an agenda in this respect—she loved her Count Sartini—this is more a portrayal of Esther's complex character. She's a liberated woman with her own opinions. She's a different version of the strong, smart female characters I love to portray. Such women should be ruling the world—it would be a far better place, I'm sure. The count's point of view is the correct one: we cannot possibly know what comes after, so we had better make sure we make the most of our time on this planet and help others do the same. You can spin this any way you want within your own credo.

The nexus between al Qaeda, South American terrorists, and cartels is well documented. See, for example, Paul Williams' *The Al Qaeda Connection.* It's not much of a stretch to assume similar connections for ISIS, especially considering their more international approach to financing their nefarious activities, involving opium as well as petroleum. Hopefully this will not continue to the time of this novel, but right now the situation is bleak.

Neo-Nazis and the current swing to the right in Europe has some of its genesis in the reactions to the wave of refugees from troubled areas in the Middle East in recent years, but fascism in Europe isn't new by any means. It tends to rear its ugly head in stressful times like these, but there are always those who are ready to take advantage of bigotry and hate. And there are always mercenaries who will do nearly anything for money. While this story is fiction, I have followed Clancy's maxim— good fiction has to seem real.

The G. B. Shaw quotes remind us that this Irish writer was a great observer of human nature who often spoke his mind.

Esther Brookstone almost seems like a disciple in that regard. Her relationship with van Coevorden is a bit like Henry Higgins's relationship with Eliza Doolittle in a more mystical way, and she realizes that. I have employed some of the lively idiom from our good friends "across the pond," so one more Shaw quote is appropriate: "England and America are two countries separated by a common language." I'd like to ask my U.K. readers to let me know if I have used the Queen's English and local slang correctly. I studied the differences in detail while writing this novel, but I've never lived in the U.K., so I'm sure errors remain, and I apologize for that. They are all mine, no one else's.

You could not have enjoyed this novel without the expertise of the wonderful publishing team at Penmore Press: editors Susan Wenger and Chris Page, cover artist Christine Horner, copy editor Terri Lynn Carter; and webmaster Midori Snyder, who is also an accomplished author. And, above all, I want to thank principal editor Michael D. James, another accomplished author in his own right, who kept the whole publishing process moving along. I thank them all for their patience and understanding.

My wife has also encouraged me throughout my writing career. Without her patience, understanding, and cheerleading, I would not have stuck with it.

Steve Moore
February 14, 2017
Montclair, NJ

About the Author

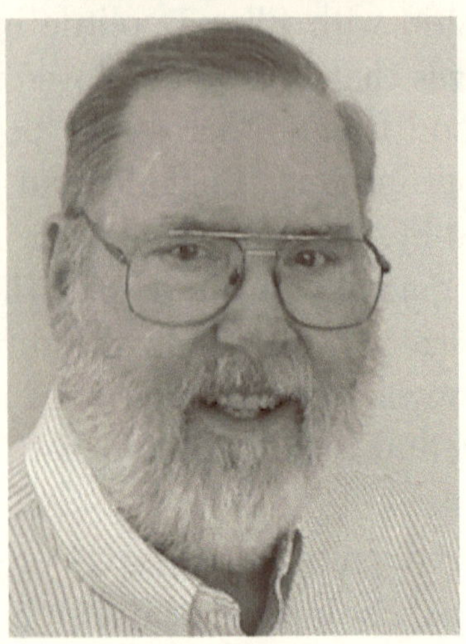

Steve Moore writes sci-fi, mystery, and thriller novels, novellas, and short stories, blog articles, and book and movie reviews. At last count, he has written twenty-one novels, one a novel for young adults—this tally includes four series. He also has three short story collections. His stories reflect his keen interest in the diversity of human nature that he has observed in his different abodes across the U.S. and in South America as well as in his Latin and European travels for work and pleasure. His interests include music, physics, mathematics, forensics, genetics, robotics, and scientific ethics. He also has an active blog which includes op-ed comments on current events and their meaning to the U.S. and the rest of the world, and opinions about writing and the publishing business of interest to readers and writers alike. He and his wife now live just outside New York City. For more details, visit him at his website http://stevenmoore.com and follow him on Facebook and Goodreads where he participates in many discussions with readers and writers.

IF YOU ENJOYED THIS BOOK
Please write a review.
This is important to the author and helps to get the
word out to others
Visit

PENMORE PRESS
www.penmorepress.com

All Penmore Press books are available directly through our website, amazon.com, Barnes and Noble and Nook, Sony Reader, Apple iTunes, Kobo books and via leading bookshops across the United States, Canada, the UK, Australia and Europe.

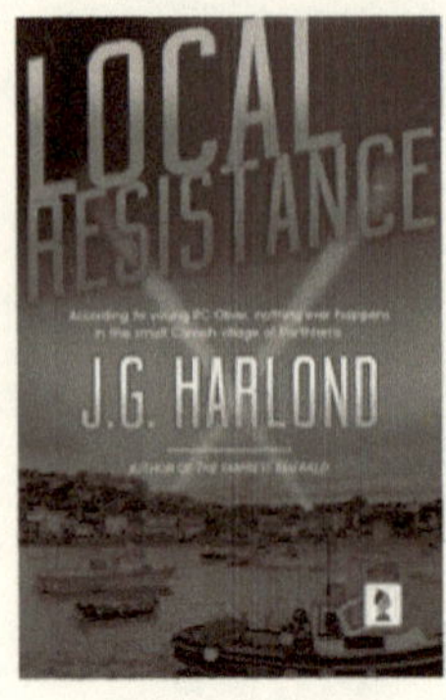

Local Resistance

by

Jane Harlond

WWII in England, Cornwall smugglers, Intelligence agents, detective story, locals and war in the UK, German navy operations on the coast of the UK. Murder thriller. Espionage.

On a stormy night in March 1941, Maisie Rose Hawkins leaves her drunk husband, Stan, out in the rain—and he disappears. Detective Sergeant Bob Robbins and young PC Laurie Oliver are called out to investigate and discover that Stan's small fishing boat is gone, the rope sawn through. As Bob searches for answers, it becomes apparent that in this small Cornish village where everyone knows everything about everybody, nobody quite knows the truth.

Beneath the surface of village life, a fierce battle is being waged against wartime deprivations. Shopkeepers quietly evade rationing restrictions. Food inspector Archibald Bantry, charged with enforcing those restrictions, dies in a suspicious car crash. Various leads connect a sea cave full of smuggled black-market goods to the missing Stan Hawkins. And what seems like the work of local malcontents becomes more complex and dangerous when Bob stumbles on the truth in a disused copper mine, where a much deadlier affair is underway.

"Uncanny happenings and warm characterization. . . . The realities of wartime life in this novel combine with a lovely sense of place to create a distinctly Cornish mixture of secluded charm and the unsettlingly mysterious." —Robert Wilton, prize-winning author of the Comptrollerate-General historical thrillers.

PENMORE PRESS
www.penmorepress.com

Historical fiction and nonfiction
Paperback available for order on line
and as Ebook with all major distributers

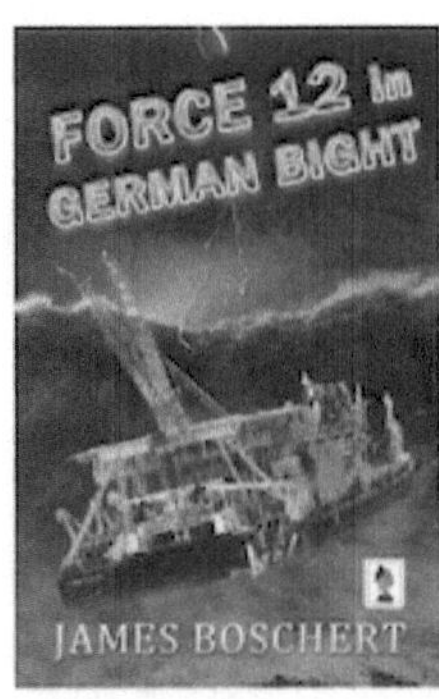

Force 12 in German Bight
by
James Boschert

Considering that oil and gas have been flowing from under the North Sea for the best part of half a century, it is perhaps surprising that more writers have not taken the uncompromising conditions that are experienced in this area – which extends from the north of Scotland to the coasts of Norway and Germany – for the setting of a novel. James Boschert's latest redresses the balance.

The book takes its title from the name of an area regularly referred to in the legendary BBC Shipping Forecast, one which experiences some of the worst weather conditions around the British Isles. It is a fast-paced story which smacks of authenticity in every line. A world of hard men, hard liquor, hard drugs and cold-blooded murder. The reality of the setting and the characters, ex-military men from both sides of the Atlantic, crooked wheeler-dealers, and Danish detectives, male and female, are all in on the action.

This is not story telling akin to a latter day Bulldog Drummond, nor a James Bond, but simply a snortingly good yarn which will jangle the nerve ends, fill your nose with the smell of salt and diesel oil, your ears with the deafening sound of machinery aboard a monster pipe-dredging ship and, above all, make you remember never to underestimate the power of the sea.

–Roger Paine, former Commander, Royal Navy .

PENMORE PRESS
www.penmorepress.com

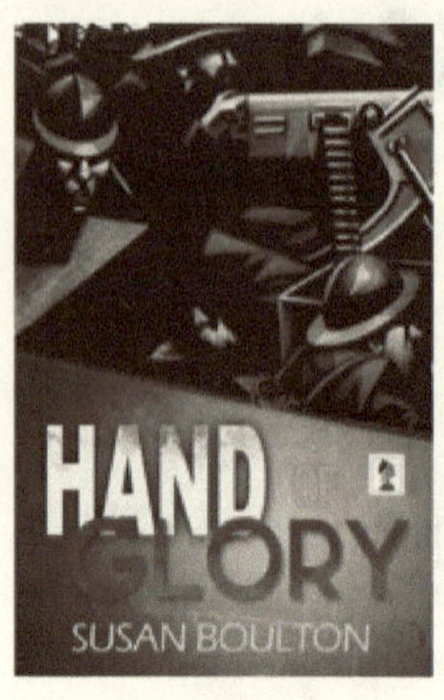

HAND OF GLORY
BY
SUSAN BOULTON

"And all that awake now be as the dead, for the dead man's sake . . ."

In Passchendaele near the end of the Great War, Captain Giles Hardy is trapped on barbed wire, wounded in mind and body, convinced he should be dead. But Giles's true battle begins after he's rescued and sent home. In the small town of Stafford, he struggles with terrifying visions of the atrocities he's witnessed—and a recruit he served with.

The visions lead Giles to a man who exploits the grief of the bereaved with the help of a Hand of Glory, a mythical tool of thieves. A new friend, Agnes Reed, and the ghost of an old one, Corporal George Adams, aid Hardy in his investigation. Now he must catch the thief, destroy the hand, and lay to rest the men who will otherwise never leave the fields of Flanders.

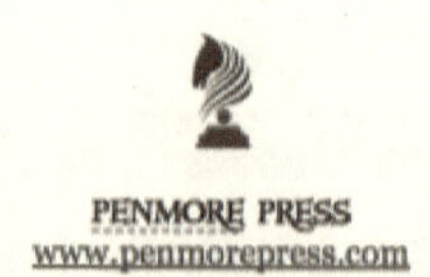

PENMORE PRESS
www.penmorepress.com

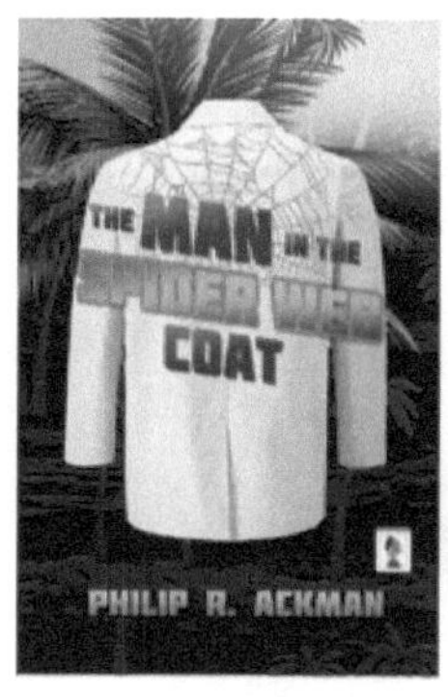

THE MAN IN THE SPIDER WEB COAT
BY
PHILIP ACKMAN

Titus Buchanan, a professor who runs a think tank at Williams College, believes he's figured out how to stage a successful revolution. When the United Nations adopts a historic vote spelling the end of colonialism, Buchanan seizes the opportunity to test his theory. His laboratory will be the Splendid Islands, a collection of palm-fringed cays scattered across three quarters of a million square miles of the South Pacific. Its inhabitants will be his lab rats.

But complications arise. The Splendids belong to New Zealand, and New Zealand has no intention of giving them up. The United States has its own secret "space age" agenda for the islands. The Queen of England is bound to support New Zealand, but she doesn't want Britain to fall out with the Americans, who favor independence. Meanwhile, the islanders, gripped with revolutionary fever, have ideas about self-rule. Reverend Geoffrey Brown, originally recruited by Buchanan to run the revolution, joins forces with an unlikely crew of locals and sets out to match wits with powerful opponents.

PENMORE PRESS
www.penmorepress.com

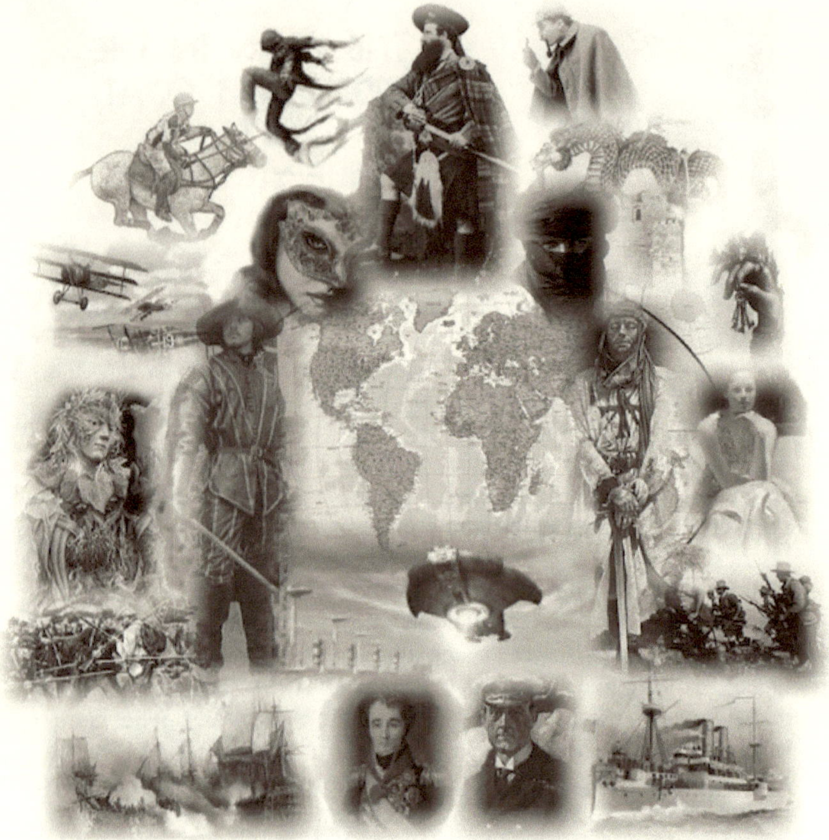